ETHICS UNBOUND

Ethics Unbound

Chinese and Western Perspectives on Morality

Katrin Froese

The Chinese University Press

Ethics Unbound:
Chinese and Western Perspectives on Morality
By Katrin Froese

ISBN: 978-962-996-496-2

The Chinese University Press
The Chinese University of Hong Kong
Sha Tin, N.T., Hong Kong
Fax: +852 2603 7355
E-mail: cup@cuhk.edu.hk
Website: www.chineseupress.com

Printed in Hong Kong

For my parents, Christa and Arnold Froese

CONTENTS

ACKNOWLEDGEMENTS

I would like to thank the sponsors at the Killam Trusts for funding a fellowship that enabled me to commit an entire semester to the writing of this book. A supportive work environment cultivated by my colleagues in Religious Studies and Philosophy remains invaluable to me. In particular, I would like to thank Virginia Tumasz for encouraging me to develop courses in the Comparative Philosophy of Religion so that I could further develop my interests in cross-cultural philosophy. I am grateful to the anonymous reviewers solicited by The Chinese University Press, who provided constructive and insightful feedback on the manuscript. Last but not least, I would like to thank Wanda Huang for hosting me in Hong Kong on numerous occasions but, above all, for our travels to China which provided the inspiration to pursue this field of study in the first place.

ABBREVIATIONS

Abbreviations are used in the citation of primary sources.

CONFUCIUS

A	*The Analects of Confucius: A Philosophical Translation*. Trans. Roger T. Ames and Henry Rosemont. New York: Ballantine Books, 1998.

All references to Confucius are by chapter and section number.

DAODEJING

DDJ	*Tao Te Ching*. Trans. D. C. Lau. London: Penguin Books, 1963.
DDJ Ch	*Daodejing* 道德經. Beijing: Beijing daxue chubanshe, 1995.

All references to the Daodejing are by section number.

HUAINANZI

AR	*The Art of Rulership: A Study in Ancient Chinese Political Thought*. Trans. Roger T. Ames. Honolulu: University of Hawaii Press, 1983.
HN	*Huainan honglie jijie* 淮南鴻烈集解. Beijing: Zhonghua shuju chubanshe, 1989.
HN Chan	"The Taoism of Huai-nan Tzu." In *A Sourcebook in Chinese Philosophy*. Trans. Wing-Tsit Chan. Princeton: Princeton University Press, 1963.
YD	*Yuan Dao: Tracing Dao to its Source*. Trans. Roger T. Ames and D. C. Lau. New York: Ballantine Books, 1998.

KANT

CJ	*Critique of Judgment*. Trans. J. H. Bernard. New York: Hafner Publishing Company, 1968.
CPrR	*Critique of Practical Reason*. Trans. H. J. Paton. New York: Harper and Row, 1964.
FMM	*Foundations of the Metaphysics of Morals*. In *Kant Selections*. Ed. Lewis White Beck. New York: Macmillan Publishing Company, 1988.
LP	*Lectures on Pedagogy*. In *On Education*. London: Kegan Paul, 1897.
MP	*The Metaphysical Principles of Virtue*. New York: Bobs Merrill and Company, 1964.
OH	"Idea for a Universal History from a Cosmopolitan Point of View." In *Kant Selections*. Ed. Lewis White Beck. New York: Macmillan Publishing Company, 1988.
R	*Religion within the Bounds of Bare Reason*. Trans. Werner S. Pluhar. Indianapolis: Hackett Publishing Company, 2009.

KIERKEGAARD

CA	*The Concept of Anxiety: A Simple Psychologically Orienting Deliberation on the Dogmatic Issue of Hereditary Sin*. Trans. Reidar Thomte. Princeton: Princeton University Press, 1981.
CUP	*Concluding Unscientific Postscript to Philosophical Fragments*. Ed. and trans. Howard V. Hong and Edna H. Hong. Princeton: Princeton University Press, 1992.
EO I	*Either/Or Part I*. Ed. and trans. Howard V. Hong and Edna H. Hong. Princeton: Princeton University Press, 1987.
EO II	*Either/Or Part II*. Ed. and trans. Howard V. Hong and Edna H. Hong. Princeton: Princeton University Press, 1987.
FT	*Fear and Trembling*. Ed. and trans. Howard V. Hong and Edna H. Hong. Princeton: Princeton University Press, 1983.
SUD	*The Sickness Unto Death: A Christian Psychological Exposition for Upbuilding and Awakening*. Trans. Alastair Hannay. Princeton: Princeton University Press, 1980.
TC	*Training in Christianity and the Edifying Discourse Which Accompanied It*. Trans. Walter Lowrie. Princeton: Princeton University Press, 1944.
WL	*Works of Love*. Trans. Howard V. Hong and Edna H. Hong. Princeton: Princeton University Press, 1998.

LIEZI

Lie *The Book of Lieh-tzu: A Classic of Tao*. Trans. A. C. Graham. New York: Columbia University Press, 1990.

MENCIUS

M *Mengzi*. Trans. Bryan W. Van Norden. Indianapolis: Hackett Publishing Company, 2008.

M Ch *The Works of Mencius. In The Chinese Classics*. Taipei: SMC Publishing, 1998.

All references to the Mencius are by section number.

NIETZSCHE

BGE *Beyond Good and Evil*. In *Basic Writings of Nietzsche*. Trans. Walter Kaufmann. New York: Modern Library, 1968.

BT *The Birth of Tragedy*. In *Basic Writings of Nietzsche*. Trans. Walter Kaufmann. New York: Modern Library, 1968.

GM *On the Genealogy of Morals*. In *Basic Writings of Nietzsche*. Trans. Walter Kaufmann. New York: Modern Library, 1968.

OTF "On Truth and Falsity in an Extra-Moral Sense." In *Early Greek Philosophy and Other Essays*. Trans. M. A. Mügge. *The Complete Works of Friedrich Nietzsche*, vol. 2. Ed. Oscar Levy. New York: Russell and Russell, 1964.

TI *Twilight of the Idols*. Trans. R. J. Hollingdale. Middlesex: Penguin, 1968.

WP *The Will to Power*. Trans. Walter Kaufmann and R. J. Hollingdale. Middlesex: Penguin, 1968.

Z *Thus Spoke Zarathustra*. Trans. R. J. Hollingdale. Middlesex: Penguin, 1968.

All references to Nietzsche are by section number; P stands for Preface.

ROUSSEAU

DOI	*Discourse on the Origins of Inequality*. In *The Basic Political Writings*. Ed. Peter Gay. Indianapolis: Hackett Publishing Company, 1987.
E	*Emile*. Trans. Allan Bloom. New York: Basic Books, 1979.
SC	*On the Social Contract*. In *The Basic Political Writings*. Ed. Peter Gay. Indianapolis: Hackett Publishing Company, 1987.

ZHUANGZI

Zh	*The Book of Chuang-tzu*. Trans. Martin Palmer. New York: Vintage, 1968.
Zh Ch	*Zhuangzi duben* 莊子讀本. Taipei: Sanmin shuju, 1998.

All references to the Zhuangzi are by chapter and page number.

INTRODUCTION

Many thinkers across divergent philosophical and religious traditions bemoan a seemingly precipitous decline in moral standards. Often, the corrupt and ethically moribund world that they inhabit is compared unfavorably to a golden age, when ethics enjoyed its rightful place at the apex of human existence and human beings were able to live in harmonious concord, rather than being ravaged by warfare and conflict. It is no coincidence that our imagination is fed by the fantasy of a perfect moral world, located in the distant past. If we did not saddle ourselves with the responsibility of making our own humanity, questions of a moral nature would not preoccupy us. Due to our capacities for speech, thought, and emotion, which allow us to reflect upon and also distance ourselves from our immediate environs, our place in the world cannot be taken for granted. Morality is an integral part of the process of making a place for ourselves in this world, and we rely on tales of moral perfection to ensure that our efforts do not cease. The irony which not only underlies but drives our moral being is that we would not be moral creatures if our position in the cosmos were secure, but that we rely on dreams of moral fulfillment for our efforts at moral development to continue.

Cultural diversity renders impossible a single definition of ethics. According to some Western approaches, ethics is considered to be universal in scope, and basic principles of humanity are assumed to cut across linguistic and cultural divides. However, the simple equating of Western thought with legal formalism is too facile because it ignores the subtlety of the impetus underlying such formalism itself. For a thinker such as Kant who perhaps epitomizes formalism, the possibility of universality acts as the "impossible possibility" that catalyzes human beings to embark on a quest of constant moral self-making. We ought to act as though our actions could be universalized (*FMM* 254),[1] all the while recognizing that they never will be universalized. The pursuit of truly "universal" maxims to orient our conduct is ceaseless.

Confucian thinkers do not base ethics on abstract principles, which they associate with a rigid legalism, but rather claim that virtue is a process of harmonizing relationships between individuals, taking into account the cultural milieu in which one is situated. This implies that what may be considered ethical in one community may be unethical in another. Furthermore, ethics does not simply offer guidance to individuals on how to act, but is also part of the process of community formation. Individuals who are situated differently within the social order may have different ethical responsibilities. This does not preclude a notion of a common humanity. Someone who is practiced in the art of being virtuous has developed the capacity to extend herself to include others, which would serve her well, even in communities of strangers. Harmony rather than universalism is the goal and while this is in some ways more flexible, it can also bring with it a conservatism that demands respect for existing social orders and conventions. It is no coincidence that Confucian philosophy demonstrates a penchant for hierarchy and deference.

Despite the changing nature of the ethical terrain across and within different cultural traditions, it does seem to be closely associated with what it means to be a human being, as a member of a larger community, as well as within the world of nature and within the cosmos as a whole. Negotiating these interrelationships is no easy task. Some ethical approaches, such as that of Kant, insist that ethics separates human beings from the natural world and that the human community is explicitly defined against nature (*CPrR* 29).[2] Other thinkers, such as Mencius, hold that social integration cannot be separated from the process of integration into nature. Ethics is concerned with *making* oneself part of a larger

---

1 Immanuel Kant, *Foundations of the Metaphysics of Morals*, in *Kant Selections*, ed. Lewis White Beck (New York: Macmillan Publishing Company, 1988).

2 Immanuel Kant, *Critique of Practical Reason*, trans. H. J. Paton (New York: Harper and Row, 1964).

whole. It is a difficult undertaking because we can never take our place in the world for granted. We are saddled with the tremendous responsibility of learning to become what we are, and to make ourselves belong in a world that we already inhabit.

In Kantian thought, much emphasis is placed on making ethical decisions. This may be symptomatic of a common bifurcation between being and becoming, which sees the self as the agent who acts. In contrast, in Confucian philosophy the emphasis is on becoming an ethical person. Who I am and what I do cannot be neatly separated. Instead of placing the emphasis on making the ethical decision, more weight is placed on becoming the ethical person. Ethics is an art, and it requires practice and learning in order to acquire its skills. The hope is that ethical actions would eventually flow naturally from one's personality.

In the Confucian tradition, ethics often seeps into areas that would not often fall within the ethical domain for a thinker such as Kant, such as ritual, art, and music. Because ethics is seen as a means of participating in the harmonizing tendencies of the cosmos, rather than a matter of making the right choices, art and ritual contribute to the cultivation of harmony. The ethical project is unending because it demands a continuous extension of the self to include others and thus necessitates ongoing self-transformation. According to more formalist ways of thinking, there is often a discomfort with movement, and ethics attempts to anchor itself to principles unblemished by the ravages of time and history which can serve as guiding beacons for our activity. Thus, Kant implores us to act *as though* our maxims could become universal law. Heteronomy and change are the circumstances that ethics must overcome. Even a thinker such as Rousseau, who acknowledges that ethics is part of an ongoing process of community formation, insists that we should orient ourselves according to the relatively static and blissful equilibrium that, he alleges, defined our existence in the state of nature (*DOI* 42).[3]

Ethics is acknowledged to be a difficult undertaking in both Chinese and Western traditions, largely due to the selfish tendencies of human

3 Jean-Jacques Rousseau, *Discourse on the Origins of Inequality*, in *The Basic Political Writings*, ed. Peter Gay (Indianapolis: Hackett Publishing Company, 1987).

beings. Selfishness undermines ethics, and ethical norms are intended to counteract its influence. Confucian philosophers such as Mencius, who maintain that ethics is rooted in the natural "sprouts" of the human being, admit that careful cultivation is necessary in order to bring our ethical potential to fruition (*M* Ch 2A6).[4] Learning how to be moral while inhabiting a society that often subverts our attempts is an important part of Mencius's project. Selfishness is often generated in times of social disarray when the territorial impulse to draw boundaries around the self will be exacerbated. While selfishness or egoism is a tendency to expand the "self" by means of possession, exclusion, and dominance, ethics hopes to cultivate a broadening of horizons that includes others. Egoism and ethics therefore appear to be at loggerheads.

And yet, what is less often explicitly acknowledged is that egoism and ethics are also bedfellows, albeit uneasy ones. Ethics is indelibly linked to the quest for identity and finding a place to stand in the social, natural, and cosmic order. It is this quest for identity and place that can unleash the spiral of egoism. Egoism springs from the fact that we covet social recognition in order to carve out an "identity" for ourselves. Others always mirror reified aspects of my "self" back to me, and I may reject and/or embrace this reflection, but nonetheless, it will cause me to relate to myself "externally." In other words, I am able to turn myself into the object of my own making because I am always also relating to myself through others. Often we will try to cultivate personalities in reaction to or in accordance with an external image of ourselves. Because dissonance within the self between our experiences and others' judgments of us is common, we can become obsessed with the notion of identity to the extent that it unleashes a desire to possess oneself and others, in a misguided effort to attain unity for oneself and in the world around one. Egoism is a social and not a private phenomenon. We begin to exhibit the need to appropriate things, and other people, in order to achieve some kind of false unity. Yet, this notion of a complete self is a fiction and thus our need is seldom satiated. Egoism spirals out of control as we grasp for a self that is not to be had. A Daoist philosopher

---

4 Mencius, *The Works of Mencius*, in *The Chinese Classics* (Taipei: SMC Publishing, 1998).

such as Zhuangzi is acutely aware of this potential, since he insists that the best way to be one's self is to forget oneself. His text abounds with stories of individuals who are not perturbed by dramatic changes that befall them, such as the man who has a willow tree sprout out of his arm and simply shrugs it off as part of the transformation of things (*Zh* 18:151).[5] This demonstrates an attitude that sees the self not as something to be had, but rather as a process to be nurtured with others.

For many philosophers, ethics comprises the highest essence of our humanity. It is no coincidence that the cardinal virtue in Confucian philosophy is *ren* 仁 (human-heartedness, benevolence) and is not only homophonous with *ren* 人 (human being), but also contains this radical within it. When we accuse someone of being "inhuman," we more often than not imply that she has acted unethically. Ethics is not merely about treating others well, for it also reflects the need to mark a place for ourselves in the human order as well as in the cosmos. Ethics is part of the process of our identity-making, and this dynamic also threatens to subvert it from within. The ethical judgment of others can spur the desire for improvement, but it can also unleash an unsettling insecurity. As individuals, we want to function well in our communities so we will feel as though we *belong* to it or hold a place in it. Furthermore, as members of those communities, we also seek an identity *for* the community. By setting up the parameters by means of which individuals find belonging, and also by situating the human community within the context of other communities and the cosmos at large, ethics ensures that it is inextricably linked to our images of ourselves. This is the Achilles heel that can nudge it into the unsavory domain of the unethical.

Furthermore, our image of who we are is also indelibly intertwined with what we are *not*. Because of this, ethics can precipitate a process of moralizing which looks to exclude in order to be able to laud ourselves as ethical beings. Ethics cannot truly root out the unethical, for it also feasts on it. It is too simplistic to claim that self-righteous moralizing is a deviant offshoot of morality; it is only a more sinister embodiment of its dynamic. By no means is this a reason for rejecting ethics altogether,

5 Zhuangzi, *The Book of Chuang-tzu*, trans. Martin Palmer (London: Vintage, 1968).

but it does imply that ethics must be continuously placed under scrutiny in order to remain cognizant of the potentially unethical strains that percolate beneath the surface.

The dependence of ethics on what it militates against becomes obvious even in Kant, who tries to distance ethical behavior from the dynamic of recognition. The desire for public approval is hardly an ethical motivation in his eyes. And yet, he recognizes that the need for belonging cannot simply be ignored and therefore brings in a God (whose existence he does not affirm) to suggest that morality, harmony, and happiness will eventually coincide (*CPrR* 137). It is God, not another human being, who stamps ethics with tacit approval. In other words, Kant reluctantly concedes that if we remain unconvinced that ethical conduct will be recognized and can provide a "home" for us in the future, it is hard to muster the motivation to practice morality. Yet, Kant's unease in introducing God to buttress morality is expressed by his insistence that God is not a condition for morality, but merely its *postulate*. That is to say, God offers a hypothetical possibility, and may or may not exist. We ought not to act morally because we expect divine recompense, but nonetheless God hovers over the horizon as a nebulous yet bright future in order to instill us with hope.

Despite Kant's hopes for perpetual harmony, his morality still feeds on an enemy, and his chosen combatant is nature, both in what he refers to as its heteronomous or unpredictable form and as the arbiter of inexorable physical laws to which human beings must submit. Moral decisions are to be made on one's own, removed from natural desires and also oblivious to the gaze of others (*FMM* 278). The highest human expression of freedom is the ability to create the laws to which one willingly succumbs. These decisions must even be free from the interference of others, in order to fiercely guard the autonomy of the self. Although Kant does his best to try to shield the self from selfish, *particular* interests, individual autonomy becomes paramount, in order to preserve a sphere of decision-making that one can call one's own, apart from others and nature. Morality becomes an exercise in individual freedom, which for Kant is the most important aspect of our individual and human identity. Furthermore, he makes it very clear that this freedom is exercised against nature.

Other thinkers see nature in a more favorable light, and use it to try to offset the dangers of social convention. Mencius looks to nature to ground ethics, and extricate ourselves from a situation of moral stagnation and decay. Both Mencius and Confucius recognize the danger of simply taking one's cues from others, but they do not dispense with the practice of invoking role models, insisting that one must be careful to choose the *right* people to emulate. Rousseau spurns the idea of looking to role models and instead turns to nature as a substratum that can provide an ethical foundation in times of ethical disarray. However, while Mencius sees nature as already imbued with meaning and sees no conflict between the natural and social world, Rousseau maintains that ethics is necessary because we have departed from the natural equilibrium of the prehuman and presocial animal. The lost harmony of our ancestors awakens in us the need for morality in order to re-create this state at a social level. It thus provides us with a catalyst for ethical activity but also reveals the inadequacy of any moral system, because the alleged natural equilibrium can never be recaptured. That which enables us to be moral also continuously throws our morality into question. For Rousseau, ethics always rests on an uneasy foundation but this tension is also what makes it productive and allows for it to become the expression of human freedom.

Despite the powerful hold that ethics exercises over us, its laudable nature is by no means taken for granted by all. There are dissident voices within both the Chinese and Western traditions that question the unassailable authority that ethics has enjoyed. Because morality is related to questions of belonging, and because it charts out a place for itself in relation to that which is deemed either immoral or amoral, it can also foster a desire to seek and root out its enemies. A preoccupation with highlighting the immoral nature of others becomes a means of resting on our own laurels, assured of our own goodness. Political rhetoric is all too often invoked in order to brand forces of evil in the world, thereby assuaging us by convincing us that all is well with *us*. Instead of worrying about our own ethical comportment, we become well-practiced in the art of ferreting out the unethical nature of others. For this reason, Confucius insists that we must recognize that we always have further to go in the ethical domain (*A* 9:19).[6] We can never rest content that we have arrived. If unchecked, ethical judgment not only runs roughshod over the particular, but can precipitate a witch hunt. Ethics, in other words, can surreptitiously metamorphize into the unethical.

Because of the connection between ethics and its opposite, some religious and philosophical traditions, such as Daoism, celebrate a time when ethics was not necessary. However, it is important to recognize that their antipathy to ethics does not stem from a position according to which "anything goes" in a meaningless and chaotic universe. Rather, these thinkers have ethical concerns about ethics. For Daoists, the fact that we need to think about either rules of conduct or appropriate forms of behavior is already indicative of a downfall from a harmonious existence when ethics was not yet necessary. Thus, the good is not only irrevocably connected to the bad, but may in fact foster it, because ethics can only work by a process of exclusion, which divides the acceptable from the unacceptable. Furthermore, norms of behavior only need to be established when human beings become incapable of accommodating differences. Focusing on Confucian virtues, the *Daodejing* 道德經 recognizes that striving for these virtues often masks the pursuit of public recognition, which is why it holds up the model of a sage who tries to remain invisible (see *DDJ* Ch 49).[7] Ethical proclamations breed hypocrisy. In an ideal world, we would not need ethics, and the "ten thousand things" would flourish in their diverse splendor, not in spite of but through their differences. Each being would provide an opening for another, rather than trying to mold others into an appropriate shape.

Nietzsche is a Western thinker who is even more radical in his condemnation of ethics. For him, ethics is symptomatic of beings that are addicted to knowledge to the extent that we assiduously try to render ourselves and the world amenable to comprehension. This is the epitome of human arrogance, because we attempt to reconfigure the world in *our image* as human beings, as we become desperate to see nothing but our own reflection wherever we go. This means that we also seethe

---

6 Confucius, *The Analects of Confucius: A Philosophical Translation*, trans. Roger Ames and Henry Rosemont (New York: Ballantine Books, 1998).

7 *Daodejing* (Beijing: Beijing daxue chubanshe, 1995).

with resentment against the natural world, which does not so willingly offer itself up to the tentacles of knowledge, and we try to sever our connection to nature. Ethics for Nietzsche is about assimilation. Brutality and violence often underlie the ethical quest as we make ourselves and others into creatures that can be known. Human beings pit themselves against the natural world that they inhabit and that also inhabits them, trying to extirpate passions and desire. In turning against nature in this way, we also direct this fury against ourselves. For Nietzsche, ethics always has a violent underbelly and unleashes a spiral of a consumptive knowledge that swallows everything in its wake. The true challenge is learning to remain open to beings and things that do not resemble oneself and to sounds which are unfamiliar. He does not deny that this will result in conflict as well as friendship, but confrontation with difference is less hypocritical than forcibly blotting it out. The zealous guarding of homogeneous boundaries suffocates unique and particular individuals, since we depend upon "foreign" influences in order to engage in the process of self-becoming that is so important to Nietzsche. In one sense, the challenge that he offers is not altogether different from that of Daoist thinkers, because he advocates a movement beyond good and evil that allows us to affirm existence in its entirety rather than seething with resentment, because the world as it is is not as it should be. Yet, at the same time, there is no denying that Nietzsche is obsessed with fostering the endless creativity of self-making. According to Nietzsche, we need the radically other, both as jousting partner and as lover, to become and create ourselves. In this sense, there is a latent danger in his philosophy that the obsession with individual creativity can encourage an openness to others for the sake of oneself, and thus result in a return to the very egoism that he hopes to go beyond.

Kierkegaard also worries about the uniformity that ethics can promote. Nothing is more reprehensible to him than the judgmental bourgeois citizen, pompously satisfied that he has achieved the correct family structure, owns the right amount of property, and holds a respectable career (*EO II*).[8]

8 Søren Kierkegaard, *Either/Or Part II*, trans. Howard V. Hong and Edna H. Hong (Princeton: Princeton University Press, 1987).

Others who do not imitate this prototype are simply scorned. It is no coincidence that the character Wilhelm, who exemplifies this in Kierkegaard's work, is indeed a judge. Kierkegaard highlights the position of the stranger who cannot so easily be accommodated into existing ethical frameworks. For him, religious faith in God, who is truly radically other, is necessary if we are to be able to embrace the unknown and unfamiliar. The difficult nature of this task is revealed by his insistence that it requires a leap of faith, and a plunge into the unknown. Only God, makes possible the kind of love that is not based on possession, but rather a love of the particular for its own sake. Nothing irks Kierkegaard more than the universalizing tendencies of ethics, which abstracts from difference. This does not mean that Kierkegaard rejects ethics outright, for he recognizes that it satisfies a very human need to live in a comfortable abode, but faith is required to periodically shake us out of our slumber, and prevent our ethical decision-making from simply degenerating into ethical judgmentalism.

Thinkers such as Nietzsche and Kierkegaard do not simply hope to overturn or dismiss ethics. Their efforts to expose its darker face also aim to resuscitate it by engendering a genuine openness to other beings. They point out that the real challenge inheres not in spurning the other, which is easily done, but in embracing him. Nonetheless, the question of creating a unique self-identity is central to both philosophers, and the other is still perceived as other to the self. Even the language of "otherness" defines the "other" in relation to the "self" and thus alludes to the self's centrality. This is why Daoist thinkers take a step that even Kierkegaard and Nietzsche would be hesitant to take. Zhuangzi advocates a forgetting of the self, encouraging us to abandon the quest for identity of any kind, for this is the best way to care for the self (*Zh* 6:58). Instead of looking in the mirror in order to elicit the praise of others, sages offer themselves up as mirrors in order to allow others to become what they are. The sage also changes as a result of the transformation of others. The mirror is not a symbol of perpetual self-reflection and narcissism, but rather of mutual transformation. It takes on a different hue depending on whom it encounters. The ideal ruler in the *Daodejing* is invisible and thus not held up as a figure to be emulated. Instead, he or she is adept at teasing out the unique characteristics of others without giving the impression of doing anything at all. Zhuangzi's sage on the other hand, goes even further, and usually repudiates politics. The position of ruler already promotes a hierarchy with which Zhuangzi is uncomfortable. His stories are replete with individuals who hold no official positions and cling to no identity. Many of them are social outcasts and thus freed from the shackles of moral convention. Because they are unconstrained by traditional roles, they attract others toward them, allowing for many to flourish in their nonassertive presence. They become leaders, precisely because they neither instruct nor judge. Confucian ethics is viewed with the kind of cynicism that Nietzsche directs at Christian morality, namely as a form of social and political control. Instead, Zhuangzi advocates interrelationships which are not based on preexisting notions of how a person should be, but rather seek out ways of engaging with others in a spontaneous and open manner. If the preoccupation with self-identity is abandoned, then ethical guidelines would become obsolete. Benevolence and justice would not be extolled but would happen spontaneously. This is a tall order indeed, but for Daoist thinkers, it is the only hope for the flourishing of the ten-thousand things.

* * *

In this book, I engage with thinkers from Chinese and Western philosophical traditions who uphold the sanctity of ethics, as well as examining those who maintain that ethics rests on a fundamentally unethical foundation. Instead of conducting a survey of ethical approaches in China and the West, I build a dialogue between Western and Chinese thinkers in order to forefront some of the assumptions that underlie the respective traditions. The first part of my book explores approaches from Chinese and Western traditions that insist on the primacy of ethics. The second part explores thinkers who question the status that ethics enjoys, exposing its sinister aspects, and advocating the need to go beyond ethics.

Chapter One looks into the thoughts of Kant and Confucius, since both are thinkers for whom ethics is the primary concern. While Kant insists that we imagine a world that transcends nature wherein the purity of form prevails, Confucius remarks that ethics is a particularly human way of integrating into the world. Both thinkers impute to human beings a special place within the cosmos, insisting that human beings are owed dignity and respect by virtue of being human. However, Kant assumes that each individual represents humanity as a whole, while for Confucius, developing our interconnectedness is the principal activity of humanization. For both, morality is always in process and it is rather difficult to live up to our human potential.

Chapter Two compares the thought of Mencius with that of Rousseau, because they both maintain that harmonization with nature is an essential part of cultivating virtue. However, they view our relationship with nature very differently. Rousseau maintains that the process of socialization is necessarily indicative of a departure from nature and that human beings in the state of nature were naturally asocial. Morality becomes a culturally mediated attempt to imitate the harmony within the state of nature at the social level. The process is fraught with tension, because the state of nature is beyond our grasp. Mencius, on the other hand, attributes to human beings a natural sociality that must be properly nourished in order to grow to fruition. Through judgment and reasoning, we are able to extend this natural sociality to those who are more removed from us. Like Rousseau, he is worried about the effects of convention divorced from its natural roots; for Mencius, morality is an extension of the natural process, while for Rousseau, it is necessary because we have departed from nature.

Chapter Three begins the second part of the book by examining works by Kierkegaard and Daoists. Both are critical of the universalist bent of ethics, suggesting that it is closely connected to the conventional pursuit of knowledge. Kierkegaard sees faith as the movement beyond ethics that allows us to affirm the particular, but God is needed to wrest us from the ego-self in order to open ourselves to the radical alterity of the other. In Daoist thought, the need to celebrate the *de* 德 of unique virtues of the ten-thousand things is extolled. The sage does not need to have recourse to morality because he is able to provide the opening that allows the *de* of others to be expressed. It is significant that Kierkegaard's thought demands an external God, in the face of whom we are made acutely aware of our finitude to wrest us from the ego-self, for this indicates that we are very much riveted to the self we have to let go. There is no radical other in Daoist thinking because there is no preoccupation with self-identity which is prevalent in Kierkegaard's writings.

Chapter Four juxtaposes Nietzschean and Daoist pleas to go beyond good and evil. Morality promotes the kind of egoism that allows human beings to exercise dominion over nature, silencing the multiplicity of the cosmos. Language and the reification of the concept are the means by which morality operates, hindering a genuinely spontaneous interaction with the environment and situating the human being at the center of all existence. According to both Daoist thinkers and Nietzsche, the process of labeling something good necessitates exclusion of the bad. Good is always constructed against evil, so it depends upon the very dynamic it purports to destroy. Nietzsche and Daoist thinkers share the need to affirm life in all its diversity. However, there is also a marked difference between these modes of thinking. The Daoist sage is blissfully unconcerned with his or her identity and thus is able to wander through life, undergoing constant transformations that would make most people tremble. Meanwhile, Nietzsche indicates that we will always be drawn to the bounded, but that we must periodically collapse our bounded nature in order to relish in the unbounded. Thus, we are concerned with preserving the self, but we must alternate between protecting it and letting go of the constraints of individuation.

In the concluding chapter, I argue that even the most vociferous critics of ethics do not advocate its complete abandonment. Instead, I maintain that they encourage us to recognize its limits, and the unethical tendencies it might inadvertently foster. Because ethics is often part of a process in which we try to build what Kierkegaard refers to as a "comfortable abode," it can easily transform from a process of continuous cultivation to a desire for the acquisition of "ethical properties" which are recognized by others. Critics of ethics want us to be aware of the dangers of this dynamic, which is why they suggest we must venture beyond ethics to keep it vibrant.

PART I

THE ESTEEM OF ETHICS

CHAPTER ONE

Taking a Stand: The Moral Philosophy of Confucius and Kant[1]

Kant and Confucius share a commitment to morality, which they see not only as the ultimate duty of human beings, but also as the highest expression of our humanity. Both thinkers take upon themselves the challenge of instructing human beings on how to take a moral stand in the midst of moral decline. Morality is not necessarily the outgrowth of civilization and in fact, as Rousseau has famously argued, ethical conduct slips by the wayside as we become more civilized. Philosophers of almost every age bemoan the deplorable state of morality in their own eras and believe that they are witnesses to moral depravity as a result of years of decay and neglect. Kant notes that culture and refinement do not go hand in hand with morality: "To a high degree, we are, through art and science, *cultured*. We are civilized—perhaps too much for our own good—in all sorts of social grace and decorum. But to consider ourselves as having reached *morality*—for that, much is lacking" (OH 422).[2] In words that ring eerily true, he wonders whether we will find ourselves in a "hell of evils" which will eventuate in the annihilation of civilization "through a barbarous devastation" (OH 421). Confucius is also dismayed by the precipitous decline in moral standards and reflects back with longing for previous eras when virtuous leaders such as the Duke of Zhou and the sage-kings Yao and Shun acted as moral inspiration for their people.

---

1 Part of this chapter was originally published as an article in *Dao: A Journal of Comparative Philosophy* VII, no. 3 (2008): 257–268.

2 Immanuel Kant, "Idea for a Universal History from a Cosmopolitan Point of View," in *Kant Selections*, ed. Lewis White Beck (New York: Macmillan Publishing Company, 1988).

How we take a moral stand constitutes a marked difference between the two thinkers. According to Kant, in considering any action I am about to take, I must imagine that I am part of a world in which each individual human being is an end in herself, apart from the world of nature. Furthermore, I must act *as though* my act could be based on a universalizable maxim. This is intended to guard against actions that are motivated primarily by the pursuit of self-interest, but also pits individuals against the world of nature of which they are a part. Conversely, in Confucian philosophy, my position is always determined by my relationships with others and thus is necessarily fluid. I not only imagine another in my place but also consider how my place is effected as a result of my relationship with others, and how my own moral horizons might be continuously expanded. Nevertheless, this expansion of moral horizons does have limits because it takes place within the framework of a social hierarchy and within the context of a particular culture that is necessary to retain social order.

Morality and Nature

Kantian moral philosophy, with its emphasis on the universalization of the moral law, appears to be a profound moral purism. His categorical imperative stipulates that "I ought never to act in such a way that I could not also will that my maxim should be universal law" (*FMM* 254). Focusing on the act of universalization, Roger Sullivan notes that Kantian thought is fuelled by the "demand for consistency and non-contradiction" that makes reciprocity possible.[3] However, I would argue that if one acknowledges the central role that Kant imputes to willing within his philosophy, one develops a slightly different image of his ethics. Willing, in Kant, is an act that involves overcoming empirical and natural inclinations. When he opens *Foundations of the Metaphysics of Morals* with the suggestion that nothing "could be called good without qualification except a GOOD WILL" (*FMM* 248), he is not arguing that moral purity

3 Roger J. Sullivan, *An Introduction to Kant's Ethics* (Cambridge: Cambridge University Press, 1994), p. 46.

be held in the utmost esteem, but rather acknowledges that morality is based upon an enduring tension with the empirical and natural world. When acting morally, I must *imagine* a world in which the universality of my maxims were possible and act on this basis, but at the same time realize that if such a perfect moral order existed, then the need for morality would be obviated. Kant's ethical philosophy is based not on contempt for contradiction but rather on a love of it. Morality can never be perfectly realized, for if it could, it would not exist. This is why, in framing our maxims, we must think *as though* we could universalize them all the while, recognizing that we will never be completely successful in our efforts because nature will remain an enduring impediment to our success.

Indeed, since we are divided beings, whose empirical inclinations and desires threaten to tarnish the moral law, we will never acquire what Kant refers to as the pure holy will, for it is a will upon which empirical elements have no sway:

> This holiness of will is, however, a practical ideal which must necessarily serve as a model which all finite rational beings must strive toward even though they cannot reach it. . . . The utmost that finite practical reason can accomplish is to make sure of the unending progress of its maxims towards this model. . . . This is virtue, and as a naturally acquired faculty, it can never be perfect, because assurance in such a case never becomes apodictic certainty and as a mere opinion it is very dangerous.
>
> (*CPrR* 33)

As Paul Saurette points out, "we must recognize the distance between the perfection of the law and our fallibility" which then imbues us with the humility that is central to Kant's moral theory.[4] Kant's emphasis on humility may seem somewhat surprising, given the high premium he places on autonomy and reason. However, it is the very awareness of the distance between our own imperfection and the moral law that can provide the impetus to improve upon the world rather than merely remaining satisfied with the status quo. Furthermore, humility also can

4 Paul Saurette, "Kant's Culture of Humiliation: Politics and Ethical Cultivation," *Philosophy and Social Criticism* 28, no.1 (2002): 61.

help to rein in the selfishness that, for Kant, is the greatest obstacle to morality. As Richard Kroner suggests, morality "is meaningful only as long as we are imperfect."[5]

Kantian philosophy is characterized by a very ambivalent attitude toward nature. Kant asserts that moral law is necessarily distinct from natural causality, which he describes as the "direct opposite of freedom" (*CPrR* 29). Nonetheless, the certitude of natural law is something he wishes to replicate in moral law. He exhorts us to design a second "moral nature" which imitates the more robust and inexorable physical laws of "first nature": "Ask yourself whether, if the action which you propose should take place by a law of nature of which you yourself were a part, and could regard it as possible through your will" (*CPrR* 70). We must manifest our independence from nature by authoring our own laws, rather than succumbing to those which are forced upon us: "For as an end in himself, he is destined to be a lawgiver in the realm of ends, free from all laws of nature and obedient only to those laws which he himself gives" (*FMM* 278). As Kroner suggests, because it is not given to us but rather created, this is not a world that can be understood by theoretical means.[6] We must imagine a parallel moral universe that is like nature but at the same time distinct from it. Because morality is defined in opposition to the causal world of nature, moral worth depends upon the impossibility of creating the perfect moral world. Nature will always interfere with our efforts. If the perfect world already existed, it would not have to be made, and therefore would not be an expression of our freedom. If the realm of the "ought" could be collapsed into the world of the "is," the "ought" would cease to exist.

Since Kant's philosophy is predicated on a division within the self that impels us to overcome our heteronomous drives, he delights in the notion of mastery over the self. This is reflected in the effusive odes to duty that are sprinkled throughout his texts:

> Thus the first proposition of morality is that to have genuine moral worth an action must be done from duty. The second proposition is: an action done

---

5 Richard Kroner, *Kant's Weltanshauung* (Chicago: University of Chicago Press, 1956), p. 24.

6 Ibid., p. 3.

> from duty does not have its moral worth in the purpose which is to be achieved through it but in the maxim whereby it is determined. The third principle, as a consequence of the two preceding I would express as follows: Duty is the necessity to do an action from respect for the law.
>
> (*FMM* 253)

Duty represents the triumph over nature within ourselves. We act as though reason could stand on its own. Nonetheless, we can never know if duty alone is indeed the impetus behind our actions; thus, our efforts are endless. As H. J. Paton points out, "a completely good and perfect will would never act for the sake of duty; for in the very idea of duty there is the thought of desires and inclination to be overcome."[7]

Kant's moral legalism is a conscious fantasy wherein we imagine a world of completely autonomous and self-originating agents. It is the impossible possibility that encourages us to mold ourselves into moral beings. However, this drive may also spring from a profound frustration regarding our inability to really *know* the noumenal world. In his *Critique of Pure Reason*, Kant famously remarked that our alleged "knowledge" of the world arises out of the manner in which the mind structures our experiences; thus, the world as it is, or the thing-in-itself, always eludes us. This limitation, in Kant's view, is also the wellspring of our freedom which enables us to create a moral universe independently of empirical constraints. While *a priori* structures of the mind help us to wade through an overabundance of shifting empirical data, they are nevertheless dependent upon external phenomena. Through morality, we set up a refuge from the world of nature wherein we become self-originating with an unadulterated rationality as its own precondition. However, we never have direct access to the noumenal sphere, for this would spell the end of human freedom. If we were to gain such access, Kant remarks that:

> Instead of conflict which now the moral disposition has to wage with inclinations, and in which, after some defeats, moral strength of mind may be gradually won, God and eternity in their awful majesty would stand unceasingly before our eyes. . . . The conduct of man, so long as his nature remained as it

7 H. J. Paton, *The Categorical Imperative* (London: Hutchison, 1967), p. 46.

> is now, would be changed into mere mechanism, whereas in a puppet show, everything would gesticulate well but no life would be found in the figures.
> (*CPrR* 152)

Freedom is not absolute, but rather arises out of the position we occupy straddled uncomfortably between the noumenal and phenomenal aspects of our being. But if morality is to survive, we must *imagine* the possibility of complete noumenal freedom, even though it remains eternally beyond our grasp. The Kantian moral universe depends upon imagination as much as it does on reason.

Some of Kant's ethical writings suggest that reason must constantly do battle with the muddied world of nature, which is the source of our moral woes. However, when one delves more widely into his corpus, including the *Critique of Judgment*, the possibility is raised that reason in interaction with nature can have disturbing effects. He implies that reason infuses chaos into the world of nature because of its totalizing tendencies: "But now the mind listens to the voice of reason which—for every given magnitude, even for those that cannot be entirely apprehended, although (in sensible representation) they are judged as entirely given—requires totality. It does not even exempt the infinite from this requirement" (*CJ* 93).[8] This taste for totality can generate the impulse to carve out the world in our image. Kant notes that human beings find "natural things of advantage for their own designs" which, he remarks, are often foolish, "for his reason knows how to give things a conformity with his own arbitrary fancies for which he was not at all predestined by nature" (*CJ* 214). This passage interestingly suggests that reason can be responsible for excess and imbalance. Nature, in turn, is infused with a kind of purposiveness reflected in the harmonious order of the whole: "For a thing to be a natural purpose, in the first place it is requisite that its parts are only possible through their reference to the whole" (*CJ* 220).

The *Critique of Judgment* raises the specter of a somewhat different relationship between nature and reason than Kant describes in his ethical writings. Reason synthesizes what might otherwise be inchoate ex-

8 Immanuel Kant, *Critique of Judgment*, trans. J. H. Bernard (New York: Hafner Publishing Company, 1968).

periences. But in so doing, reason comes up against its own limits, and its desire to operate unobstructed in its quest for totality can unleash a desire for freedom. Kant exposes the destructive underbelly of our lust for freedom which is unique to human beings: "The love of freedom is naturally so strong in man that when once he has grown accustomed to freedom, he will sacrifice everything for its sake. . . . Owing to his natural love of freedom it is necessary that man should have his natural roughness smoothed down; with animals, their instinct renders this unnecessary" (*LP* 3).[9]

When we act in accordance with moral maxims, we imagine a world in which the purity of reason prevails and it encounters no resistance. In this way, we are able to tame our own destructive impulses because reason in the moral realm can assert its sovereignty in a manner that is impossible in the empirical realm. In fact, Kant notes that "without the development of moral ideals, that which we prepared by culture call 'sublime' would present itself 'to the uneducated man as merely terrible'" (*CJ* 105). Thus, morality assures us of the superiority of reason and mitigates our fears in the face of something larger than we can imagine. By claiming in morality a domain for itself and upholding it as the height of human dignity, we are able to diminish the frustration that emerges through reason's encounter with the world. Because we keep acting as though reason were a self-enclosed sphere, and as though it were already independent of nature, we can then begin to resist the impulse to use others and nature to further our own ends. The imaginary "purity" of reason is not only to protect ourselves from natural desires and impulses, but also to protect the world from our reason.

The ingenuity of Kantian philosophy inheres in the fact that he recognizes the need for contradiction that sustains morality. It is always in the making because it will always meet resistance. Kant undermines the "realist" position that the empirical world is amoral and therefore we should adapt to the way the world is, rather than engaging in a futile pursuit of what it should be. Kant recognizes that only human beings can be moral as a result of the uneasy position they occupy ensconced in the

9 Immanuel Kant, *Lectures on Pedagogy*, in *On Education* (London: Kegan Paul, 1897).

world of nature and yet imbued with an insatiable desire to overcome it. But it is not just nature that is to be overcome. The interaction of reason within the world of nature also poses a grave threat to morality.

The resistance of nature to our moral efforts renders morality admirable, but also flies in the face of the powerful need for human happiness. Kant tacitly acknowledges that this is perhaps the weakest strand in his moral theory. The necessary faith in rationality is severely tested if moral reason must relentlessly wage battles with the surrounding world: "To be in need of happiness and also worthy of it and yet not to partake of it could not be in accordance with the complete volition of an omnipotent rational being" (*CPrR* 110). The highest good is when virtue and happiness coincide. Virtue is not a perfect good in itself and "this happiness is also required" in order to complete reason (*CPrR* 110). Reason demands not just a rational universe, but a harmonious one. The highest good eludes us because its realization depends upon the perfection of moral virtue. In a somewhat startling move, Kant then insists that "the highest good is practically possible only on the supposition of the immortality of the soul" which "derives from the practically necessary condition of a duration adequate to the perfect fulfillment of the moral law" (*CPrR* 137). Furthermore, only God can ensure that happiness and virtue exist in a relationship that satisfies reason's yearning for proportion. Since Kant does not want us to act morally because of God's sanction, he insists that God is a mere postulate of reason, refusing to make truth claims about his existence. This is a desperate attempt to preserve the autonomy of reason. It turns out that reason depends upon faith, which Kant insists emerges out of the needs of reason.

For Confucius, this kind of dilemma does not arise, because there is no attempt to separate virtue from nature in Kant's fashion. The universe does offer a patterned order, and nature is inscribed with meaning, although it cannot be known, nor can it be reduced to human discourse: "We can learn from the Master's cultural refinements, but do not hear him discourse on subjects such as our 'natural disposition' and 'the way of *tian* 天 [heaven]'" (*A* 5:13). Spirituality and naturalness are included in the meaning of *tian* and cannot be disentangled. Although *tian* is often translated as heaven, this translation is rather misleading. Roger Ames and Henry Rosemont point out that *tian* is often used in conjunction with *di* 地 (earth) to indicate that it is not independent of this world,[10] but both transcendent and immanent. There is neither a differentiation between creator and created, nor the assumption that *tian* is separate from human beings. *Tian* creates all things not through the willful act of an omnipotent being, but rather through constant generation, which imbues us with a sense of pattern, order, and harmony. As human beings, we are part of this process of generation.

Like Kant, Confucius is known for an ethical philosophy that is centered upon human beings. According to Kant, human beings *give* meaning to the cosmos through morality. Confucius views things differently and suggests that human beings participate in an already meaningful cosmos in a *human* way through morality, which is also a process of spiritualization. This by no means suggests that human beings simply passively acquiesce to the order of things. As Confucius points out, while nature seems to function spontaneously, human beings do not: "Does *tian* speak? And yet the four seasons turn and the myriad things are born and grow within it. Does *tian* speak?" (*A* 17:19). *Tian*'s silence does not imply it is bereft of meaning. It takes many years of moral practice for virtue to be so refined that it comes naturally. Only at seventy years old does Confucius claim to have come close (*A* 2:4). By refusing to discourse on matters of *tian*, Confucius is not implying that we neglect it; instead, we must correlate with its patterns in an active and human way, and he repeatedly draws upon *tian* for metaphors of harmony, remarking that "*tian* has given life to and nourished excellence in me" (*A* 7:23).

We participate in the agency of *tian* rather than being, as in Kantian thought, the lone champions of freedom. Julia Ching points out that while freedom and autonomy are preoccupations of Western thinkers such as Kant, they do not figure prominently in the Chinese tradition.[11] For this reason, in Confucian thinking, there is no need to construct an imaginary parallel universe which is self-contained.

---

10 Roger T. Ames and Henry Rosemont, "Introduction," in *The Analects of Confucius: A Philosophical Translation* (New York: Ballantine Books, 1998), p. 46.

11 Julia Ching, "Chinese Ethics and Kant," *Philosophy East and West* 28, no. 2 (1978): 162.

According to Confucius, harmony must take on a specifically human form through the use of ritualized patterns and social relationships (*li* 禮). *Li* is one of the most salient markers of our humanity: "Achieving harmony is the most valuable function of observing ritual propriety. But when things are not going well, to realize harmony just for its own sake without regulating the situation through observing ritual propriety will not work" (*A* 1:12). A process of careful observation and active membership in a cultural community is necessary for human beings. Culture is not pursued for its own sake but is part of human participation in a larger, harmonious cosmos. Human beings who do not heed *li* are forsaking the particularly human way of integrating into *tian*. *Li* is a means of strengthening the sense of social and spiritual integration and also a method of ensuring continuity with the past. Harmony for human beings means nothing without participating in the social dynamics and relationships of a particular place: "Excellent persons do not dwell alone; they have neighbours" (*A* 4:25). Furthermore, memory and continuity are important in sustaining the human community. This is why Confucius remarks that a filial son would continue the customs of the father for three years, and why it is so important that individuals be familiar with the *Book of Songs* if they are to know where to stand. If Kantian philosophy depends upon tension and often Herculean efforts of the will, Confucian philosophy endeavors to ensure an enduring sense of historical connectedness and integration. Each person in social ceremonies coordinates actions harmoniously with others and if it is carried out well, no force or compulsion is necessary. It is like learning a piece of music in such a way that eventually it appears effortless.

In fact, music is a central part of the Confucian tradition. David Hall and Roger Ames point out that the term for culture, namely *wen* 文, means to inscribe and pattern.[12] Music is perhaps the best example of how cultural sociality functions, because it both depends upon tradition and demands the creative interaction of unique particulars. If music reverts to simple mimesis, then it rings hollow: "In referring time and again

---

12 Roger T. Ames and David Hall, *Thinking from the Han: Self, Truth and Transcendence in Chinese and Western Culture* (Albany: State University of New York Press, 1998), p. 33.

to making music, how could I just be talking about bells and drums?" (*A* 17:11). Music depends upon the uniqueness of each note in relation to others. There is no universal that subsumes the particular; instead, a confluence of particulars interact, which are preceded by the whole and also create it through their interplay. Dynamic harmony is important, signifying the importance of the particular in transmitting and performing ritual: "Much can be realized with music if one begins by playing in unison, and then goes on to improvise with purity of tone and distinctness of flow, thereby bringing all to completion" (*A* 3:23). This passage is interesting because the Chinese text reads: 樂其知也，始作，翕如也，從之，純如也，皦如也，繹如也以成 (*yue qi zhi ye, shi zuo, xi ru ye, cong zhi, chun ru ye, xi ru ye, yi ru ye yi cheng*). *Chun* 純, translated as purity of tone, can be read as pure and unmixed, implying a differentiation of tones as well as the purity that results in playing the notes together. *Xi* 皦, translated as distinctness of flow, has the connotation of sparkling, which highlights the interaction of distinct but not separate things. *Yi* 繹 suggests continuation. This passage implies that the delicate interplay between unity and difference leads to completeness. However, it is important to note that the passage begins by stressing the importance of harmony (*xi ru ye* 翕如也). Difference is not pursued for its own sake: "I find inspiration by intoning the songs, I learn where to stand from observing ritual propriety, and I find fulfillment in playing music" (*A* 8:7).

The problem with an approach focusing so heavily on *li* is that harmony can be founded in a narrow parochialism connecting the development of virtue tightly to entrenched social roles. This would be anathema to Kant, for whom morality is universal and independent of local customs. Confucius would vociferously disagree, for the extension of the self within one's locality provides the groundwork which makes it possible to enter unfamiliar terrain and treat others with a similar sort of decorum and respect. One cannot learn what it means to treat others as human, unless one is part of a human community oneself.

Li also serves to keep human beings within bounds and refrain from overstepping the limits: "Having gone astray, to fail to get right back on track is to stray indeed" (*A* 15:30). The Chinese text reads: 過而不改，是謂過矣 (*guo er bu gai, shi wei guo yi*). *Guo* 過 also suggests excess, and it is not straying from the path that is criticized, but the failure to transform in order to get back on track. Imbalance rather than change is the enemy. *Li* is supposed to constitute a dynamic process of cooperation with others, instead of a set of dogmatically prescribed rules.

If there is an overriding need on the part of human beings to structure experiences and know the world in the Kantian system, it is necessary in the Confucian understanding to accord with the way or the dynamic process of things, even to the point of accepting death: "If at dawn you learn of and tread the way, you can face death at dusk" (*A* 4:8). Things that one cannot know do not generate any resentment or frustration: "The master had nothing to say about strange happenings, the use of force, disorder or the spirits" (*A* 7:21). The sage experiences no antipathy or tension in relation to the world around him or her: "Exemplary persons in making their way in the world are neither bent on nor against anything; rather they go with what is appropriate" (*A* 4:10). The sage strides through the world calmly: "The exemplary person is calm and unperturbed; the petty person is always agitated and anxious" (*A* 7:37).

Acting in harmony with the way of *tian* as the sage does is no easy task. Although Confucius himself does not offer an explicit account of why this is the case, a possible answer can be pieced together from some of his sayings. The primary obstacle that Confucius confronts in his environment is the pursuit of personal advantage, which causes not only internal imbalance but continued warfare and political strife: "Exemplary persons cherish their excellence; petty persons cherish their land. Exemplary persons cherish fairness; petty persons cherish the thought of gain" (*A* 4:11). While the exemplary person tries to extend the self to accord with the cosmos and include others, the petty person tries to extend the self by appropriating other things and people. Although antithetical, these two processes are related. The petty person tries to make the cosmos synonymous with the self by engulfing it. The virtuous person tries to perpetually broaden the self in order to attune to the cosmos. Each of these processes implicitly assumes that unlike other natural beings, human beings must consciously transform themselves in an attempt to become one with the world.

Speech both arises from and produces social interaction, making possible dissonance within *tian*. As Confucius's own repeated juxtapositions between the virtuous and petty persons illustrate, speech invites a process of comparison that enables human beings to entertain the possibility of becoming something other than they are. Through this comparison, we are also reminded of our inadequacies. The ensuing vulnerability impels some to greedily appropriate, and others to incessantly improve upon themselves by always seeking out harmonious relationships *with* others.

Speech is both beneficial and necessary, but also perilous because it can undercut the harmony of *tian*. In a humorous passage, Confucius tacitly pokes fun at his own garrulous nature: "The master said, 'I desire not to speak.' Zigong responded: 'If you do not speak, how will we, your little followers, find the proper way?' The master responded: 'Does *tian* speak? And yet the four seasons turn and the myriad things are born and grow within it. Does *tian* speak?'" (*A* 17:19). Confucius reflects with longing upon a time where speech and the deliberate cultivation of virtue were not necessary. Now, even in order to *not* speak, Confucius must speak. He hopes that we can somehow attain nature's unspoken harmony, but recognizes that he must do so through speech, which is always rather clumsy: "All under *tian* have long since lost their way and *tian* is going to use your master as a wooden bell-clapper" (*A* 3:24). The kind of spoken and performed harmony that human beings engage in is rarely, if ever, in complete accord with nature as reference to the "wooden" bell clapper suggests. Only decades of practice offer any hope of rendering morality natural.

Li as a form of social communication is closely related to speech, since it encompasses nonverbal forms of expression. It must be deliberately cultivated, and offers individuals a social vocabulary in addition to boundaries demarcating what is acceptable from what is not: "Do not look at anything that violates the observance of ritual propriety; do not listen to anything that violates the observance of ritual propriety; do not speak about anything that violates the observance of ritual propriety; do not do anything that violates the observance of ritual propriety" (*A* 12:1). *Li* is supposed to complement and extend nature, as exemplified in the interpretation of a passage from the *Songs* that describes a woman's makeup:

> What does the song mean when it says:
> Her smiling cheeks—so radiant,
> Her dazzling eyes—so sharp and clear,
> It is the unadorned that enhance colour?
> The master replied: "The application of colour is to the unadorned."
> "Does this mean that observing ritual propriety comes after?" asked Zixia.
> The master replied: "Zixia, you have stimulated my thoughts. It is only with the likes of you that one can discuss the *Songs*."
>
> (*A* 3:8)

The woman's makeup must be tailored to the unadorned contours of the face and cannot simply be forced upon it. Ideally, artifice supplements and enhances nature: "When one's basic disposition [*zhi* 質] overwhelms refinement [*wen* 文] the person is boorish. When refinement overwhelms one's basic disposition the person is an officious scribe. It is only when one's basic disposition and refinement are in appropriate balance that you have the exemplary person" (*A* 6:18).

Li appears to involve a dynamic interplay between the external and internal, whereby the external requirements of custom are internalized and also transformed in the process through the individual's participation in them. A balance must be struck between the need to maintain social boundaries and their continuous transformation. Human beings make themselves "natural" by purposively training themselves to the point where *li* becomes spontaneous, just as a good pianist must engage in tedious repetition before being able to play so well that the music emerges from her fingers almost effortlessly. The naturalness of human beings is cultivated consciously and deliberately.

The problem with *li* is that our cultural accoutrements can be treated as external possessions, used to wield influence and gain social standing. Because *li* depends very much on social recognition, it can easily devolve into a quest for reputation: "Scholars of old would study for their own sake [*wei ji* 為己], while those today do so to impress others [*wei ren* 為人]" (*A* 14:24). The self is viewed as a vessel in need of praise from others. *Li* then remains an external appendage and therefore alien. Because integration is seen in terms of possession rather than participation, it is ultimately dissatisfying and unleashes an insatiable desire for more. If *li* is properly incorporated into one's being, then I transform as well as being transformed by *li*; but in doing so, I can never undermine the overall harmony of social relationships: "If people can recite all of three hundred *Songs* and yet when given official responsibility, fail to perform effectively, or when sent to distant quarters, are unable to act on their own initiative, then even though they have mastered so many of them, what good are they to them?" (*A* 13:5). Confucius repeatedly warns against blindly following tradition and praises Zengxi who, when asked what he would do if his worth were finally recognized, says he would take several boys to bathe in the Yi river and return home singing (*A* 11:26). Reputation is of no concern to him. Although *li* prescribes limits, it must not function as an enclosed sphere wherein we dogmatically repeat familiar and socially approved actions.

Confucius remarks that it is easy to follow the prescriptions of custom, but it is much more difficult to become an exemplary person: "In the niceties of culture I am perhaps like other people. But as far as personally succeeding in living the life of the exemplary person, I have accomplished little" (*A* 7:33). Confucius's emphasis on sincerity indicates that he is all too cognizant of the perils of language when it is treated as an external adornment, for this makes deception possible. This is why he repeatedly reminds us of the need to live up to one's word. He remarks that the "ancients were loath to speak because they would be ashamed if they personally did not live up to what they said" (*A* 4:22).

For Kant, the schism between human beings and nature is not only irreparable, but enables human beings to be moral in the first place. According to Confucius, human beings are not separate from nature, but they can fail to correlate with it effectively. Human beings must transform in order to harmonize with nature that already is. This is why Confucius insists that "it is the person who is able to broaden the way, not the way that broadens the person" (*A* 15:29). Human beings do intentionally what nature does spontaneously. When Confucius indicates that he desires not to speak, he recognizes the effort that human beings must now make, hoping to imitate the effortless harmonization of nature. But, by *telling* us that he wants to be silent, he also acknowledges that human beings cannot escape their own intentionality. It is the nature of human beings to strive to become natural and this always also marks them apart from nature, and transforms them into spiritual beings at the same time. Human beings must do intentionally what nature does naturally. Years of practice are needed to *become* natural and Confucius holds little hope that most people can accomplish this: "The common people can be induced to travel along the way, but they cannot be induced to realize it" (*A* 8:9). Morality is a process of actively cultivating what nature already is. We need artifice and culture in order to become natural, but this same artifice can also interfere with the process of "naturalization."

Becoming Human

The moral universe which Kant envisions presupposes that one must bestow upon human beings respect and dignity based solely on their humanity, which is defined by the capacity to reason. To be moral, "it is required that reason only presuppose itself" (*CPrR* 19). Reason differentiates human beings from nature and confers on them a special status that is central to Kant's moral worldview. By virtue of reason, each person is a representative of humanity as a whole and must be treated as such. We must act toward human beings as though they were a complete world unto themselves and not a means to another's end. Morality is the condition under which alone a rational being can be an end in himself, because only through it is it possible to be a "lawgiving member in the realm of ends" (*FMM* 277). Kantian morality is based on common rather than shared ground.

The respect owed to all human beings is based on his or her potential qua rational being. This is the case even if they refuse to exercise their rationality, falling short of the ideal of humanity. One must treat others as though the perfect moral universe already existed, while recognizing that it does not.

Kant prevails upon us to act in accordance with duty alone, and while this sounds austere, it is intended to safeguard human beings from selfish motives. Undoubtedly, there are problems with this approach, for it does not necessitate care for another human being. For example, it would not be morally acceptable to lie to a person, even if he or she is an assassin who is preparing to kill another and my falsehood could prevent this tragedy. I could not will that lying be universalized because this would constitute an affront to the dignity of humanity, which is represented in the assassin. But in this case, out of respect for the universal law, I may not be respecting the victim as an end in him- or herself. Treating a person as such may require attentiveness to his or her particular situation. Yet, taking another's particularity into account is tantamount to succumbing to the heteronomy of nature: "Thus all material principles, which place the determining ground of choice in the pleasure or displeasure to be received from the reality of any object whatsoever, are entirely of one kind. Without exception they belong under the principle of self-love or one's own happiness" (*CPrR* 20–1). According to Kant, morality cannot be based on how another is connected to me, but rather must be based on the common humanity that we all share. Catherine Chalier notes that it is the universality and humanity in an abstract sense that is respected rather than the "singularity of every human person." [13] Therefore, it is possible to act morally toward someone, even while holding them in utter contempt, provided my actions are based on moral duty alone.

Often criticized for his relative silence on questions of substance by thinkers such as Charles Taylor, who attributes his proceduralism to a reluctance to speak of substantive notions of the good,[14] Kant himself makes no attempt to conceal this formalism: "If a rational being can think of its maxims as practical universal laws, he can do so only by considering them as principles which contain the determining grounds of the will because of their form and not because of their matter" (*CPrR* 26). There are several reasons for his position. He has hinted in the *Critique of Judgment* that selfishness can arise out of the encounter between

---

13 Catherine Chalier, *What Ought I to Do?: Morality in Kant and Levinas*, trans. Jane Marie Todd (Ithaca: Cornell University Press, 2002), p. 30.

14 Charles Taylor argues that the shift to proceduralism reflects a peculiarly modern emphasis on individual freedom: "Beyond the common weight of modern epistemology on them, it is clear how for both the stress on the procedural is bound up with their allegiance to modern freedom. To make practical reason substantive implies that practical wisdom is a matter of seeing an order which in some sense is in nature." See Taylor, *Sources of the Self: The Making of Modern Identity* (Cambridge: Cambridge University Press, 1989), p. 86.

reason and matter, since this can generate the desire to recast the world in one's own image. Even if form cannot be completely isolated from matter, actions which attempt to preserve the purity of form provide at least a partial check against the often totalizing tendencies of reason to sculpt the world, according to our own selfish ends: "He must concede that the ground of obligation here must not be sought in the nature of man or in the circumstances in which he is placed but a priori solely in the concepts of pure reason. . . . All moral philosophy rests solely on its pure part" (*FMM* 245–6). Furthermore, if Kant were to lay out a blueprint for moral behavior for us to follow, we would not be acting as autonomous agents. Thus, Kant's commitment to form serves two main purposes: it provides a check against the slide into moral opportunism that arises when I try to tailor an action to suit my needs; on the other hand, it upholds the autonomy of the individual by allowing scope for individual judgment.

In the Kingdom of Ends, each person constitutes a whole unto him- or herself. The virtue of such a position is that no individual can legitimately be sacrificed for another, because in denying one individual his or her status as an end, we dismantle the entire moral edifice. We are connected to each other through the universal reason that we all share. Morality is derived from a relationship that one has with reason. The disadvantage of this position is that the social dimension of Kantian philosophy is introduced surreptitiously and arises from common judgments independently arrived at. At the same time, the dignity of the individual is imputed to her as a rational being that is apart from the world she is in. Kantian morality will always rest on a profound tension between the world as it ought to be and the world as it is. The virtue of this stance is that it is intended to protect us from a sinister pragmatism that simply adapts to existing circumstances. Kant provides a justification for moral idealism that ought to be pursued even if the world as it is always falls far short of our moral vision. If the universe were already a moral one, we would not have the freedom to make it so. This deflates the kind of Machiavellian argument which insists that the only realistic approach is to adapt to the world as it already is.

Confucius also makes his morality contingent upon locating human beings at the center of the cosmos. However, rather than viewing each individual as a representative of the whole, the whole is the social order of which each person is a part. Julia Ching points out that Chinese ethics are relational, while Kantian ethics always refers back to the self.[15] While Kantian ethics is based on the virtue of respect, Confucian ethics is based on the virtue of care. Confucius advocates the extension of the self to include an increasingly broad spectrum of people, and it is appropriate that their fate be experienced as intertwined with one's own. In order to accomplish this, one must start by attempting to broaden the immediate concern one has for members of one's family or circles of friends, so that one can eventually include even the stranger. Personal concern for another is the central node from which morality has the potential to radiate; therefore, one must maintain this center if further extension of one's moral horizons is possible. When Confucius is told about a man who turns in his own father for stealing a sheep, he insists that such an action would not be laudable in his own state and that a father should cover for his son (*A* 13:18). However, Confucius is not pretending to provide moral counsel for any state but specifically emphasizes that such an action would be considered inappropriate in his own. The ethical son would help his father to escape. Family ties are the locus of moral relationships. If one allows the root of the family to wither, then one's entire moral fiber may be weakened. For Kant, this would be a highly unethical act, for I should envision a world in which such actions were sanctioned by universal law. According to Kantian logic, I would surely not want to legitimize through universal law the protection of criminals in one's family. However, the Confucian thinker would take a very different approach, arguing that no one can take the place of the son's relationship to his father, since the role of every person within the family is unique. Therefore, the son may be the only individual with the duty to shield his father from the force of the law. From a Confucian perspective, it would not be inconsistent to claim that while it is the duty of the son to facilitate the father's escape, it would be the duty of the minister to have the man arrested. Chad Hansen points out that the prescriptive legalistic

15 Ching, "Chinese Ethics and Kant," 169.

approach of Kant is alien to the Confucian thinker, and argues that because of this, there is no Confucian understanding of moral responsibility because it "does not need one."[16] This does not mean that there is no sense of moral responsibility, because Confucius clearly stipulates that certain actions are appropriate under certain conditions.

Kant does not advocate indifference to others. He suggests that if human beings are ends in themselves, they must contribute to the happiness of others, for only in this way can they uphold the dignity and autonomy of human beings. Each human being is a representative of humanity, and as such, has a responsibility to all others:

> Humanity might indeed exist if no one contributed to the happiness of others, provided he did not intentionally detract from it, but this harmony with humanity as an end in itself is only negative, not positive, if everyone does not also endeavor as far as he can, to further the purposes of others. For the ends of any person, who is an end in himself, must as far as possible be also my ends, if that conception of an end in itself is to have its full effect on me. (*FMM* 274)

Nevertheless, the reasoning in use here is not entirely devoid of self-interest. If the conception of an end in itself is to have its full impact on me, then I must further the happiness of others. Kantian philosophy is predicated on the necessity for each human being to represent the universal. There is no such assumption in Confucian philosophy, which assumes that each person is a part of an infinite web of relationships. These relationships must be affirmed on an ongoing basis.

The virtue associated with this process of perpetual extension is *ren* 仁. If rationality is tantamount to humanization in Kantian moral terms, then *ren* epitomizes what it means to be a human being in Confucian understanding. The interconnectedness of human beings is the Confucian counterweight to selfishness. The purpose of morality is to extend the self so that it is not defined by its separateness from others, but rather includes them as part of the self. To be a Kantian moral person, I must imagine any other in my place, whereas for Confucius, my place

---

16 Chad Hansen, "Freedom and Moral Responsibility in Confucian Ethics," *Philosophy East and West* 22, no. 2 (1972): 172.

includes others. Weiming Tu points out that "a characteristic Confucian selfhood entails the participation of the other and that the reason for this desirable and necessary symbiosis of selfhood and otherness is the Confucian conception of the self as a dynamic process of spiritual development." [17]

Ren encompasses all other virtues and refers to the art of becoming human. It is not easy to render into English and is sometimes translated as love, benevolence, or human-heartedness; Confucius himself is claimed to have said that it means to "love others" (*A* 12:22). The word is composed of the characters for person (*ren* 人) and for two (*er* 二), suggesting that one cannot be a person in isolation and pointing to the indelibly social aspect of our being. The self must include others, and extending one's horizons in this way is an endless project of self-development. It is impossible to provide an all-encompassing definition for *ren* since it is multidimensional and incorporates physical, aesthetic, spiritual, and social aspects of one's comportment. Kwong-Loi Shun suggests that in the *Analects*, it is used both more narrowly to refer to one desirable quality among others, and to refer to an ethical ideal that includes all desirable qualities.[18] Like Kant, Confucius suggests that one must work hard at developing the most fundamental human virtues, but this involves an element of social integration.

In Kantian philosophy, I would imagine putting another in my place in order to determine how to act, while in Confucian ethics, one already experiences the other as part of oneself. Kant would be weary of such a position, for it leaves one open to the possibility of pursuing one's personal interest. *Ren* is not so much a perfected state of being as it is a continuous extension of the self, so that who I am is constantly developed in relation to another. It means that I begin to take the concerns of another as my own. The fact that I may not be the same person two years from now that I am today is not resented but rather expected.

---

17 Weiming Tu, "Selfhood and Otherness in Confucian Thought," in *Culture and Self: Asian and Western Perspectives*, ed. Anthony J. Marsella, George A. De Vos and Francis L. K. Hsu (New York: Tavistock Publication, 1985), p. 231.

18 Kwong-Loi Shun, "*Ren* and *Li* in the *Analects*," in *Confucius and the Analects: New Essays*, ed. Bryan V. Norden (Oxford: Oxford University Press, 2002), p. 53.

Regarding such self-extension as the essence of human activity, the moral domain in Confucius is much more far-reaching than in Kant. While Kant insists on separating custom from morality, virtually all of our actions fall into the ethical domain in Confucius, since at every moment we are members of a larger society which needs to be not only affirmed but revitalized on an ongoing basis through cultural, social, and political means. At times, Confucian judgment shows an extraordinary degree of rigidity: "If the Ji clan's use of the imperial eight rows of eight dancers in the courtyard of their estate can be condoned, what cannot be?" (*A* 3:1). Thus, we are engaged in ethical behavior when we are engaged in the customs and rituals of a community, including the performance of dance or the practice of archery. We must determine and act out our specific roles in order to be genuine parts of the whole. Undoubtedly, social integration is dependent upon hierarchy. Each person has an appropriate role within the social context, and the duties associated with these roles must be followed: "Indeed, if the ruler does not rule, the minister not minister, the father not father, and the son not son, even if there were grain, would I get to eat of it?" (*A* 12:11). This constitutes one of the most profound differences between Kant and Confucius, for this emphasis on specific roles would be anathema to Kant. Confucius would be uncomfortable with the individualism inherent in Kantian philosophy and place more emphasis on what the community does together, rather than on the individual's decision.

The centrality of the human being is common to both Confucian and Kantian philosophies. However, for Kant, this centrality is based on rationality and the assumption that each individual is a representative of humanity as a whole, while for Confucius, our humanity is more closely associated with our interconnectedness. This means that for Kant, where one stands in relation to others should not be a deciding factor when making a moral decision, while for Confucius, one's particular relationship to others will closely determine how we should act towards them. Kant would consider the contextual nature, which is a necessary part of developing one's *ren*, as highly problematic, while Confucius would argue that the abstract recognition of human worth that is prevalent in Kantian philosophy too distant and unlikely to develop genuine concern for others. Despite disagreements, they share an understanding that the humanization of human beings is a perpetual process that we can ill afford to neglect, even for a moment. We must continuously engage in a process of becoming what we are, while realizing that we will never completely live up to our *human* potential.

Moral Education

Since the art of becoming human is a difficult undertaking, both Kant and Confucius devote considerable attention to moral education. Yet, while Kantian education is concerned with training an individual to make the right kinds of decisions, Confucian education focuses on what kind of person one should become. Sor-Hoon Tan notes that the importance Confucius attributes to moral character is more in keeping with the virtue ethics extolled by MacIntyre, than it is with the deontological position adopted by Kant.[19] My efforts to cultivate my personhood must be unceasing: "As in piling up earth to erect a mountain, if, only one basketful short of completion, I stop, I have stopped. As in filling a ditch to level the ground, if having dumped only one basketful, I continue, I am progressing" (*A* 9:19). It is not the result of the action or the proximity to an intended goal that is significant, but rather the process of moral growth itself. Even if I have almost completed the task of making a mountain, what matters is not my achievement but the fact that my development has stopped. If I continue to grow, regardless of how distant my objective may be, I am engaged in the process of humanization.

The importance that Confucius attributes to moral growth means that learning is a central aspect of his ethical philosophy. Knowing is a kind of ethical attunement to one's social environs. The notion of knowledge for its own sake, predicated on the concept of a detached observer, is alien to Chinese ways of thinking. Instead, the task of *xue* 學 (learning) is, as Roger Ames and David Hall point out, "a process of becoming aware rather than a conceptually mediated knowledge of a

---

19 Sor-Hoon Tan, "Imagining Confucius: Paradigmatic Characters and Virtue Ethics," *Journal of Chinese Philosophy* 32, no. 3 (2005): 409.

world of objective fact."[20] It is no coincidence that it is the first concept introduced in the *Analects*: "Having studied, to then repeatedly apply what you have learned—is this not a source of pleasure?" (*A* 1:1). The act of learning itself is not merely a passive reception of data, but involves the integration of stimuli into the cognitive maps that we have formed based on past experiences and emotional responses. Therefore, even the art of learning is creative.

There is no indication, in Confucius, of an inherent tension between the ethical and happy life, for harmonious integration brought about through continuous learning is bound to augment happiness rather than diminish it. For Kant, morality is something that involves self-overcoming by virtue of resistance in the face of desires and pleasures. While Kant demonstrates an otherworldly approach to morality in the sense of trying to adjust the world as it is to standards of perfection, Confucius advocates seeking and fortifying the harmonious potential in the existing world. Furthermore, the notion of happiness in Kant is predicated on a notion of complete rational self-sufficiency, which allows us to choose to act based upon our moral maxims. The notion of moral self-sufficiency would not even enter Confucian consciousness since happiness is related to harmonization achieved between individuals rather than in isolation.

Through learning, one becomes cognizant of the loci of meanings that one is enmeshed in. It is not a means to the acquisition of knowledge, but rather is an opening-up of oneself that assists in one's harmonious integration into the world. Moral behavior does not issue from innate rationality, but rather demands assiduous study and cultivation. There is no claim akin to the Kantian one that in legislating the moral law for myself, I legislate for all of humanity; instead, moral education is ongoing: "A person can be said to truly love learning who, on a daily basis, is aware of what is yet to be learned, and who, from month to month, does not forget what has already been mastered" (*A* 19:5).

An awareness of how the self fits into a larger whole is of primary importance to Confucius, and thus critical reflection without taking

20 Roger T. Ames and David Hall, *Thinking Through Confucius* (Albany: State University of New York Press, 1987), p. 44.

into account the cultural context and the contributions that others have made threatens to disrupt the social order. Learning is linked to a kind of social pragmatism, which ensures that other virtues are not applied in excess. It also ensures social continuity as we defer to the wisdom of those who have gone before us:

> The flaw in being fond of acting authoritatively without equal regard for learning is that you will be easily duped; the flaw in being fond of acting wisely without equal regard for learning is that it leads to self-indulgence; the flaw in being fond of making good on one's word without equal regard for learning is that it leads one into harm's way; the flaw in being fond of candour without equal regard for learning is that it leads to rudeness; the flaw in being fond of boldness without equal regard for learning is that it leads to unruliness; the flaw in being fond of firmness without equal regard for learning is that it leads to rashness.
>
> (*A* 17:8)

This conception of learning differs substantially from the kind of moral development that Kant envisions, for it exhibits sensitivity to the particularity of circumstance.

Following Confucius, interpreters such as Zhu Xi emphasize the importance of role models and hierarchy in the process of learning: "*Xue* means to emulate. Human nature in all cases is good, but in becoming aware of goodness, there are those who lead and those who follow." [21] According to Zhu, it is impossible to improve on oneself without observing and taking to heart the superior ethical conduct of others. Role models are particularly important in a world beset by moral decay. However, blind emulation is not enough in order for effective learning to take place. Sor-Hoon Tan notes that following the examples of paradigmatic characters requires a creative imagination that is able to understand why a character acted in certain ways. Only then can we adapt the example to *new* circumstances.[22]

Confucius is willing to allow for gradations of morality, because ethical virtue must be learned and depends on the authoritative person

21 Daniel Gardner, *Zhu Xi's Reading of the Analects* (New York: Columbia University Press, 2003), p. 31.

22 Tan, "Imagining Confucius," 419.

or sage whom others can emulate when pursuing their own moral journey: "Zizhang asked about the way of the truly efficacious person. The Master said, 'Not following in the steps of others, one does not gain entrance to the inner chamber'" (*A* 11:20). The emphasis on emulation and harmony implies that there is a hierarchical dimension to Confucian thought which cannot be ignored.

Learning must be accompanied by *si* 思 (reflection) and *zhi* 知, sometimes translated as knowing or realizing, which allows one to adapt ideas and models to the unique situations one encounters: "Learning without due reflection leads to perplexity; reflection without learning leads to perilous circumstances" (*A* 2:15). Reflection without learning is considered to be more dangerous, as reflection alone, without regard for what has come before, disrupts equilibrium.

Zhi is a process of recognizing and drawing out the moral potential of the world. In order to facilitate such an emergence, one must both be receptive to one's environment while at the same time contributing to it. Moral living could not take place if the self were simply a product of its social environment, nor could it occur if the self was absolutely independent and only extrinsically related to the community in which he or she lives. Learning can be seen as a process of "taking in," while reflecting can be seen as adapting what one has learned to the unique circumstances one faces and bringing out its inherent harmony. The two processes of learning and reflection in conjunction with each other make *zhi* possible: "He inquired about realizing, and the Master said, 'Realize others.' Fan Chi did not understand and so the Master explained, 'If you promote the true into positions above the crooked, you can make the crooked true'" (*A* 12:22). In this case, knowing or realizing others is conceived of as an activity for transforming the world, and not as a passive act of recognition. In a Confucian world, there could be no imaginary Kingdom of Ends that inspires one to act *as though* it exists. Instead, the Confucian reply to the Kantian moral imperative might be to search for and cultivate the world as it should be within the world as it is. Knowing the world is also a process of transforming it by recognizing the potential inherent in it.

Although there must be a perpetual confluence of learning, reflecting, and realizing, on at least one occasion Confucius implies that reflection unaccompanied by learning is more dangerous: "Once, lost in my thoughts, I went a whole day without eating and a whole night without sleeping. I got nothing out of it, and would have been better off devoting the time to learning" (*A* 15:31). This is indicative of Confucius's penchant for humility and social deference. He is weary of undisciplined reflection that does not take into account the ritualistic patterns and hierarchical structures of society.

While the creative dimension of Confucian thought cannot be denied, it always takes place within a context of moral hierarchy. The sage is an individual who embodies the highest moral excellence and has a responsibility to transmit his knowledge while furnishing an example for others. Confucius himself remarks that his commitment to teaching is what defines him: "How would I dare to consider myself a sage or an authoritative person? What can be said about me is simply that I continue my studies without respite and instruct others without growing weary" (*A* 7:34). The *Shuowen* lexicon 說文解字 defines *sheng ren* 聖人 (sage) as deriving from the ear radical, implying it has the connotation of listening and communicating with.[23] The sage is both receptive to others and an effective communicator. Confucius himself notes that at sixty his ear "was attuned" (*A* 2:4). The emphasis on hearing and communication rather than sight is significant, for it represents a more integrated posture toward one's environment than sight, which is associated with greater distance and detachment. Furthermore, such attunement also demands an awareness of the social structure of which one is a part.

The Confucian approach to morality is not one of problem-solving, but rather one of integrating oneself into one's environment. Individuals must not only be treated with respect, but also have a place to which they belong if virtue is to find fruitful soil in which to grow. A sage ruler such as Yao is praised for his creative contribution to cultural development and not simply for moral goodness: "How great indeed was Yao as a ruler! How majestic! Only *tian* is truly great and only Yao took it as his model. How expansive was he—the people could not find the words

23 The *Shuowen* lexicon entry reads: 通也，從耳呈聲.

adequate to praise him. How majestic was he in his accomplishments, and how brilliant was he in his cultural achievements" (*A* 8:19). *Ren* cannot flourish in an environment where a sense of community is absent.

David Hall and Roger Ames have described the Confucian order as an aesthetic one, meaning that it is not buttressed by an appeal to transcendent principles, but rather that "togetherness" arises out of the combination and interaction of unique particulars. The Kantian moral order would be described as rational, meaning that we adjust our behavior to comply with predetermined patterns such that any individual can be substituted for another.[24] Because individual differences are assumed to be intractable and divisive, only a framework which, within certain parameters, demands that we all act in the same manner can hold the society together. In the Confucian understanding, *li* provides the network of meanings that link people not only to the whole that is their current social order, but provides a sense of continuity with the past. Yet, Confucius is not advocating a blind acceptance of tradition. Continuity can only be furthered if new patterns are formed that help reconstitute social bonds. *Li* must be continuously reinterpreted so that its meaning can be preserved.

Li enables one to take one's place or stance within society. In order to achieve this, one must also appropriate *li* for oneself by contributing to its extension. *Li* extends the self and the self extends *li* in a cycle of continuous reinforcement. *Li* must be accompanied by *yi* 義, sometimes translated as right conduct or appropriateness: "The exemplary person gives first priority to appropriate conduct" (*A* 17:23). *Yi* implies that each individual must disclose meaning based on particular circumstances, otherwise *li* becomes moribund. At the same time, one's behavior must also be appropriate in the evaluation of others so as to preserve social coherence: "But I am different from all of these people in that I do not have presupposition as to what may and may not be done" (*A* 18:8).

Undoubtedly, *li* is intended to disclose the hierarchical order within any given society, and taking one's place also means that one is to assume the appropriate rung on the hierarchical ladder: "The ruler must rule, te

24 Ames and Hall, *Thinking Through Confucius*, p. 134.

minister minister, the father father and the son son" (A 12:11). Each individual is situated in a complex web of relations that bestow obligations based on status. Without assuming the status that befits one, there would be social chaos. Indeed, Confucian social order is extremely dependent upon hierarchy as a way of transmitting and cultivating virtue: "The excellence of the exemplary person is the wind, while that of the petty person is the grass. As the wind blows, the grass is sure to bend" (A 12:19). Confucius assumes that not all will attain levels of virtue that permit the creative adaptation of *li*. The characteristics and behavior of the petty person are often compared in the *Analects*. Coupled with the importance of position on the hierarchical ladder, this indicates that social recognition is an important aspect of Confucian morality. After all, a hierarchy can only function through such recognition. Although Confucius would vehemently deny that the exemplary person would act virtuously in order to elicit public approval, this kind of moral system cannot help but be fueled in part by the dynamics of approval and repudiation. By tacitly encouraging behavior that impels individuals to bolster their public image, Confucian morality may unwittingly produce the kind of egoism that it hopes to avert, by making people concerned with their reputation.

The importance of public appearance in Confucian philosophy becomes evident in accounts of filial piety, which is central in patterns of Confucian sociality. When asked what filial conduct entails, Confucius replies that it means not to disobey (A 2:5). Underpinning the whole edifice of filial piety is the father-son relationship, which is decidedly patriarchal in structure. The father acts as a hinge between the ancestors and the present, thereby representing continuity. His authority does not reside solely in himself but in the relations he represents. This does not mean that blind obedience is called for on the part of his children. One may gently disagree with one's parents: "In serving your father and mother, remonstrate with them gently. On seeing that they do not heed your suggestions remain respectful and do not act contrary. Although concerned, voice no resentment" (A 4:18). However, one should never bring such disagreement into the public domain, as is evidenced by the example where Confucius insists that a filial son would not inform his ruler of his father's thievery. Since harmony within the family is the lynchpin for larger social order, in the case where the duty to one's ruler and duty to one's family conflict, one's family assumes greater importance. Such emphasis on the proper role does mean that social hierarchy is strictly enforced. Although the Confucian individual does not see him- or herself as an individual apart from the whole, there is no doubt that the emphasis on public image can lead to a concern for one's outward appearance which easily fosters selfish behavior.

Kant describes a world wherein the individual may not know his or her position in order to determine what the appropriate moral response might be. The Confucian individual cannot think of him- or herself apart from his or her place within the social order because the self is always relationally defined. Thus, awareness of my place is always relative to the place of another. Without this, I am lost and cannot properly speak or communicate:

> Once when my father was standing alone and I hastened quickly and deferentially across the courtyard, he asked me, "Have you studied the *Songs*?" I replied "Not yet," to which he remarked, "If you do not study the *Songs*, you will be at a loss as to what to say." I deferentially took my leave and studied the *Songs*. On another day, when he was again standing alone, I hastened quickly and deferentially across the courtyard. He asked me, "Have you studied the *Rites*?" I replied, "Not yet," to which he remarked, "If you do not study the *Rites*, you will be at a loss as to where to stand."
>
> (*A* 16:13)

Thus, Confucian philosophy would attribute moral degeneration, not merely to individual weakness but to a flawed social order that leaves human beings rudderless and without a sense of purpose and longing. The formalized rituals are sacred, not because they have any intrinsic universal worth but because they are the social fabric which imbue one with a sense of social purpose. *Li* creates the whole to which we belong. While Confucian philosophy is often associated with social rigidity, social norms and customs themselves are context-dependent and do not represent general moral principles. One could argue that *li* developed without *ren* would lead to empty mimicry.[25] However, some Confucian

25 There is some debate as to whether or not *ren* is merely the observance of *li*, or whether

concerns regarding propriety might seem pedantic, particularly when we are unfamiliar with the original context in which they were performed: "He would not sit unless the mats were properly placed in accordance with custom" (*A* 10:12).

If Confucius holds that carefully orchestrated behavior is a necessary part of moral training so that individuals learn what it means to be part of a community, Kant puts a much greater onus on the individual to make the right moral decisions, particularly in his earlier works such as *Foundations of the Metaphysics of Morals*. While Kant is also concerned with the formation of moral character, he asserts that this consists of the ability to follow through on plans or rules that one has set for oneself. Making a moral decision involves dialogue with oneself. In order to speculate on how I should treat others, I need to reflect on how I would wish others to treat me. Karyn Lai points out that such theories of morality focus on what "each person qua moral agent does, rather than on what the community as a whole does together."[26]

Kant's moral philosophy is often directed at the situation of the moral conundrum. Moral dilemmas arise because I find myself in a world peopled with others like me who are also ends in themselves. Therefore, I cannot simply pursue my own happiness at their expense. If I am to be an end in myself, then others must treat me as such. Thus, it is no surprise that Kant frames this "principle of humanity" as the "supreme limiting condition on the freedom of action of each man" (*FMM* 275). The paradox of Kantian morality is that because each person is a rational world unto himself, we must contribute to the wellbeing of others in order to preserve the individual dignity of each and every person. The social aspect of morality is therefore introduced through the back door and is derived from the need to assiduously protect human autonomy.

Kant's philosophy is tailored to react to the moral crisis when others impinge on our horizon in a way which we may not have anticipated.

---

ren takes precedence over and informs *li*. Kwong-Loi Shun adopts a position between the two, arguing that *ren* is "shaped by existing *li* practices." At the same time, "it is not totally determined by *li* because advocacy of the ideal allows room for departing from or revisiting an existing rule of *li*." See Shun, "*Ren* and *Li* in the *Analects*," p. 67.

26 Karyn L. Lai, "Confucian Moral Thinking," *Philosophy East and West* 45, no. 2 (1995): 249.

This is evident from the way in which he outlines his moral scenarios. One example is a man in desperate straits who is "forced by need to borrow money" (*FMM* 268). Suddenly, he is in a situation where he needs others in order to relieve his own suffering. He has to decide whether or not to promise to repay his debts, knowing full well that he will be unable to. Making false promises would be in accordance with his own "future welfare" and "self-love," but he could not want this universalized since this would make borrowing as an institution impossible: "No one would believe what was promised to him but would only laugh at any such assertion as a vain pretence" (*FMM* 269). His moral imagination extends as far as thinking of the broader repercussions on himself as a member of a society in which his action were to become the basis of a universal law: "The universality of law which says that anyone who believes himself to be in need could promise what he pleased with the intention of not fulfilling it would make the promise itself and the end to be accomplished by it impossible" (*FMM* 269).

Kant also considers a man who is leading the good life and encounters the suffering of others. He cannot remain indifferent to their agony, because the situation might arise when "he would need the love and sympathy of others, and in which he would have robbed himself, by such a law of nature . . . of all hope of the aid he desires" (*FMM* 270). Once again, Kant is describing a moral calculation whereby I imagine myself in place of the other and the other in my own place.

The kind of reasoning that Kant describes in these writings suggests that education does not play a key role in his ethical philosophy, because it seems that lack of grooming or education is no excuse for moral frailty. He also points out that "imitation has no place in moral matters" (*FMM* 259) and that every rational being should be capable of making moral decisions on his or her own. However, upon reading some of his later writings, we get a very different image of his understanding of morality. These works lend credence to the suggestion I made earlier that his "pure ethics" is intended to be a prescriptive ideal that underwrites the ethical system, rather than an accurate account of how morality actually works in the public domain. In fact, in order for the universality of every individual to be imprinted onto the individual's psyche, we must be furnished with evidence of this in our daily lives. Reason's maxims are developed in a social setting, with centuries of experience to back them up.

Robert Louden has convincingly argued against the charges of empty formalism levied against Kant, claiming that these are based on an "ignorance of the second part of his ethics" which focuses on the "massive infusion of empirical knowledge" that is necessary if human beings are to become ethical.[27] Kant himself makes reference to two parts in his moral system, noting that the "empirical part may be called more specifically practical anthropology," while "the rational part" is referred to as "morals proper" (*FMM* 244–5). The pure philosophy of his moral theory must be accompanied by efforts to determine what makes it "effective in concreto in the conduct of his life" (*FMM* 245). The purity of ethics is a fantasy that enables us to become moral, but we need empirical background, and knowledge of human nature in order to actively use our moral judgment and to recognize the universality of other beings.

Like Confucius, Kant insists that education is necessary in cultivating morality, for by nature, the human being "is not a moral being at all" (*LP* 102). In fact, human beings seem to be characterized by a kind of unsocial sociability:

> Man has an inclination to associate with others, because in society he feels himself to be more than men (i.e. as more than the developed form of his natural capacities). But he also has a strong propensity to isolate himself from others, because he finds in himself at the same time the unsocial characteristic of wishing to have everything go according to his own wish. Thus he expects opposition on all sides, because, in knowing himself, he knows that he, on his own part, is inclined to oppose others.
>
> (OH 418)

Out of this discord, nature has willed that human beings produce concord. The project of eventually producing such harmony is a collective one to be achieved through meticulous education: "Education can only advance by slow degrees, and a true conception of the method of educa-

27 Robert Louden, *Kant's Impure Ethics: From Rational Beings to Human Beings* (New York: Oxford University Press, 2000), p. 168.

tion can only arise when one generation transmits to the next its stores of experience and knowledge" (*LP* 11).

The awkward relationship between discord and concord arises out of the totalizing tendency of reason, which recognizes the universal nature of the self. Because of this, human beings have a desire to have everything go their way, but they also covet the recognition and admiration of others. Yet, if reason whets in me the desire to be a universal individual, then I must also recognize the universality of other individuals. This is why education is so important, since I am not inclined to come to this recognition on my own. Education helps to keep the more antisocial dimension of reason in check by buttressing its social dimension.

The fact that human beings are "contradistinguished from themselves" (*MP* 28)[28] means that they require extensive training in order to develop the moral disposition that allows them to choose the good all the time: "His disposition must be so trained that he shall choose none but good ends, good ends being those which are necessarily approved by everyone, and which may be the same time be the aim of everyone" (*LP* 13). This is why Kant insists that children not be punished when they have violated a moral law, but rather be subjected to disapproval (*LP* 35). The outward disapproval of others functions similarly to reason within the self as an inner watchdog. Punishment, on the other hand, leads children to pursue the more utilitarian course of avoiding the pain associated with it.

Meanwhile, Kant recognizes that morality is also mixed up with impulses that may be embedded in our nature, seemingly suggesting that it is not reason alone which makes us moral:

> There are such moral qualities, that if one does not possess them, there can be no duty to acquire them. These are moral feeling, conscience, love of one's neighbour and respect for one's self. There is no obligation to have these, because they are subjective conditions of susceptibility to the concept of duty and are not objective conditions of morality. . . . Though it cannot be regarded as a duty to have these predispositions, yet every man has them, and it is by means of them that he can be obligated. The consciousness of them is not

---

28 Immanuel Kant, *The Metaphysical Principles of Virtue* (New York: Bobs Merrill and Company, 1964).

> of empirical origin but can only follow upon the consciousness of a moral law—upon its effects on the mind.
>
> (*MP* 57–8)

This statement is confusing because Kant notes that these are natural predispositions that enable a person to become moral, but at the same time asserts that they are the effects of the moral law upon the mind. Furthermore, Kant now suggests that each individual represents within him- or herself "humanity," and therefore must assiduously work to develop "the crude dispositions of one's nature . . . since thus the animal is first raised to man; therefore it is a duty in itself" (*MP* 50). What is most human is our dormant potential which must be brought to the surface through education and cultivation.

The purity of reason may be a necessary fiction that furnishes human beings with a sense of responsibility and the determination to become moral. Indeed, Kant remarks that pure virtue "completely free from the influence of an incentive foreign to duty" is "commonly personified poetically under the name 'the wise man,' as an ideal which one ought constantly to approach" (*MP* 41). He appears to suggest that this is the ideal that will inspire us to tirelessly pursue the course of morality. The Kantian wise man is the personification of the idea of pure virtue, while the Confucian sage describes an ideal type of person. We must imagine the possibility of reason unsullied by "foreign influences" so that we are incited to obey rules we set for ourselves. In reality, the rules we develop will be constructed out of the layers of experience that several generations have offered us.

The educational process is primarily an art of training the will, so that we have the fortitude to carry through on the maxims that we posit for ourselves. The importance that Kant attributes to education also constitutes an important concession. The ideal of a completely self-legislating moral being that does not rely on imitation for the development of morality may be an impossibly difficult dream to realize. Only the sage can act in this manner. Confucius is not motivated by the fantasy of a perfect self-sustaining moral universe. Education is a central aspect of his philosophy, because constant learning and moral development are not means to an end but themselves ideals that are not dependent upon dreams of moral perfection. It is seen as part of the larger process of harmonization and attunement. Thus, education and social integration go hand in hand for Confucius. Although Kant also recognizes the importance of education, the ideal pure moral world that becomes the impetus behind our moral striving would have no need for it. Education is necessary because of our indelible moral imperfections. For Confucius, the ideal is the process of education itself, whereby one recognizes that one is constantly engaged in the activity of becoming moral.

Moral Troubles

Kantian moral philosophy rests on a fantasy in which human beings are insulated from the world of nature within a Kingdom of Ends, wherein the pure laws of reason prevail and the restrictions of the phenomenal realm can be relegated to irrelevance. Ambiguity is ever-present but struggled against, since our natural inclinations will always interfere with the dictates of reason. It is the struggle which elicits Kant's highest praise as attested to by his insistence that there is nothing good but the good will. The will must always do battle against heteronomous and egotistical desires; therefore, Kant tacitly acknowledges that good requires the non-good in order to be affirmed as such. Morality is only possible in the realm of finite creatures, who act as though they were living in a world which they had shaped by virtue of their pure reason, while recognizing that they will never do so.

For Kant, the form of a pure rationality, unblemished by empirical drives and heteronomous desire, is the only stable bulwark in the world of human relations. Without form to structure such change, we would be lost in a dizzying whirlwind of stimuli. Kant does not suggest that we can eradicate change, but rather that we adopt a rule-based approach that lends form to our actions, while recognizing that the content will vary. I must act as though my actions could be universalized, while recognizing that they can never be. Yet, if I act as though they could become universal moral law, then I am erecting a shield against my own selfish tendencies. Not just reason but imagination is at work here. Change cannot be eradicated but managed by viewing it against a backdrop of permanence. Heteronomous desire can hurtle the self in a multitude of directions, representing the occasional chaos of the material and empirical realm that elude the repose and stability sought by the human mind.

Thus, while for Kant, it is up to human beings to provide the form that structures these perceptions, for Confucius, the form is already an intrinsic part of the natural world: "The master was standing on the riverbank and observed: 'Isn't life's passing just like this, never ceasing day and night?'" (*A* 9:17). The river is an apt metaphor for it signifies a steady process of transformation which nevertheless contains a strong element of constancy. The river is both never the same and always the same. The alternation between day and night connotes the kind of repeated and harmonious order esteemed by Confucius. Because harmony is already in the world, and it is up to human beings to draw on this potential, Confucius does not see human beings as alienated from the world they are in.

Because Confucian philosophy recognizes the world as one of dynamic flux, ambiguity is simply taken for granted. It is always a part of the moral domain when unique particulars interact with each other, and is not something that can or should be extirpated. Therefore, one must learn the art of morality as one would any craft, through the observation of virtuous figures who are practiced in it and by applying what one has learned to the unique situations one finds oneself in. For Kant, the moral project is one of attempting to protect the purity of form within the messy world of nature.

Yet, the purity of the moral law alone cannot act as the guarantor of morality, nor can it protect human beings from the vicissitudes of reason. In *Religion within the Bounds of Bare Reason*, Kant tacitly acknowledges the vulnerability of his moral system in his efforts to offer an account of moral evil. He faces a conundrum because he wishes to reserve the right to call a person "evil," even going so far as to label it an aspect of human nature, yet he does not want to exclude the possibility of the evil individual's eventual redemption. The evil personality is thus most likely a "perversity of the human heart, because it reverses the moral order (*umkehren*) in regard to the incentives of a *free* power of choice" (*R* 33).[29] Thus, Kant notes that evil is only possible in the wake of moral freedom because the evil person, while fully cognizant of the moral path, deliberately chooses to not only ignore it but rather actively subvert it. The German word *umkehren* has connotations of turning upside down as well as turning away. The same appetite for freedom that draws people toward morality now also makes evil alluring, because people derive satisfaction from deliberately subverting the moral law. What proves to be so startling in Kant's account of moral evil is that it is indeed rational, for he views it as the outcome of a freely chosen "ground of maxim-making" which acts as a kind of "supreme maxim." Kant does not want to attribute evil to an absence of autonomy, so he is forced to highlight its "rational" foundation because he had inextricably wedded autonomy to rationality. Autonomy from nature through the moral law now becomes a desire for autonomy from the moral law. Kant hints at what he dare not say—morality may make evil possible. Evil is not merely acquiescing to "undisciplined inclinations," but choosing to do so on a consistent basis in full awareness of the moral maxims which the evil super-maxim militates against.

Confucius does not make reference to the evil person but rather to the petty person or small person (*xiaoren* 小人). Thus, what Kant calls evil, Confucius would more likely attribute to a lack of learning and proper moral education. Kant's evil is much more pernicious than the self-aggrandizing behavior of the *xiaoren* because it is deliberately, willfully, and often gleefully chosen, not ignorant of the moral law but fully aware of it. The *xiaoren* is most often portrayed as lacking in comparison to the *junzi* 君子 (exemplary person): "Exemplary persons associating openly with others are not partisan; petty persons being partisan do not associate openly with others" (*A* 2:14). The original reads: 君子周而不比，小人比而不周. *Bi* 比 is an interesting word choice in this context, because it can mean to "approve," "be partial to," and also "compare." This suggests that the petty person is mired in comparison and partiality, and thus cannot easily surround him- or herself with others (*zhou* 周). And

29 Immanuel Kant, *Religion within the Bounds of Bare Reason*, trans. Werner S. Pluhar (Indianapolis: Hackett Publishing Company, 2009).

yet, Confucius engages in a process of comparison in order to reveal the characteristics of the petty and exemplary persons. Morality cannot be transmitted without having recourse to comparative tactics, but this very process may inadvertently spark the small-minded selfishness that morality hopes to transcend. Nature does not approve or disapprove of actions whereas human beings do. In order for our actions to be harmoniously coordinated within the realm of *li*, they must be acknowledged by others. Because this desire for acknowledgement cannot easily be excised from morality, it can spawn competitive behavior that encourages us to stray from the process of becoming moral.

Neither Confucius nor Kant would hold that being moral comes easily to human beings. According to both thinkers, the seeds of morality are already within us, but it is no easy task to make sure that they grow to fruition. In Kant, our will is needed to ensure that reason reigns supreme, while for Confucius, the kernel of our humanity must be actively worked upon in order to grow: "Exemplary persons concentrate their efforts on the root, for the root having taken hold, the way will grow therefrom" (*A* 1:2). Resistance to ethical behavior that may initially be experienced will fade over time as body-mind become attuned and integrated in the surroundings. A truly virtuous person, such as the sage, reaches a point where he does not have to do battle with either himself or with others, as he becomes ethically more advanced: "From fifteen, my heart-and-mind was set upon learning; from thirty I took my stance; from forty I was no longer doubtful; from fifty I realized the propensities of *tian*; from sixty my ear was attuned; from seventy I could give my heart-and-mind free rein without overstepping the boundaries" (*A* 2:4). The openness of his early years enabled him to discover for himself where he fitted into the social order and through a process of careful adjustment become accustomed to his position. As he grows older, greater levels of integration are achieved, resulting in an attunement to the rhythms of *tian*. Thus, only at the age of seventy, following years of training and learning, could moral behavior become spontaneous and natural.

Despite Confucius's emphasis on harmony, he intimates that we would not need morality if we could take our place in the world for granted. Although the rule-based approach of Kant would be anathema to him, he insists that human beings require a particular space that they belong to, which is governed by customs and rituals that each person participates in. Human beings are moral creatures, because they intentionally need to mark a space as their own in order to live in harmony with the cosmos. This is true of Kantian philosophy as well, but this space must be stamped by reason, while for Confucius, it must bear the insignia of custom and social ritual. However, the dependence on local and cultural context in Confucian thought could foster a parochialism that becomes problematic when we confront a stranger whose rituals cannot so easily be accommodated with our own. The consecration of ritual depends upon recognition, and this craving for social recognition can, if one is not careful enough, become the primary motivation for acting morality. Although Confucius in no way wishes to make such approval a condition of morality, his system cannot function without it, because the legitimacy of rituals and patterns of social relationships depend upon it. Although this is a potential weakness of the Confucian system, it is also its greatest strength. Confucian philosophy recognizes that the seeds of morality must be sown within a strong community wherein individuals can nurture their concern for others and where concepts of self include rather than exclude the other. Being part of a larger whole is the soil in which virtue grows. Yet, at the same time, the cultivation of Confucian ethics depends very much on a hierarchy led by exemplary figures who transmit virtue. A delicate dance is required to ensure that politics does not usurp the place of virtue in such a hierarchical order, so that the hierarchy is not experienced as coercion.

Kant also insists that human beings need a space of their own, and recognizing the distinct nature of humanity is inextricably intertwined with what it means to be a moral being. However, the project of moralization is universal and must span across generations and civilizations. Even the strife that we experience discloses a purpose in nature which follows "a lawful course in gradually lifting our race from the lower levels of animality to the highest level of humanity, doing this by her own secret art and developing in accord with her law all the original gifts of man in this apparently chaotic disorder" (OH 421). It is nature's way of bringing us "to that which reason could have told them at the beginning" (OH 420). Despite Kant's repeated emphasis on the purity of the moral law, his corpus also attests to his recognition that we must be trained to become moral. Nevertheless, this training enables us to realize the fantasy of a being capable of positing universal moral maxims on its own.

For Kant, morality springs from a paradoxical relationship with the world that we inhabit. We are at odds with nature and at the same time part of it. This ambiguity forces us to actively choose the moral law. While this may be an unrealizable goal, it ought to be a perpetual driving force of human behavior. According to Confucius, we are already part of the world of *tian*, but it is incumbent upon us to extend this harmonious potential and integrate into social orders within which we can create harmonies of our own. Human beings have a particular way of being in the cosmos which necessitates a ritualized sociality and customs that tie them to very specific places. For Confucius, it is the recognition of this specificity that is the mark of morality and also makes it possible to care for others, by extending one's horizons. Kant would balk at this emphasis on local context. Confucius, in turn, would be suspicious of Kant's abstract formalism. Despite these profound differences, both thinkers would agree that we must learn to be moral because of the peculiar position human beings are in. They insist that we can never rest on our laurels, thinking that we have reached morality, because morality is always in process. It is a horizon we aim for but never fully reach.

CHAPTER TWO

Organic Virtue: Reading Mencius with Rousseau[1]

For both Kant and Confucius, moral development bequeaths upon human beings a unique place within the cosmos. In the case of Confucius, human beings must attune themselves to the patterns of *tian* in a distinctly human way, relying heavily upon *li*, while for Kant, nature must often be struggled against in making moral decisions. Mencius and Rousseau are two thinkers who maintain that reflection upon nature is a key component of exercising moral judgment. Mencius is much more confident in the possibilities for harmony between nature and artifice than Confucius, suggesting that even the most common person can work towards it. Rousseau wrote in an era when reason was being upheld as the essence of humanity, and in contrast to many of his contemporaries, he offers a trenchant critique of our rationality which, when unchecked, can contribute to the alienation from nature and consequently a spiraling moral decline. Attunement to nature is necessary to ensure that reason does not spill over. Mencius is also concerned that a corrupt civilization can cause human beings to stray from their potential for goodness which, he affirms, is inherent in the disposition of each human being.

The natural substratum can be drawn upon even in times of moral degradation to provide a basis for moral renewal that can help turn the tide in favor of virtue. No matter how depraved we become, the roots in nature that incline us toward morality can never be eradicated. Thus, both Mencius and Rousseau insist on the moral improvement of each

---

1 Parts of this chapter were originally published as an article in *Asian Philosophy* 18, no. 1 (2008): 83–104.

human being. Nevertheless, an assiduous process of learning and acculturation is necessary if we are to make use of the preliminary building blocks at our disposal. Neither Rousseau nor Mencius would claim that the natural world is moral in and of itself, but both would assert that our intellect, emotions, and will must heed and strengthen the impulses associated with nature, and build their moral edifice upon them. However, Rousseau demarcates human beings from nature more sharply than Mencius, since in his view only human beings creatively contribute to nature in a manner which gives it meaning. For Mencius, the constant self-perfection of the ethical human being is evidence of our participation in a creative and already meaningfully ordered cosmos. Continuity within the natural order of things is an integral part of being moral.

Nature as Morally Neutral

In order to gain an understanding of Mencius's and Rousseau's conceptions of the realm of nature, I will compare Rousseau's account of the protohuman with the Mencian use of the notion of *qi* 氣, which is central to much of Chinese cosmology. While these concepts, upon first glance, may appear to have little in common with one another, they each provide clues to the reasons underlying the dynamic process-oriented approach to morality that both thinkers espouse. The protohuman is the prehuman animal which, in Rousseau's view, becomes a focus for nostalgia and longing with the potential to provide the subterranean impetus for the unending process of becoming moral. *Qi* in Mencius is akin to dynamic energy that not only reverberates through the cosmos, but is the "stuff" of all beings. There is no demarcation between substance and process according to the cosmological outlook based on *qi*. Moral virtue is the particularly human way of participating in its flow, as Mencius insists that we must nourish our vast flood-like energy.

Rousseau is a rather atypical figure within the Enlightenment tradition. He does not take nature to be an impediment to moral development, but insists that we must take our cues from it. The tendency to divorce the two can have disastrous consequences, as the opening of *Emile* dramatically proclaims: "Everything is good as it leaves the hands of the Author of things; everything degenerates in the hands of man. . . . He turns everything upside down, he disfigures everything; he loves deformity, monsters" (*E* 37).[2] Rousseau makes explicit reference to a process of civilization, which has become too hasty and not heeded the primordial world of nature that still resounds within us. Such imbalance can have deleterious results because our striving becomes more frenetic, as we become increasingly alienated from nature in an attempt to compensate for our loss. An ever-widening chasm between human beings and nature is created. Thus, Rousseau insists that the balance between nature and civilization must be maintained and the effort to harmonize the two must be ongoing. The continuous cultivation of such a balance constitutes the essence of morality.

Rousseau begins the *Discourse on the Origins of Inequality* with the claim that human beings are naturally good. However, this natural goodness does not necessarily spur human beings to come to the aid of each other and therefore perhaps the term "morally neutral" is a more appropriate designation for this condition. Rousseau makes it very clear that in their presocial environment, human beings are indifferent toward each other and thus, while they have no inclination to inflict harm, are not inherently social beings. In keeping with the Enlightenment tradition, Rousseau takes the asocial individual as the norm, implying that socialization is primarily a cultural process superimposed onto nature. He sets up a hypothetical state of nature, in order to imagine what the precivilized human being may have been like. All our ills could have been avoided by preserving the "simple, regular and solitary lifestyle prescribed us by nature" (*DOI* 42). Because this state is not social, the human being is not yet saddled with an ego. While Rousseau is not imploring us to go back to the world of nature, he is suggesting that this state will always be greeted with pangs of nostalgia and that we should try to re-create this kind of contentment, albeit at a social level.

Rousseau remarks that the advent of reason ushers in a departure from nature that requires morality as an antidote. The "man who meditates is a depraved animal" (*DOI* 42) in need of a cure from the ills he soon

2 Jean-Jacques Rousseau, *Emile*, trans. Allan Bloom (New York: Basic Books, 1979).

heaps upon himself: "This distinctive and almost unlimited faculty is the source of all man's misfortunes; that this is what, by dint of time, draws him out of that original condition in which he would pass tranquil and innocent days; that this is what, through centuries of giving rise to his enlightenment and his errors, his vices and his virtues, eventually makes him a tyrant over himself and nature" (*DOI* 45). Our relationship to nature prior to civilization was one of contentment. Yet, at the same time, human beings are not creatures of the cosmos in the way that other beings are, because of their capacity for self-perfection and freedom: "Nature commands every animal, and beasts obey. Man feels the same impetus, but he knows he is free to go along or to resist; and it is above all in the awareness of this freedom that the spirituality of his soul is made manifest" (*DOI* 45). Unlike Confucian thought which does not sharply differentiate between the agency of human beings and the patterns of the cosmos, Rousseau adopts a Cartesian-like dichotomy between human beings and the mechanisms of nature: "In any animals I see nothing but an ingenious machine to which nature has given senses in order for it to renew its strength and to protect itself, to a certain point, from all that tends to destroy or disturb it. I am aware of precisely the same things in the human machine, with the difference that nature alone does everything in the operations of an animal, whereas man contributes, as a free agent, to his own operations" (*DOI* 44). In Confucian thought, the cosmos is imbued with meaning and it is the responsibility of human beings to harmonize with its rhythms. For Rousseau, human beings impute meaning to the cosmos.

Rousseau is one of the first Western thinkers to consider the possibility that reason may be destroyed by its own excesses, maintaining that nature can help put our reason into perspective: "Dissatisfied with your present state for reasons that portend even greater grounds for dissatisfaction for your unhappy posterity, perhaps you would like to be able to go backwards in time. This feeling should be hymn in praise of your first ancestors, the criticism of your contemporaries and the dread of those who have the unhappiness of living after you" (*DOI* 39). Rousseau's teleology is interesting, for it demands a conscious reflection and "imitation" of a hypothetical harmonious time prior to the socialization of human beings which is allegedly buried in each consciousness. There is nothing inevitable about the path that human beings must choose if they are to catch a glimmer of their lost contentment. Because the pre-social bliss can never be returned to but must simultaneously furnish us with a direction for our striving, it forces us to exercise our freedom.[3] We never arrive at the goal and thus, the unsatisfactory nature of the human condition also ensures our constant perfectibility.[4]

Rousseau sketches the figure of the protohuman who represents an undifferentiated relationship to our surroundings where we are not yet cognizant of a separate self. The contentment of the protohuman is due to the fact that he or she has not yet experienced the torment of individuation: "His soul, agitated by nothing, is given over to the single feeling of his own present existence, without any idea of the future, however, near it may be, and his projects, as limited as his views hardly extend to the end of the day" (*DOI* 47). While the protohuman does not rush to the aid of others, he or she also has absolutely no inclination to do them harm. Although we can never return to the blissful state of nature, it is always the subject of our longing. Morality in Rousseau's thought becomes a socially and culturally mediated effort to recapture the sense of harmony that has since been lost. Because the protohuman is not yet a self, and has no genuine interaction with others, his relationship with nature is in complete equilibrium, and there is no need for morality. Our natural state is one of complete independence.

The paradox that lies at the heart of Rousseau's moral philosophy is that the hope for reinvigorating a social morality inheres in the reflection upon the asocial protohuman who is governed primarily by instinct. Capable of procuring everything he or she needs, this creature wants for nothing: "His desires do not go beyond his physical needs. The only goods he knows in the universe are nourishment, a woman and rest; the

3 Asher Horowitz remarks that the cultural re-creation of the self is always indicative of an attempted return to the natural world. See Horowitz, *Rousseau, Nature and History* (Toronto: University of Toronto Press, 1987), p. 52.

4 The notion of *perfectibilité* in Rousseau does not mean that human beings arrive at perfection, but rather is akin to the activity of constant improvement that is spurred on by dreams of completeness.

only evils he fears are pain and hunger" (*DOI* 47). Rousseau uses the term *amour-de-soi* to refer to this blissful state. Although this is often translated as self-love, it is more akin to contentment with one's existence since a concept of self does not yet exist. Hence, this refers to our way of being in the world prior to the formation of an ego. In relation to the insecurity that is unleashed in social settings, this prehuman creature seems complete. The protohuman is content simply as she is, because she has not yet subjected herself to the trials and tribulations of self-reflection. Nevertheless, this primordial *amour-de-soi* continuously haunts us by stamping our psyche with a sense that the golden age has been lost. Paradoxically, it has always been there and yet has never been there. At times, Rousseau suggests that this protohuman existed and yet on other occasions, he hints that this is a thought experiment:

> I will suppose him to have been formed from all time as I see him today: walking on two feet, using his hands as we use ours, directing his gaze over all of nature, and measuring with his eyes the vast expanse of the heavens. When I strip that being, thus constituted, of all the supernatural gifts he could have received and of all the artificial faculties he could have acquired only through long progress; when I consider him, in a word, as he must have left the hands of nature. I see an animal less strong than some, less agile than others, but all in all, the most advantageously organized of all.
>
> (*DOI* 40)

This passage suggests that Rousseau *imagines* a creature, stripped of all its cultural and social trappings, who would bear little resemblance to what we commonly perceive as human.

Rousseau repeatedly remarks on the protohuman's independence because it is not subject to the servitude of others. Therefore, he implicitly identifies independence as the natural state of humankind: "It is clear, from the little care taken by nature to bring men together through mutual needs and to facilitate their use of speech, how little she prepared them for becoming habituated to the ways of society, and how little she contributed to all that men have done to establish the bonds of society. It is impossible to imagine why, in that primitive state, one man would have a greater need for another man than a monkey or a wolf has for another of its respective species" (*DOI* 51). Indeed, even the protowoman, who by nature must care for her young, puts her own needs ahead of those of the child. Rousseau claims that at first she "nursed her children for her own need and then, with habit having endeared them to her, she later nourished them from their own need. Once they had the strength to look for their food, they did not hesitate to leave the mother herself" (*DOI* 48). He questions the natural sociability of human beings and insists that the act of raising and nurturing children satisfies the natural and independent urges of the mother. He relies upon an arbitrary coincidence between the needs of the mother and those of the child.

For Rousseau, we become moral beings because we have departed from nature and long for the lost equilibrium. Fostering our connection to nature is thus an integral part of the moral process. Mencius would agree with Rousseau that the roots of morality are to be found in nature and they must be properly attuned in order for virtue to develop. However, Mencius does not demarcate as strongly between nature and artifice as Rousseau, for they are always already intertwined. His frequent use of agricultural metaphors throughout his texts is telling since it aptly symbolizes this entanglement.[5]

In order to illuminate the relationship between nature and virtue that underwrites Mencius's ethical perspectives, it is necessary to understand the notion of *qi* that is central to much of Chinese philosophy and forms the cornerstone of Mencius's natural and cosmological orientation. *Qi* is not inherent in anything but akin to a kind of energy in all things and changes its concentration or quality, depending on the way in which things relate to each other. James Behuniak points out that *qi* "refers to the vital energies that channel their way through the dispositions and configurations of dynamic environments."[6] The shape that *qi* assumes depends on the localized climate in which we find ourselves, just as different habitats spawn different types of vegetation. Thus, in

---

5 Franklin Perkins underlines the fact that the metaphors Mencius employs are agricultural rather than wild. Virtue, therefore, demands a conducive natural environment, but also necessitates proper ritual and cultivation in order to develop. See Perkins, "Mencius, Emotion and Autonomy," *Journal of Chinese Philosophy* 29, no. 2 (2002): 212.

6 James Behuniak Jr., "Disposition and Aspiration in the *Mencius* and *Zhuangzi*," *Journal of Chinese Philosophy* 29, no. 1 (2002): 70.

Chinese cosmology, there is no opposition between the one and the many, for *qi* flows through all things while changing shape in order to give rise to multifarious particulars. It is infinitely malleable and is the source of both unity and difference.

Qi is morally neutral and must be properly channeled for moral purposes by human beings. Franklin Perkins points out that our nature in Mencius is not so much good as it is "propelled toward the good."[7] In the case of Mencius, *qi* is connective and therefore cannot legitimize the absolute independence of a being such as Rousseau's protohuman. *Qi* in itself is neither good nor bad but human attentiveness to the flow of *qi* results in good, while efforts to contain it culminate in vice.

If *qi* on its own cannot be imbued with moral values, then why does the attentiveness to *qi* culminate in moral virtue? First of all, *qi* is connective rather than divisive, and flowing rather than stagnant. Therefore, if we promote connectivity with other human beings, we contribute to its flow. When we tend to our own interests to the exclusion of others, we stymie the flowing nature of *qi*. Thus, moral behavior and expanding the realm of care is a way of participating in the flux and movement of the cosmos. Selfishness is akin to impeding the flow. Ironically, our selfishness may constitute an attempt to house the vastness of *qi* within ourselves, and this is bound to fail because the expansiveness of *qi* depends upon interconnection rather than containment.

Immoral behavior is usually due to selfishness which can be regarded as producing an unhealthy effort to block *qi*. Amassment and acquisition are among the most nefarious means of obstruction: "Why does your majesty use that word 'profit'? . . . If your majesty says, 'What is to be done to profit my kingdom?' the great officers will say, 'What is to be done to profit our families?' and the inferior officers and common people will say, 'What is to be done to profit our persons?' Superiors and inferior will try to snatch this profit the one from the other and the kingdom will be endangered'"[8] (M 1A1). Seeking one's own advantage or *li* 利 manifests an attempt to harness the vast flood-like energy for oneself. When *qi* is

7 Perkins, "Mencius, Emotion and Autonomy," 211.

8 Mencius, *Mengzi*, trans. Bryan W. Van Norden (Indianapolis: Hackett Publishing Company, 2008).

contained in this way, it creates discord and imbalance like water that overflows its banks. Confucian thinkers see a kind of equilibrium inherent in the cycles of transformation that *qi* undergoes, and harmonious social living is the human contribution to maintaining this balance. *Qi* is creative energy that is part of the cosmos. In Mencius, there is no opposition between the creative capacities of human beings and the relatively static state of nature as is described by Rousseau. Humans do not introduce freedom and creativity into a mechanistic universe, but rather participate in its creative rhythms. The attempt to amass advantages for oneself interrupts the flow of *qi*, similar to stagnation.

Selfish behavior is the ill-fated attempt to become complete unto ourselves. Nevertheless, the fact that the selfish individual is often buoyed by the misfortunes of others demonstrates that even her warped sense of self-sufficiency is defined in relation to the position of others. Selfishness is inherently contradictory because it demands the recognition of those we are trying to exclude. The selfish person has an insatiable appetite, because he or she needs others while at the same time wanting to excise them from his or her domain. For Mencius, the fact that we are not complete unto ourselves is not the wellspring of anguish as it is in Rousseau. Instead, erroneously striving for such completeness can only exacerbate our anguish.

Mencius insists that there must be a balance between the spontaneity of *qi* and cultivation. This becomes evident in his description of the passion-nature or flood-like energy (*haoran zhiqi* 浩然之氣; *M* Ch 2A2). When Mencius claims that "I am good at cultivating my floodlike *qi*" (*M* 2A2), he refers to an energy that permeates all beings but that must be properly cultivated through *ren* 仁 (love, humanity, benevolence) and *yi* 義 (appropriateness), in order to assume a distinctly human and moral form: "It is *qi* that is supremely great and supremely unyielding. If one cultivates it with uprightness and does not harm it, it will fill up the space between heaven and earth" (*M* 2A2). Virtue is often described as fluid and flowing, implying that the process of cultivating it can never cease: "Confucius said, 'The flowing progress of virtue is more rapid than the transmission of royal orders by sages and couriers'" (*M* 2A2).

Qi impels Mencius to espouse a process-oriented understanding of morality that depends upon equilibrium. Rousseau's morality is also dynamic but as moral beings, we are spurred on by the impossible possibility of recapturing the lost *amour-de-soi*. Thus, the moral journey will always be marked by a degree of frustration since the realm of prehuman innocence is lost to us forever. In Mencius, the moral process maintains the flowing nature of *qi*, and thus there is no ineradicable tension between the moral journey and the natural rhythm of the cosmos. For Rousseau, morality always reminds us of the rift between human beings and nature. He invokes the relatively static point of origin of the protohuman that becomes the impossible object of our moral striving. Because of this, morality will always be haunted by the specter of dissatisfaction. In Mencius, the continuous expansion of moral horizons is also extolled, but because *qi* is forever flowing, it cannot spark nostalgia for a lost innocence.

Roots of Virtue and Vice

According to Rousseau, our relationship with the natural world is predicated primarily on the satisfaction of need. The connection with others necessitates morality, which becomes a surrogate for the primordial self-sufficiency of the protohuman. Because morality can never completely compensate for our loss, it will always be fragile. Social interaction necessarily upsets nature's equilibrium and we must assiduously work to restore it. In Mencius, morality has somewhat firmer roots. His understanding of *qi* suggests that interconnection is primary and it would not occur to him to sketch an image of a self prior to its social relationships. Instead, he makes it clear that the social dimension of our being is part of our nature from the very beginning, and makes far greater use of organic metaphors that attempt to anchor Confucian teachings firmly in the natural world, albeit an already cultivated one.

The language surrounding the four "sprouts" of virtue is indicative of Mencius's organic concept of virtue. The suggestion that the seeds of virtue are within all of us reduces, to some extent, the prominent role accorded to learning and education within the Confucian system. It enables Mencius to assert that everyone has the potential to become a moral sage, provided they engage in the activity of internal reflection: "Thus, all things which are the same in kind are like to one another—why should we doubt in regard to man, as if he were a solitary exception to this? The sage and we are the same in kind" (*M* 6A3). The four sprouts form the pillars of Mencian morality: "The feeling of compassion is the sprout of benevolence. The feeling of disdain and shame is the sprout of appropriateness. The feeling of deference is the sprout of propriety. The feeling of approving and disapproving is the sprout of wisdom. People having these four sprouts is like having four limbs. To have these four sprouts, yet to claim that one is incapable of virtue is to steal from oneself. To say that one's ruler is incapable is to steal from one's ruler" (*M* 2A6). Foremost among these sprouts is the feeling of commiseration, which renders human beings unable to witness "the suffering of others" (*M* 2A6). It is the basis for *ren* 仁, which is perhaps the cardinal virtue in the Confucian tradition.

Because Mencius maintains that the seeds of human virtue are to be found within everyone, he is insistent that there is hope for even the most self-seeking despots to chart a better course for themselves. Compassion provides the greatest hope for such a moral rebirth. The nascent moral potential can never be obliterated completely and will occasionally surface even among the cold-hearted. For example, Mencius insists that any human being would worry if a small child fell into the well and would be moved to help without consideration of personal advantage or public approval. The primordial instinct for survival is tapped into and the child's distress seems to temporarily denude us of all social convention that could interfere with our impulse to aid another. An impending death quickly renders all acculturation insignificant. Based on such examples, Mencius attempts to teach King Xuan to modify his behavior, for the king could not bear to see the frightened appearance of an ox that was going to its slaughter and so exchanged it for a sheep. Mencius suggested that this feeling of benevolence should be extended to the people, and the failure to do so simply marks a refusal to properly tap into one's disposition: "In the present case your kindness is sufficient to reach animals, but the effects do not reach the people?" (*M* 1A7). Emotions alone are not adequate guides because they are often evoked by circumstances beyond our control. However, reason can be used to train the sentiments so that they are eventually transferred to analogous circumstances and become important barometers of moral virtue. Mencius employs this example to prove to the king that the sprout of compassion is present and that it is his responsibility to extend it to his populace.[9] Mencius suggests that the moral sprouts are never completely annihilated in any human being but they must be continuously worked upon in order to grow. Edward Slingerland notes that self-cultivation cannot be "rushed in Mohist fashion" simply through the application of external principles.[10] Instead, we must train our sentiments, just as we are capable of training our taste to prefer healthy food over junk.

The only other sprout that Mencius discusses in detail is that of shame and dislike which give rise to *yi* 義. *Yi* is linked to acting appropriately in circumstances and demands adaptability. While *ren* is linked to affective concern, *yi* often involves restoring lost balance and exercising appropriate judgment. Shame or disdain relate to the emotion that surfaces when one either ponders or performs an action that meets with social disapproval. It also arises when one is spurned by others. This suggests that the desire for public recognition and social integration are important pillars of any social order. Jiyuan Yu points out that *yi* is often linked to ritual but at the same time surpasses it, because it demands an ability to make judgments when no prescriptive standard can be invoked.[11] Shame engenders feelings of social isolation, suggesting that lack can be a powerful moral catalyst. How we are viewed in the eyes of others is an important component of morality.

Chung-Ying Cheng notes that in the writings of Mencius, *yi* is used

---

9 Philip J. Ivanhoe notes that Mengzi is encouraging the king to see that he has a "moral sense, to feel its power and to extend it to his people." He claims that rather than pointing out an inconsistency in his moral feelings, he is exhorting the king to experience a like reaction with respect to his people. See Ivanhoe, "Confucian Self Cultivation and Mengzi's Notion of Extension," in *Essays on the Moral Philosophy of Mengzi*, ed. Xiusheng Liu and Philip J. Ivanhoe (Indianapolis: Hackett Publishing Company, 2002), pp. 230–1.

10 Edward Slingerland, *Effortless Action: Wuwei as a Conceptual Metaphor and Spiritual Ideal in Early China* (New York: Oxford University Press, 2003), p. 155.

11 Jiyuan Yu, "The Moral Self and the Perfect Self in Aristotle and Mencius," *Journal of Chinese Philosophy* 28, no. 3 (2001): 243.

in conjunction with *ren* and assumes a much more prominent place than in the philosophy of Confucius.[12] However, without a solid basis of *ren*, it would be difficult to develop *yi* properly: "Benevolence is people's peaceful abode. Righteousness is people's proper path" (*M* 4A10). *Yi* is the art of engendering appropriateness at all times, suggesting that human beings cannot always rely on preexisting harmony, but rather must actively pursue it. This passage posits an interesting relationship between *ren* and *yi* because it suggests that those who experience the comfort and security of love or *ren* are more likely to travel along unknown paths without straying off course. *Ren* connotes the affective feeling of connectedness, which cannot be undermined if we are to take appropriate action in various circumstances. We need to be enveloped in a strong community if we are to develop the skills that allow us to generate balance. Judgment and reason cannot function independently of emotion. Without *ren* as an affective pillar, it is very difficult to exercise our judgment well because we are not rooted in the community.

In another passage, Mencius suggests that *yi* may be more important than life itself. *Yi* is based on the repugnance toward things that we cannot bring ourselves to do because they often constitute an affront to the dignity of human beings:

> People all have things that they will not bear. To extend this reaction to that which they will bear is benevolence. People all have things that they will not do. To extend this reaction to that which they will do is righteousness. If people can fill out the heart that does not desire to harm others, their benevolence will be inexhaustible. If people can fill out the heart that will not trespass, their righteousness will be inexhaustible. If people can fill out the core reaction of refusing to be addressed disrespectfully, there will be nowhere they go where they do not do what is righteous. If a noble speaks when he may not speak, this is tricking someone with speech. If one does not speak when he should, this is tricking someone with silence. These are both in the category of trespassing. (*M* 7B31)

The negative dimension of experience is stressed here, suggesting that lack in Mencius is also an important catalyst to morality, as it is in Rous-

12 Chung-Ying Cheng, *New Dimensions of Confucian and Neo-Confucian Philosophy* (Albany: State University of New York Press, 1991), p. 237.

seau. The adverse reaction to being improperly addressed derives from the shame experienced when one is not granted proper recognition. It seems that in this case, appropriateness pertains to a way of behaving that bestows dignity upon all individuals as respected members of the social body. Mencius notes that a beggar will be reluctant to receive a small bowl of rice that is offered with an insulting gesture, but that human beings have no problems accepting "ten thousand 'barrels of grain' for the sake of beautiful mansions or concubines (*M* 6A10). If it is shameful to be treated like a social outcast, then it is also shameful to accept monetary rewards in order to tend to one's own interest, because this is also an affront to oneself as a member of the community. To feel complete as a human being, one must have a meaningful place within the social order as a whole. The need for virtue exists because one's place in the community cannot be taken for granted. *Ren* and *yi* are the central virtues according to the Mencian moral vision because *ren* represents a connectedness between human beings, while *yi* is the continuous cultivation of balance that underwrites this connection.

Rousseau shares with Mencius the belief that compassion or *pitié* is the most primordial moral sentiment. In fact, Rousseau's words are remarkably similar to those of Mencius when he refers to an "innate repugnance to see his fellow men suffer" (*DOI* 53). Rousseau's description of compassion begins to chisel away at the myth of complete independence that he associates with the protohuman, and suggests that even his philosophy cannot work without acknowledging a "natural" social dimension:

> It is therefore quite certain that pity is a natural sentiment which, by moderating in each individual the activity of the love of oneself, contributes to the mutual preservation of the entire species. *Pitié* is what carries us without reflection to the aid of those we see suffering. *Pitié* is what, in the state of nature, takes the place of laws, mores, and virtue, with the advantage that no one is tempted to disobey its sweet voice.
>
> (*DOI* 55)

The phenomenon of compassion implies that there is an instinctive sense of integration with all other beings that allows us to participate in their pain and impels us to diminish it: "Such is the pure movement of nature prior to all reflection. Such is the force of natural pity, which the most depraved mores still have difficulty destroying" (*DOI* 54). It is powerful because it is instinctive, which is why Mencius asserts that in crises, it will surface very quickly. Like Mencius, Rousseau claims that all other social virtues flow from compassion and that its echo, even in the most corrupted soul, constitutes the hope for moral regeneration. The desire that another being not suffer is equivalent to a desire that "he be happy" (*DOI* 54). It also suggests that our own contentment is irrevocably tied to that of others, something that Rousseau is, on other occasions, reluctant to admit.

Shame also plays an important role in Rousseau's philosophy, but he is much more cautious with respect to its impact than Mencius. He would agree with Mencius that it is a potential catalyst for virtue, but would also warn that it is often the wellspring of vice. Virtue and vice have the same roots and this is why morality will never come into being without its opposite. Shame is a function of *amour-propre*, a comparative evaluation of the self. How others see us is a vital part of our self-image and our integration into the community. *Amour-propre* has the potential to unleash tremendous insecurity that can, when properly channeled, facilitate moral cohesion but may also unleash the disintegrating spiral of egoism, which enfeebles the community. It can either steer us toward improvement or plunge us into vice.

According to Mencius, shame arises when one has done something to exclude oneself from the community, or is devalued by others; for Rousseau, the interaction with others inevitably generates such feelings of lack. In fact, the development of *amour-propre* ensures that the moral order will always be fragile, and Rousseau might insist that a healthy dose of compassion is necessary as a counterweight to the insecurity that *amour-propre* generates.

Amour-propre emerges with the increased use of language, which incites people to make comparisons: "People become accustomed to considering different objects and to make comparisons. Imperceptibly they acquire the ideas of merit and beauty which produce feelings of preference" (*DOI* 63). The differences between myself and others impel me to reflect on myself as a separate being who longs for the "restoration" of the lost fullness of the protohuman. As a comparative understanding of the self, it also focuses our attention on what we perceive ourselves to be lacking. In Rousseau's view, social interaction introduces lack into our consciousness and forever deprives us of *amour-de-soi*, ensuring that we will never experience the unadulterated satisfaction with our own existence. The nostalgia for a lost contentment coupled with the perception of lack leads to the formation of an ego, along with its potentially ravenous appetite for recognition.

Incipient feelings of inadequacy impel us to constantly solicit the affirmation of others. Selfish tendencies are exacerbated when we too eagerly covet their recognition. *Amour-propre* for Rousseau is intrinsically connected to reason: "Reason is what engenders egocentrism, and reflection strengthens it. Reason is what separates him from all that troubles him and afflicts him. Philosophy is what isolates him and what moves him to say in secret, at the sight of a suffering man, 'Perish if you will; I am safe and sound'" (*DOI* 54). Reason allows us to relate to another abstractly: "Although it might be appropriate for Socrates and minds of his stature to acquire virtue through reason, the human race would long ago have ceased to exist, if its preservation had depended solely on the reasonings of its members" (*DOI* 55). Because reason allows for the possibility of an abstract and distant relationship to others, it must be controlled by counterbalancing it with emotions such as pity. Indeed, this is not entirely dissimilar to the balance that Mencius believes is necessary between *ren* and *yi*. According to Rousseau, we must nourish the animal side of humanity to prevent humanity's slide into barbarism.

Rousseau makes the case that in earlier, allegedly primitive communities, the community as a whole would grant the coveted recognition, and in this way the individuals would continuously be welcomed into the social fold. In so doing, the community would act as a surrogate for the completeness of the protohuman experience: "People grew accustomed to gather in front of their huts or around a large tree; song and dance, true children of love and leisure became the amusement or rather the occupation for idle men and woman who flocked together. Each one began to look at the other and to want to be looked at himself, and public esteem had a value" (*DOI* 64). Although there was competition for the esteem of one's fellow human beings, this was mitigated by the overall equality and the fact that the community as a whole provided recognition. Community bonds were repeatedly strengthened and formed through this process, offsetting the contrary pull of selfishness. However, the community was fragile because it drove a wedge between the world of nature and the "natural" independence of the protohuman. Furthermore, it was inevitable that some people were able to achieve greater recognition than others: "And this was the first step toward inequality and at the same time, toward vice" (*DOI* 64).

Once relationships of inequality started to creep into social orders, a tremendous sense of insecurity set in, quickly dissolving the trust that would uphold social bonds. This development was accelerated by agriculture and metallurgy. The division of land into plots impelled human beings "to say *this is mine*" (*DOI* 60), an announcement signaling the exclusion of others. With metallurgy, labor became increasingly specialized and human beings stumbled on the possibility of making a profit: "The farmer had a greater need for iron, or the blacksmith had a greater need for wheat; and in labouring equally, the one earned a great deal while the other barely had enough to live" (*DOI* 67). Insecurity gives rise to the need for moral virtues and civility: "From this came the first duties of civility, even among savages, and from this every voluntary wrong became an outrage, because along with the harm that resulted from the injury, the offended party saw in it contempt for his person, which often was more insufferable than the harm itself" (*DOI* 64). The affront to dignity described here is very similar to the repugnance experienced by Mencius's beggar who is offered rice with an insulting gesture. Social decorum is necessary because iniquitous relationships undermine the security of individuals. Politeness becomes a way of masking inequality.

The tension created by iniquitous relations is compounded by a growing rift between artifice and nature, which furthers the profound sense of alienation endemic to many societies. We attempt to fill the gaping void within us through possession, not only in terms of material goods but also by trying to force others to comply with our demands.[13]

---

13 Pierre Burgelin maintains that I become the owner of attributes and characteristics

This may be part of a misguided attempt to regain independence, since it reflects a desire to bring everything into the enclosure of the self. In reality, it merely exacerbates our dependence, because such possession only has meaning if recognized by others. The quest for independence results in its opposite, and thereby compounds a burgeoning sense of dissatisfaction.

When Rousseau labels nature "good," this is more of a comment on the accelerated degeneration he witnesses in social orders, which have abandoned their natural moorings. Nature in itself is neither good nor bad, but an attempt to imitate it and integrate oneself into it leads to good, while a widening of the schism between ourselves and nature leads to vice. Once we have wandered too far from the path of nature, we engage in a kind of frenetic striving in a misguided attempt to recapture the "wholeness" of *amour-de-soi*. The civilizing process becomes a moral one, if it is attentive to our natural roots and strives to achieve balanced human interconnectedness that takes into account what Rousseau considers to be our presocial origins.

Human interconnection becomes the "substitute" for integration into the state of nature. Nevertheless, it is important to recognize that we can never feel completely at home within any community, because the blissful state of the protohuman can never be re-created. Once the path of civilization has been embarked upon, the self-sufficient and contented protohuman is lost to us forever. At the same time, this fuels what Rousseau refers to as our perfectibility and provides the impetus for the assiduous re-creation of a community which can never be taken for granted. Harmony must be continuously re-created because it is always under threat.

According to Rousseau, we would not be moral beings if we were not also selfish beings. Both are symptomatic of the loss which accompanies our departure from the state of nature. When we are selfish, we

once they are recognized by society as mine. He thereby equates possession with individuation. However, this ignores the fact that in primitive societies, human beings were recognized not for their possessions but rather for their activity. Individuation is not necessarily linked to possession. See Burgelin, *La Philosophie die l'Existence de Jean-Jacques Rousseau* (Paris: Presses Universitaires de France, 1952), p. 253.

try to compensate for our own insecurity by either denigrating others or excluding them, in an effort to act upon the misguided belief that we can be complete on our own. Morality uses social harmony to offset this lost sense of completeness. However, when compared to the independent contentment of *amour-de-soi*, it always remains an insufficient substitute.

The fact that Mencius identifies emotions based on sentiments of lack such as shame suggests that even in his philosophy, imbalance can become a powerful moral impetus. If balance was always automatically generated, we would not need morality. Yet, when this imbalance is too pervasive, the cultivation of virtue becomes exceedingly difficult. This is why Mencius suggests that unfortunate circumstances spawn cruel behavior in the youth, while good circumstances are more likely to produce reliability. The youth do not have the necessary moral backbone that may help adults weather times of distress. Furthermore, they may lack the "tranquil abode of *ren*" which furnishes human beings with the fortitude to overcome injustice rather than escalating it. Mencius admonishes us to refrain from deliberately reproaching those one is close to, since this leads to alienation that can undermine morality: "Fathers and sons did not demand goodness of one another. If the one demands goodness of the other, then they will become estranged. There is nothing more inauspicious than for them to become estranged" (*M* 4A18). The Chinese text reads 責善則離 (*ze shan ze li*; *M* Ch 4A18), or "demanding the good leads to separation." Mencius, like Rousseau, recognizes the powerful role that psychological factors play in spawning either virtue or vice. If children and parents become estranged from each other, then *ren* will become unstable, and it is very difficult to develop one's virtues without being enveloped in a strong community. If a child's moral fiber is to be strengthened, then he cannot have overly critical and demanding parents.

By reading Mencius in conjunction with Rousseau, one can see that both morality and selfishness arise in part from a sense of lack and imbalance within social orders. Rousseau would argue that they will always exist as uneasy bedfellows so long as we find ourselves in societies which necessarily constitute a departure from nature. We must ensure that morality prevails by being cognizant of the specter of selfishness that will always haunt us. While Mencius also acknowledges the threat of selfishness, he would insist that we are naturally interconnected beings. The insecurity that generates vice occurs when we lose sight of this interconnectedness. For Rousseau, this insecurity is ineradicable precisely because we are naturally solitary beings.

Artifice and Spontaneity

The relationship between artifice and convention is central to both Rousseau's and Mencius's account of morality. Human beings have the capacity to either heed and extend natural patterns or disregard them, and consequently fall into vice. At the same time, both recognize nature as a potential source of imbalance, in need of taming by human beings. Rousseau argues that meteorological tempests may have contributed to the socialization of human beings. According to Mencius, nature must not only be incorporated in agricultural practices but tamed through them, and agriculture is symbolic of the human way of participating in the connective energy of *qi*; for Rousseau, farming marks our irreversible exit from nature. According to Mencius, our natural dispositions must be reinforced through deliberate cultivation and a constant attentiveness to balance. While *qi* itself is indifferent to the shape it assumes, his account of morality insists that we consciously build upon our natural dispositions in order to become moral beings. Flood-like energy alone does not suffice to cultivate virtue. For this, one's *xin* 心 (heart-mind) must be nurtured. "Gaozi said, 'What you do not get from doctrines, do not seek for in your heart. What you do not get from your heart, do not seek for in the *qi*.' 'What you do not get from your heart, do not seek for in the *qi*' is acceptable. 'What you do not get from doctrines, do not seek for in your heart' is unacceptable" (*M* 2A2).

There is no equivalent in the English language to *xin*. It intertwines both feeling and thoughtfulness, and suggests that we have an embedded relationship to the environment, rather than an abstract one predicated on words alone. The strongest evidence for the existence of *xin* is that we care for other human beings, for ourselves, and for our world. *Xin* is a profound testament to our interconnectedness, and while we can muffle it, it is impossible to eradicate it completely.

Mencius is widely known in the Chinese philosophical literature for his assertion that human nature is fundamentally good, largely because of the importance he accredited *xin* with. When queried about behavior, which tends in the direction of the bad as well as the good, Mencius replies: "As to what they are inherently, they can become good. This is what I mean by calling their natures good. As for their becoming not good, this is not the fault of their potential" (*M* 6A6). All the necessary building blocks for goodness exist and it is up to human beings to avail themselves of them. It is interesting to note that in this passage, the term *bu shan* 不善 (not good) rather than *e* 惡 (ugly) is used. In doing so, he points to someone who has failed to cultivate the potential for goodness within us, rather than to an inherent personality flaw.

The disposition for good must be reinforced by habit and education. Mencius asserts that in good years, children of people are "gentle" while in bad years, "most men are violent" (*M* 6A7). Immediately following this passage is an agricultural metaphor which reinforces the notion that careful nurture is required to ensure that the seed grows to its full capacity: "Consider barley. Sow the seeds and cover them. The soil is the same and the time of planting is also the same. They grow rapidly and by the time of the summer solstice they have all ripened. Although there are some differences, these are due to the richness of the soil and to unevenness in the rain and in human effort" (*M* 6A7). The agricultural metaphors which Mencius avails himself of are not accidental, for they suggest that a blend of artifice and nature defines the moral course of human beings. Agriculture is not a symbol of our departure from nature, but rather a testament to our particularly human way of being in nature. In fact, there is a sense in which nature needs human beings in order to improve upon it: "The way of the people is this: if they are full of food, have warm clothes, and live in comfort but are without instruction, then they too come close to being animals" (*M* 3A4). Indeed the mythical sage-king Yu had to prepare the land for farming, so that animals and birds were subdued and people were able to plant grain.

In one passage, Mencius describes Ox Mountain which has been shorn of its trees by grazing cattle. The wood-stuff (*cai* 材) is present in the mountain soil but requires the proper nutrients in order to grow.

Similarly, daily habits of human beings will affect one's natural disposition, and either enhance or destroy it:

> The way that they discard their genuine hearts is like the hatchets and axes in relation to the trees. With them besieging it day by day, can it remain beautiful? With the respite it gets during the day or night, and the restorative effects of the morning *qi*, their likes and dislikes are sometimes close to those of others. But then what they do during the day again fetters and destroys it. If the fettering is repeated, then the evening *qi* is insufficient to preserve it, then one is not far from an animal. Others see that he is an animal, and think that there was never any capacity there. But is this what a human is like inherently?
>
> (*M* 6A8)

It is significant that Mencius identifies the moment between night and day as the time when we are attuned to those sentiments proper to humanity. The frenzy of the day often shatters our sense of equilibrium. At dawn, when night has not yet abandoned us and the morning has not fully arrived, there is an awareness of balance and the interconnection between things, including light and darkness. This balance is fragile because it is only momentary and is quickly surpassed by the overwhelming light of day. Furthermore, night provides a temporary respite from the habits imposed upon us during the day, since it occasions a brief encounter with the formless.

Although Mencius is insistent on the need for moral cultivation and habituation, he is careful not to undermine the harmonious aspect of *qi*. Morality imposed by rigid rules or doctrinaire approaches would disrupt the balance of nature and interfere with the natural process of *qi*'s growth. Rousseau issues similar warnings that a child cannot be weighed down with a set of moral doctrines that it is then forced to obey, because it will then quickly become skilled at the art of deception. Mencius is suspicious of an externally imposed practice because it often leapfrogs nature, failing to recognize that we are engaged in its creative process. In order to shape *qi* well, one must also be attuned to nature, rather than positing a goal and then simply forcing circumstances into a human mold.

Mencius has frequent recourse to agricultural metaphors in order to illuminate the path of moral cultivation. While the art of agriculture does lend its own shape to nature, it must do so by heeding its rhythms. Agriculture is therefore a primary example of the intersection of natural and human worlds. Mencius offers the example of the man of Song who tried to compel corn to grow by pulling it up, thereby upsetting the balance of nature. A doctrinaire approach prevents the individual from being attuned to the dynamics of the moment and may undermine the activity of harmonization. Instead, balance must be aspired to at all times. In fashioning human dispositions, one should not use doctrine in order to enforce it:

> When people in the world discuss "nature" they are referring simply to what is primordial. What is primordial is based on what happens smoothly. In contrast, what I dislike about "wise" people is that they force things. If "wise" people were like Yu in guiding the waters, then there would be nothing to dislike about their wisdom. Yu, in guiding the waters, guided them where no effort was required. If "wise" people also guided things where no effort was required, there wisdom would also be great.
>
> (*M* 4B26)

A heavy reliance on words can cause us to lose sight of the spontaneous connectedness associated with *xin*. However, this does not mean that Mencius denies the important role of the will or *zhi* 志 in shaping *qi*. The will can direct *qi* but cannot establish its autonomy from it. Instead, one must see the relationship between *qi* and the will as mutually constitutive, since an accumulation of *qi* can shape the will: "Your will is the commander of *qi*. . . . When your will is unified it moves the *qi*. When the *qi* is unified, it moves your will. Now running and stumbling have to do with the *qi*, but nonetheless they perturb the heart" (*M* 2A2). Running is a participation in the flowing energy of *qi*; a fall occurs when we encounter a temporary obstacle to movement, when *qi* is obstructed. This is an interesting example because it points out that the direction movement takes will effect the flow of *qi*. We do not just passively run or fall, but rather respond to this action at both emotional and intellectual levels. Furthermore, the obstruction of prior movement sparks a desire for the continuation of movement. *Zhi* is a distinctively human way of channeling *qi*. Just as the hollows through which wind travels will affect the sounds that it emits, so can our use of the will generate different constellations with *qi*, but it cannot eliminate or ignore it. The will must be used to react in a manner that is appropriate to the particular situation. Mencius asserts that, "Flowing water is a thing which does not proceed till it has filled the hollows *in its course*" (M 7A24). Morality can be thought of as a way of opening new passages for *qi*, thereby enhancing its flow.

Joanne Birdwhistell points out that the reverence for Yu and the taming of nature, which is part of Mencius's philosophy, involves an implicit privileging of masculine over maternal metaphors. She cites the passage which refers to a man named Xu Xing who was a follower of the sage-ruler Shen Nong, the Divine Farmer. Shen Nong is associated with agricultural practices such as the cultivation of crops, but also with fertility, birth, civilization, and nourishment.[14] She points out that the occupation of Xu Xing and his followers bind sandals and weave clothes and mats, which are tasks traditionally associated with women. They come as outsiders who are attracted to benevolent government. Another set of migrants, Chen Xiang and his brother, are farmers who carry ploughs but convert to the teachings of Xu Xing maintaining that the ruler who follows the way also tills the land and cooks meals. Mencius argues against this blurring of boundaries, maintaining that the "great men govern and are fed by inferior men." [15] Birdwhistell shows that the division of labor upon which Mencius insists parallels that between husband and wife, and therefore implies that his order demands a sexual division of labor.[16] Taming nature, takes on a specifically masculinized form.

For Mencius, nature is not lost to us in the way that Rousseau describes, because human beings are always already part of it. Nonetheless, there is an implicit assumption that nature cannot be left to its own devices; it must be ordered by human beings. Furthermore, the natural cosmos is a meaningful one, enabling us to discern patterns which can serve as aids to moral living. Reason responds to cues from nature. In one example, Mencius asserts that, "There is a technique to observing water:

14 Joanne D. Birdwhistell, *Mencius and Masculinities: Dynamics of Power, Morality and Maternal Thinking* (Albany: State University of New York Press, 2007), p. 40.

15 Ibid., p. 44.

16 Ibid.

one observes where the waves come from" (*M* 7A24). The contemplation of water demands an awareness that is both intuitive and reflective. The waves represent a gentle rhythm consisting of a constant swelling and abatement; on the other hand, the waves suggest upheaval in contrast to the tranquil waters of a moonlit lake or the steady flow of a river. It is the relationship between balance and imbalance to which human beings must be attentive. Moral virtue often demands that we find possibilities for balance in the midst of moral upheaval. If we live in corrupt times, the restorative potential of nature becomes even more important.

Interpreters of Mencius have argued that he employs a teleological approach similar to that of Aristotle where human nature tends in a pre-given direction.[17] However, his teleology, unlike Rousseau's, is not fueled by the awareness that our natural beginnings are lost to us forever. Nevertheless, there is a sense in which the human capacity for abstraction and reflection can cause us to lose sight of the balance in nature which, Mencius suggests, should always be available to us. The kind of civilization that Mencius proposes is seen as one that is consistent with the harmonizing potential of nature itself. There need be no profound sense of loss because the potential for balance is always already there; we must learn to heed its voice, not only in ourselves but also in natural phenomenon, such as the movement of waves or the activity of the stars: "Consider the height of the heavens and the distance of the stars and planets. Yet if one merely seeks out their primordial state, one can sit and determine the solstice in a thousand years" (*M* 4B26). This is a striking passage because it juxtaposes the remoteness and nearness of natural phenomena. What is far, is close and what is close, is far. The stars represent a continuity with all that is and has been. This is why the distant is near—because the stars are nodes of connectedness that have spanned generations, they bring us close to what is temporally remote.

In a similar vein, morality demands that we extend our range of care to include those who are not within our immediate environs. This demands an adroit juxtaposition of emotion, and reason for emotion

17 Benjamin Schwartz, *The World of Thought in Ancient China* (Cambridge: Harvard University Press, 1985), p. 175.

can often be limited to more immediate encounters with others. We cannot only rely on our immediate sense perceptions alone, since they can pull us in a multitude of directions. In order to engage with things, we must think as well as feel, in order to bring them into accord: "It is not the function of the ears and eyes to reflect and they are misled by things. Things interact with other things and simply lead them along. But the function of the heart is to reflect. If it reflects, then it will get it. If it does not reflect, it will not get it" (*M* 6A15). Our engagement with the world must resemble the creation of harmonious melodies, which depend upon a subtle combination of reflection and spontaneity.

If moral virtue is to be inculcated in human beings, it cannot be forced but must extend and/or strengthen natural elements. Like Rousseau, Mencius is attentive to the danger inherent in abstractions of words, and thus also seems aware of the perils of reason:

> If someone's expressions are one-sided, I know that by which they are obscured. If someone's expressions are excessive, I know what they have sunk into. If someone's expressions are heretical, I know that by which they are separated from the Way. If someone's expressions are evasive, I know that by which they are overwhelmed. When these faults grow in the heart, they are harmful in governing.
>
> (*M* 2A2)

For Mencius, the social setting can create environments that propagate selfish behavior, but this is the case when, like Ox Mountain forcibly shorn of trees, the environment does not provide the occasion for flourishing. Thus, he implies that there must be an organic and mutually reinforcing relationship between nature and civilization. Indeed, one could argue that for Mencius, nature is not the substratum that is antecedent to civilization, for nature and civilization are always already entangled. Rousseau is slightly less optimistic, as he suggests that the social environment cannot but drive a wedge between human beings and their pre-social roots. Ensuring that the rift does not undermine the social order itself is a delicate balancing act; while selfishness can be controlled, it can never be curbed completely since it is part of the process of socialization.

According to Rousseau, morality is necessary when human beings have lost the natural equilibrium in nature and attempt to reconstruct a new social equilibrium based on an awareness of what has been lost. True equilibrium always escapes us, and the return to nature that we long for is impossible. Morality will always be infected with sentiments of incompleteness, which threaten to disrupt the very balance we need to cultivate.

Because Rousseau demarcates artifice and nature more sharply than Mencius, he associates morality with artifice. Since he is prescribing a moral social order for bourgeois society in which selfishness is deeply entrenched, his prescription for reviving balance necessitates the resurrection of an almost defunct community. For him, it is inevitable that the civilizing process alienates us from nature and thus spawns nostalgia for a world lost to us forever. Selfishness may be a misguided grasping for the protohuman nonself, who did not face internal divisions and who was so immersed in the natural world that he or she was complete. The selfish individual attempts to bring everything within his or her purview in a desperate attempt to ensure that nothing is exterior to the self in a mistaken attempt to restore *amour-de-soi*. Such tactics are bound to fail and so the egotistical self will be infected with a gnawing unhappiness. Ironically, the egoist may really be after the nonegotistical contentment of the protohuman.

Because Rousseau uses the independent presocial human being as his barometer, he tries to imitate this condition within the social order. The problem he confronts is that the social self is already a divided self since the capacity for comparison drives a wedge into the core of our being. A workable morality must satiate the desire for independence that is a remnant of the protohuman ancestry he assumes we all share. Recognizing that we can never return to our presocial condition, he tries to develop a form of social contract that approximates it at a social level. The fact that he must invoke the mechanism of a social contract is a testament to the atomized relationships within bourgeois society, which generate a widespread distrust. Furthermore, it implies that a great deal of artifice is needed to "return" to nature once we have become individuated beings.

Through his social contract, Rousseau tries to elicit the best of all worlds by creating both a strong community and independent individuals. Thus, he hopes to "find a form of association which defends and protects with all common forces the person and goods of each associate, and by means of which each one, while uniting with all, nevertheless obeys only himself and remains as free as before" (*SC* 148).[18] Obviously, the complete independence of the protohuman is forever beyond our grasp, and thus the closest means of imitating it is to ensure that each citizen is equally dependent on the whole. Each individual is to be both an indivisible part of the community at large, while the community is dependent upon each and every individual. Evidently, this is a most striking paradox. Each person agrees to put aside their particular will and legislate for the community as a whole of which they are members. The individual thereby becomes part of something larger than the self, while at the same time creating the conditions by which he becomes such a part. The nature of the self undergoes a transformation as a result of this interaction: "This passage from the state of nature to the civil state produces quite a remarkable change in man, for it substitutes justice for instinct in his behaviour and gives his actions a moral quality they previously lacked" (*SC* 148). Every individual obeys only himself in outlining the conditions under which he is willing to be part of the community. Not only does he become part of a larger whole, but the whole is embodied in each and every individual.

For Rousseau, it is absolutely paramount that individuals in such a society are equal, for without such equality, a gnawing insecurity further spawns selfishness: "Finally in giving himself to all, each person gives himself to no one, and since there is no associate over whom he does not acquire the same right that he would grant others over himself, he gains the equivalent of everything he loses, along with a greater amount of force to preserve what he has" (*SC* 148). Because each of us is equally dependent on the whole, nobody can undermine the independence of another. Rousseau's social contract is intended to protect us from each other, and thus is tailored to the suspicious bourgeois. Furthermore, Rousseau suggests that by legislating the terms for our membership in

---

18 Jean-Jacques Rousseau, *On the Social Contract*, in *The Basic Political Writings*, ed. Peter Gay (Indianapolis: Hackett Publishing Company, 1987).

this community, I become the whole that includes me and therefore, I universalize myself. Citizenship forces me to be conscious of the universality and of the whole, of which one is a part. The bonds of the whole must be continuously rewoven and recrafted. Each person is both part and embodiment of the whole. This is the closest we can come to the independence of the protohuman while living within society's frontiers.

Rousseau's thought suggests that the impossibility of achieving the harmonious reconciliation between nature and convention, and between self and community, necessitates constant vigilance with respect to forming the community: "If we wish to form a durable establishment, let us then not dream of making it eternal" (*SC* 194). Because social bonds can never fill the void left by the lost harmony of the protohuman, they must continually be rejuvenated. The ineradicable tension between nature and civilization spawns human creativity and also generates a restlessness, which can never be completely extirpated from the human psyche. Furthermore, Rousseau insists that the individual can have a "private will contrary from the general will that he has as a citizen" (*SC* 150). I have to be able to distance myself from the community in order to ensure that the community is consciously and deliberately formed. Rousseau's "teleology" is without terminus since it is a process that never achieves its goal. Social harmony must be perpetually renewed because it never completely satisfies.

Rousseau's moral community is spurred on by a profound sense of tension and loss accompanying the departure from our origins. Nevertheless, its failure is necessary to its success. The tension between nature and the social existence of human beings demands unceasing attentiveness to the community, and thus ensures that the community remains alive. Prodigious effort must be exerted to prevent stagnation. Once we begin to take the laws we formulate for granted, "the state is no longer alive" (*SC* 194). In contrast to the thought of Mencius, Rousseau's moral equilibrium will never succeed in producing a harmonious relationship with the natural world. Instead, the friction between nature and the social existence of human beings demands unceasing regeneration of the community.

Family

Both Mencius and Rousseau are aware that virtue directed at an abstract other is very difficult to engender without concrete relationships of intimacy. This is why the family plays a central role in both of their philosophies. Family affection and social hierarchy are the cornerstones of Confucian ethics, and are seen by Mencius as the wellspring of moral virtue. Weiming Tu points out that "families imbued with Confucian values are perhaps still the single most important social institution in imparting ways of learning to be human in East Asian societies." [19] The high premium that Mencius places on familial affection is in keeping with his notion of organically unfolding virtue that must have a solid grounding before it can flower. He is extremely critical of the Mohist approach, which places greater emphasis on external doctrines and underlines the importance of universal love. The family is the arena in which moral sentiments, such as deference and love, are first cultivated; because such affection is unlearned, they form the foundation of all subsequently acquired virtues:

> That which people are capable of without learning is their genuine capability. That which they know without pondering is their genuine knowledge. Among babes in arms there are none that do not know to love their parents. When they grow older, there are none that do not know to revere their elder brothers. Treating one's parents as parents is benevolence. Revering one's elders is righteousness. There is nothing else to do but extend these to the world.
>
> (*M* 7A15)

Upholding these feelings and extending them to include a broader spectrum of relations is the mark of a great man: "The great man is he who does not lose his child's heart" (*M* 4A12).

If these feelings are to transform into moral virtue, they must evolve into respect that moves beyond immediacy and becomes part of the ritual of the community: "Caring for the living is not sufficient to be considered a great task. Only sending off the dead may be considered

19 Weiming Tu, "Probing the 'Three Bonds' and 'Five Relationships' in Confucian Humanism," in *Confucianism and the Family*, ed. Walter H. Slote and George A. De Vos (Albany: State University of New York Press, 1998), p. 135.

a great task" (*M* 4B13). The development of the nonimmediate respect that occurs after one's parents have died is indicative of a virtue that has extended beyond the fulfillment of an immediate need. Furthermore, ancestral worship is not simply a matter of familial respect, but also marks the continuity of the larger community. According to Mencius, ideally, the link to one's parents is interwoven within the broader framework of the social order: "Treat your elders as elders and extend it to the elders of others; treat your young ones as young ones, and extend it to the young ones of others, and you can turn the world in the palm of your hand" (*M* 1A7). Mencius was critical of the Mohist Yi Zhi, for making the case that we must love universally without favoring those closest to one: "Yi Zhi said, 'According to the Way of the Confucians, the ancients treated the people like caring for a baby.' What does this saying mean? I take it to mean that love is without differentiations, but it is bestowed beginning with one's parents" (*M* 3A5). To this, Mencius's response was, "Does Yi Zhi truly hold that one's affection for one's own nephew is like one's affection for a neighbour's baby?" (*M* 3A5). Morality must be grounded in its roots if it is to develop properly. If one does not acknowledge the ethical import of familial relations, one is little more than a beast. As Sor-Hoon Tan points out, the "network of relations is like a ripple—no matter how far it extends, the energy is always greatest at the center, decreasing proportionally to the distance from the center. How far a ripple could extend depends on the amount of energy at the center."[20] The more energy is focused at the center, the more it can be directed further afield.

Mencius's account of the growth of moral feeling is very dependent on a specific local context. While one may extend one's moral concern to other human beings and broaden one's moral horizons, the root affection for the family must be maintained, since it is the concrete soil of all that comes beyond it. If it withers, one's moral character is at stake: "The core of benevolence is serving one's parents. The core of righteousness is obeying one's older brother. The core of wisdom is know-

20 Sor-Hoon Tan, *Confucian Democracy: A Deweyan Reconstruction* (Albany: State University of New York Press, 2003), p. 72.

ing these two and not abandoning them" (*M* 4A27). This also means that in a situation where one is forced to choose between loyalty to the state and loyalty to the family, for Mencius, the latter assumes priority. Like Confucius, Mencius insists that the sage-king Shun would flee with his father if his father had killed a man and was in danger of arrest. While this clearly contravenes the law, Confucian thinkers see the law as an inadequate means of inculcating virtue.

The problem with this intense concentration on familial virtue is that it can easily be accommodated in very noncommunal and fragmented societies, which prevail in the modern era. There is no necessary connection between broader public involvement and loyalty to one's own. Mencius himself cites a disturbing example, when the sage-king Shun rewards his unethical brother with a fiefdom while others, whose conduct was less reprehensible, were punished more harshly. Mencius justifies the treatment that Shun meted out on the basis of familial devotion. On the other hand, Mencius concedes that Shun was justified in not informing his parents of his marriage, thereby overlooking the requirements of custom, because his parents would have denied him the opportunity to marry, thus disrupting the continuity of the family line.

Rousseau does not view the family as a natural institution of social order, since he takes the independent protohuman as the most primordial human being. The family, like the social order itself, is the product of artifice and the bonds of affection within it are not entirely natural, but in part contrived. Nevertheless, Rousseau would concur with Mencius that the familial order provides a more immediate range of concern, which can then be extended to create possibilities for responsible citizenship. However, the lynchpin of the family in Rousseau's account is not the father-son relationship as in Mencius, but rather the husband-wife relationship as illustrated in his *Bildungsroman*, *Emile*. Morality and sex must be intertwined so that Emile's desires can be harnessed to lead him to social responsibility. The sexual relationship is to mirror the oneness within nature. Furthermore, the love for another always emerges out of a desire for self-love: "The source of our passions, the origin and the principle of all the others, the only one born with man and which never leaves him so long as he lives is self-love—a primitive innate passion which is interior to every other and of which all others are in a sense only modifications. . . . The love of oneself is always good and always in conformity with order" (*E* 208). The departure from nature leaves us with a gaping wound, because the self is now plagued with a sense of incompleteness and love constitutes a panacea for this. The paradox of Rousseau's account of love is that it constitutes an opening of the self to others that stems from nostalgia, for the contentment of a completely self-sufficient being. Seen in this way, love will always be fraught with tension, for the same lover who is destined to "reproduce" our self-contentment also disturbs it. The awareness of being "one" in love is accompanied by a disturbing awareness that one is "two"; for Rousseau, this is always a source of malaise.

When introducing Emile to the delights of love and sexual desire in *Emile*, Rousseau provides a mystical account of nature: "Stones, trees, heaps of rocks, consecrated by these acts and thus made respectable to barbaric men, were the pages of this book which was constantly open to all eyes. The well of the oath, the well of the living and seeing, the old oak of Mamre, the mound of the witness, these were the crude but August monuments of the sanctity of contracts" (*E* 321). Then, he introduces sexuality and marriage to Emile: "The idea of the exclusive attachment which makes it delicious and the idea of the duties of fidelity and of modesty which surround it and redouble its charm in fulfilling its object; if in depicting marriage to him, not only as the sweetest of associations but as the most inviolable and holiest of all contracts" (*E* 323). Thus, the union with another human being is portrayed as a union with nature itself. Through passion, Emile extends the boundaries of the self to include the other rather than just perceiving the other as a means for the reciprocal satisfaction of needs.

The fragility that tarnishes Rousseau's account of love is manifested in the relationship between Emile and Sophie: "As soon as man has need of a companion, he is no longer an isolated being. His heart is no longer alone. All his relations with his species, all the affection of his soul are born with this one" (*E* 214). And yet, Sophie must be trained to please Emile in such a way that his self-love is augmented and she becomes a mirror that reflects Emile's image back to him. Sophie is not allowed to be an independent other, since her whole education is directed at tending to the needs of her future husband. In this way, Emile's love for another really is a reflection of a kind of self-love. Emile does not have the experience of extending the self that Mencius would claim necessary for moral virtue. Instead, his relationship with Sophie is set up to facilitate Emile's perpetual return to himself. Her dependence makes his continued independence possible.

Nevertheless, there is in Rousseau the recognition that the passionate bonds to one's beloved can easily become all-consuming, rather than facilitate ethical virtues concomitant with responsible citizenship. Because of Emile's strong propensity for independence, it is Sophie who is to receive training in social niceties and accommodation to others: "Always justify the cares that you impose on young girls but always impose cares on them. . . . All their lives they will be enslaved to the most continual and most severe of constraints—that of proprieties" (*E* 369). She is the one, who at dinner gatherings, smooths over social tensions. Furthermore, her love is to be reserved for the model citizen, even though she is to remain forever hidden within the home. She entices Emile to take part in the community that might otherwise not interest him and therefore becomes the link between Emile and the broader community. It is Sophie who is responsible for the extension of Emile to include the community and thus strengthen the seeds of moral virtue within him: "Observe how the physical leads us unawares to the moral, and how the sweetest laws of love are born little by little from the coarse union between the sexes" (*E* 360). When Emile arrives late for a date with Sophie because he had been tending to a man with a broken leg, Sophie decides to marry him since he has proven to be socially responsible. The family unit that Rousseau describes is centered on Emile and the problem of integrating him into the larger society falls upon Sophie's shoulders. However, her needs are not taken into account; she simply becomes the conduit through which Emile's virtue can be adequately developed.

Rousseau assumes that children are naturally indifferent to others, and thus his ideal love relationship is one modeled along the lines of what he considers to be a healthy self-love. For Mencius, love and humility are connected and he does not assume that the child is naturally indifferent to others, insisting that the love that children have for their parents is one of the most basic human emotions. Conversely, Emile is brought up without this intimate relationship with his parents, because that would interfere with the project of turning him into a morally responsible but independent individual. He is to grow up under the illusion that he managed to meet his needs on his own, thanks to the carefully crafted interference of his tutor. According to Rousseau, an individual who is not independent cannot be moral because he would be too eager to solicit the approval of others.

The difficulty in extending Emile's range of concern from the immediate family setting to include the broader community is evident, when Emile is hesitant to leave Sophie to enter the broader world to learn about politics and the wider community. However, in order to entice Emile away from Sophie, Rousseau must invoke a promise that Emile had made earlier while in the throes of passion, namely to obey his tutor. The fact that Rousseau must invoke this promise, made almost without thinking in the midst of the impetuous passion of youth, demonstrates that the political and the personal cannot always easily be reconciled.

The choice of examples in Rousseau and Mencius provides an interesting contrast. The family in Rousseau is predicated on the relationship of desire, which seeks a lost fullness in the other who is there to close a gap. Desire is spawned out of an interesting blend of distance and proximity. The enchantment with Sophie inheres in her physical closeness; meanwhile, she can never satisfy Emile's quest for oneness. Desire plays on the difficult negotiation around sentiments of presence and loss. The parent-child relationship in Mencius, on the other hand, is not fraught with such tension. It is an example of the natural connectedness between human beings whose influence must radiate beyond one's immediate environs. For Rousseau, this broadening of connectedness is a more daunting project, because all love for others is a variation of male self-love, and thus threatens the very sense of self-sufficiency it is supposed to underwrite.

Naturalizing Civilization

Both Rousseau and Mencius stand out within their own traditions for the decisive role that nature plays in their moral philosophies. They would concur that the process of harmonization within nature is an essential aspect of the moral development of human beings. However, while Mencius would hold that the process of socialization is part of the unfolding of the natural cosmos itself, Rousseau would insist that the constant reconciliation with nature is necessary because human beings are not naturally social creatures but indifferent to others. Once they become part of communities, a rift is opened between them and nature that must be constantly tended to; otherwise, it can lead to a selfishness that threatens to undermine the social order itself. Selfishness for Rousseau is not an accidental byproduct of socialization, it is an inherent part of its dynamic. As social beings, we are separated from our natural moorings, and as natural beings, we will always regard the social order with some suspicion. Morality is part of the process of creating a relative equilibrium, so that the dualistic nature of the self does not tear us apart. We are perfectible beings because we are imperfect.

Mencius would agree with Rousseau that selfishness must be contained. The intermediate realm we occupy between the earth and heaven is fraught with danger as well as possibility, because it might impel us to harness the energy of *qi* for ourselves. Selfishness, often linked to *li* or amassment for one's own advantage, represents a misguided attempt to enjoy the vastness of *qi*. This threat is particularly acute in times where community bonds have degenerated and moral doctrines are limited to abstract words. This is why human beings must be continuously reminded of their natural sociability, most evident for Mencius in familial relationships. Like Rousseau, Mencius recognizes the potential for alienation that can occur within a social order. Nevertheless, unlike Rousseau, he asserts that affection for others and feelings of pity are indicative of a natural sociability that must be extended because left to its own devices, it does not go far enough. Reason and judgment are used to extend the range of one's feeling to include a broader social spectrum. Humility is necessary because we can never go far enough; the potential for such extension is limitless. There is no such thing as the completely moral person, as virtue is a process and not a fixed state. Morality becomes the human method of participating and contributing to the expansion of *qi*.

Because Mencius does not hold to an image of primordial completeness, there is no evidence of the poignant sense of lack, which characterizes Rousseau's thought. The latent memory of the content protohuman imbues us with a powerful sense of nostalgia and longing. Mencius, on the other hand, is not motivated by a sense of loss, but rather by the flowing nature of *qi* which cannot be arrested, even in times of moral turmoil. *Qi* continues to flow, in spite of human efforts to contain it, and provides moral nourishment if human beings are attentive to it at both emotional and intellectual levels. While both Mencius and Rousseau insist that our virtue never goes far enough, they hold to this view for very different reasons. For Rousseau, morality will always fall short because a return to the protohuman forever eludes us. For Mencius, the movement of *qi* is incessant and moral activity never ceases because we draw upon the source of *qi*, which never runs dry but opens up endless possibilities for cultivating moral connectedness. Thus, the vastness of the moral horizon in Mencius is seen as an opportunity rather than as a testament to human shortcomings.

PART II

VICES OF VIRTUE

CHAPTER THREE

Strangers to Ethics: Kierkegaard and Daoist Approaches

In the first part of this book, I dealt with thinkers for whom the moral vision was paramount, and for whom knowing one's place within the social order becomes a central component of living a life of virtue. While this does not imply that an ethical life is one which remains stagnant, it does link moral virtue to a process of familiarization. Confucius emphasizes that knowing where one stands through the ritualized practices of society is essential if moral virtue is to prevail. A meaningfully ordered cosmos demands that one assume a place within a distinct cultural community. Only this setting is conducive to developing the moral character that allows one to express humanity toward others. The Confucian vision differs profoundly from the legalistic universality of Kant's categorical imperative. Although Kant would refuse to wed morality to a particular place, his insistence on universalization suggests that I should be able to conceive of myself in the position of any other. The imaginary Kingdom of Ends is a world in which nobody is a moral stranger.

Mencius and Rousseau broaden the moral vision by insisting that nature be more carefully incorporated into it. Both would find the Kantian gap between heteronomous desires and the maxims of morality unsustainable. One could argue that, according to their philosophies, a reflection upon nature makes the movement from the familiar to the unfamiliar possible. For Mencius, expanding one's range of concern by building upon innate moral dispositions is part of the human contribution to the flowing dynamic of *qi*. In Rousseau, commitment to the community and to others is motivated in part by our nostalgia for a prehuman state of natural harmony, which fuels the attempt to re-create this harmony at a social level. The natural substratum, which both thinkers rely upon, makes the familiarization of the unfamiliar possible by shaping and also providing a check on artifice.

In the second part of this book, I will deal with thinkers who are critical of ethical systems which they assume are closely tied to convention. This makes it difficult to openly receive the unfamiliar stranger who may not be so easily incorporated into a familiar rubric. From Kierkegaard's perspective, it is precisely in dealing with a stranger that ethics is subjected to its most rigorous and excruciating tests. Kierkegaard is not content with an ethics that limits itself to an extension of the self, for this simply constitutes a broadening of horizons which remains within the purview of selfish behavior. While it is relatively easy to comport oneself ethically when dealing with another subject we either know or whose wellbeing is correlated with our own, it is much more difficult to act morally when such correlation is impossible and the otherness of the other cannot be reasoned away. In such a situation, our ethical horizons are stretched to the limit. Although Confucius would insist that moral cultivation would allow the sage to act appropriately even amongst strangers, Kierkegaard would disagree.

A nonpossessive approach to ethics is impossible without faith in God, who is the infinite intermediary between self and other, in Kierkegaard's view. God, as infinite and absolute other, also opens us up to the "otherness" of others. Kierkegaard insists that if we are truly to respond to the other as other, without attempting to reduce her to a version of ourselves, then the differentiation between self and other must be vigorously maintained. We do this only when we allow her to be stranger, without reducing her to the comforts of familiarity.

Daoist philosophies,[1] with their emphasis on the myriad things, also require a release from selfish attachments in order to provide an opening

---

1 Texts such as the *Daodejing* and the *Zhuangzi* are not likely the work of a single author. In the case of the *Zhuangzi*, only the first six chapters are likely to have been penned by Zhuangzi himself. Hans-Georg Moeller notes that in the life of ancient China, the *Daodejing* was not present in the form of a book as it is read now. Whether or not its alleged author, Laozi, actually existed is still a matter of debate. See Moeller, *The Philosophy of the Daodejing* (New York: Columbia University Press, 2006), pp. 1–3.

to the other that does not necessitate assimilation. The celebration of particularity is something that both Kierkegaard and Daoist texts share. There is a profound interconnection between beings that results from participating in the undifferentiated oneness of *Dao* 道, while at the same time affirming the unique particularity of each being in and of itself. Daoist sages, who are most attuned to *Dao*, are not concerned with their individual identity at all, but rather are as adaptive as water to the world around them. They are at home with themselves because they are not concerned with crafting an identity for themselves. Rather than asking themselves who they are, they ask where they are at a particular juncture of their lives. Unlike the Confucian sage, they revel in the fact that they have no place to stand.

Daoist philosophy rejects conventional ethics, but this does not mean it does not espouse an ethics of its own. I would argue that it is an ethics predicated on cultivating the formless, not as a negation of form but rather as an opening that allows for the flourishing of different forms. The problem with conventional ethics from a Daoist perspective is its prescriptive nature, enjoining us to do and not do certain things, or outlining what sort of person one should be. If openness is cultivated, the problem of the stranger or the "other" does not arise, because it becomes obvious there is neither a self, nor another defined in opposition to the self. From a Daoist perspective, cultivating the self means refusing to fixate on a self-identity. For Kierkegaard, self-identity is important, which is why a leap of faith in God is needed to open one's arms to the other. Radical openness is only possible for God, who is infinite—a finite being cannot be open in this way. Therefore, in order to love the other as other, the Kierkegaardian individual must first make a leap of faith towards an infinite God that cannot possibly be known. Only then can he or she cross the infinite divide that separates self and other. According to Daoist thinkers, this divide does not exist and is only formed through conventional morality. If conventional morality can fall by the wayside, then a truly open engagement with others can begin.

Kierkegaard: Ethics of Aesthetics and the Aesthetics of Ethics

Kierkegaard, like many philosophers of the late-modern and contemporary era, wages an assault against abstract philosophy which reaches its epitome in the philosophy of Hegel. Hegel's thought with its grandiose attempt to make knowledge of the world coterminous with self-recognition was, according to Kierkegaard, egoism writ large. It is no coincidence that a pernicious leveling has reduced us to the abstract phenomenon of the crowd. Selfishness leads to a selflessness born not of generosity to the other, but rather of reluctance to recognize anything other to the self. The ubiquitous abstraction of the crowd, which reduces everyone to the same common denominator, ensures that the social world is a reflection of me and I am in turn a mirror image of the social world. The crowd phenomenon for Kierkegaard is the concretization of the Hegelian abstraction, which tries to harmonize the particular and the universal rather than allowing for dissonance between them.[2] Rousseau had noted that a tension between the particular and general will is necessary in order for the common formulation of the general will to be meaningful. Kierkegaard laments an age that has all but eradicated contradiction by transforming us into living abstractions. The modern individual "does not dare to believe in himself, finds it too venturesome a thing to be himself, far easier and safer to be like the others to become an imitation, a number in the crowd" (*SUD* 186).[3]

The propensity to take refuge in a kind of Hegelian abstraction for Kierkegaard constitutes a powerful statement with respect to the lamentable state of the modern individual. His position on ethics is somewhat confusing and can only be understood against the backdrop of the late-modern context, in which we are subjected to contradictory tendencies. Modern society advocates a kind of dizzying movement that

2 Kierkegaard's critique of Hegel is somewhat unfair. Universalization is not a process of abstraction, but rather a process by which the particular makes and recognizes itself as part of a larger whole. The universal, in turn, is always revealed as a particular because it is simply a part of the unending process of *Geist* or spirit. See G. W. F. Hegel, *Phenomenology of Spirit*, trans. A. V. Miller (Oxford: Oxford University Press, 1979).

3 Søren Kierkegaard, *The Sickness Unto Death: A Christian Psychological Exposition for Upbuilding and Awakening*, trans. Alastair Hannay (Princeton: Princeton University Press, 1980).

not only escapes but defies all definition. The relentless pace means that the movement is often empty because it is impossible for us to take our bearing in the midst of this whirlwind. This in turn whets our appetite for the grip of social convention, which hopes to package existence into clearly defined types and accompanying social norms.[4] These two pulls on the self converge on the individual but do not harmonize. On the one hand, Kierkegaard portrays ethics as a realm of stultifying convention and at other times, he associates it with the responsibility for aesthetic self-creation. We are saddled with the perpetual responsibility for choosing ourselves and fashioning a being that enjoys some kind of temporal continuity in a state of polymorphous confusion. It is this uncomfortable dynamic that impels many to flee unquestioningly into the secure embrace of social convention.

Kierkegaard's most detailed description of conventional ethics occurs in the second volume of *Either/Or*, wherein Assessor Wilhelm extols the standards of conventional morality for the "benefit" of Johannes the Seducer. Unlike many of his contemporaries, Kierkegaard does not lather the aesthetic realm with affectionate praise but rather accuses it of cultivating an empty immediacy which claims to valorize the moment, yet only insofar as the moment is overcome. This is in part a response to an existential condition wherein we inhabit the liminal realm between the finite and infinite. The realm of morality satisfies our craving for the comfort and security of finitude by prescribing our social roles. Aesthetics represents the frenetic attempt to overcome boundaries by continuously outpacing ourselves, until we eventually collapse from the pressures of constant vertigo. One is constructed against the other, but neither offers us an escape from the nullity of existence.

Johannes the Seducer encapsulates the aesthetic phase of life, and is so enraptured by the infinite potential that stretches before him that

---

4 George Pattison sets Kierkegaard's philosophy in the context of the modern urban environment. The new urban culture is engaged in a process of oversimplification; on the other hand, we find ourselves in an environment dominated by the ephemeral and fleeting. The two tendencies feed off each other through their mutual resistance. See Pattison, *Kierkegaard, Religion and the Nineteenth-Century Crisis of Culture* (Cambridge: Cambridge University Press, 2002), pp. 2–3.

he has trouble committing to actuality, living his life as though it were a series of possibilities, and treating others as though they were merely characters in a narrative he has constructed. This is an example of a man who is seduced by the infinite such that every moment is cast aside: "You, however, actually live by plundering; unnoticed you creep up on people, steal from them their happy moment, their most beautiful moment, stick this shadow picture in your pocket . . . and take it out whenever you wish" (*EO II* 10). His existence is characterized by a diffuse immediacy which is thoroughly empty. As Georg Lukács noted, Kierkegaard saw "more clearly than any other the thousand aspects, the thousand-fold variability of every motive exposing the dark underbelly of sentiments that we might otherwise hold in high esteem."[5] Johannes the Seducer does not even live up to the highest potential of erotic love, and his object of fascination, Cordelia, is merely an instrument in the aesthete's unfolding plot. Setting for himself the task of "living poetically" he "egoistically enjoyed personally that which in part actuality has given to him and which in part he himself had used to fertilize actuality" (*EO I* 304–5).[6] Imitating God, he engages in a game of continuous appearance and withdrawal, which becomes the basis for his seductive power. He dangles himself in front of her and then retreats into hiding in order to increase her anticipation of that which is "yet to come." In the process, he molds her into a shape that will satisfy his erotic desires and meet her needs without paying the least attention to hers: "My practice, namely has always been imbued with the conviction that woman is essentially being-for-other" (*EO I* 432).

The world becomes his playground and his egoism knows no boundaries. Johannes ends the diary musing whether or not "one could poetize oneself out of a girl in such a way as to make her so proud that she imagined it was she who was bored with the relationship" (*EO I* 445). He creates himself out of nothing at every moment and negates his

5 Georg Lukács, "The Foundering of Form Against Life: Søren Kierkegaard and Regine Olson," in *Søren Kierkegaard*, ed. Harold Bloom (New York: Chelsea House Press, 1989), pp. 5–18.

6 Søren Kierkegaard, *Either/Or Part I*, ed. and trans. Howard V. Hong and Edna H. Hong (Princeton: Princeton University Press, 1987).

own creation, leaving only a vast emptiness at the center of his being. This he claims would furnish him "with many erotic observations" (*EO I* 445). He is completely uninterested in Cordelia's emotions or thoughts, discarding her when his project has reached its termination: "I do not wish to be reminded of my relation to her; she has lost the fragrance, and the time I past when a girl suffering the pain of faithless love can be changed into a sunflower" (*EO I* 439–40). As long as he does not yet have her, she represents the fullness of potentiality, but when he comes close to capturing his prize, she represents an enclosure that he cannot endure and threatens to put an end to his love affair with the infinite.

At the same time, Johannes lives his life at a distance, cataloging his experiences in an effort to capture the multiplicity of the world for himself. Because he is trying to encompass everything, he cannot commit himself to any particular cause and so he will eventually be trapped in his own empty egoism, which becomes "a circle from which he cannot find an exit" (*EO I* 308). He is so addicted to possibility that he remains a spectator in the face of his own existence, unable to choose any specific course of action, remaining perpetually trapped between either/or. For Kierkegaard, Johannes is a man frozen in adolescence who experiences vertigo in the face of a plethora of choices, and is unable to commit to any one of them.

This vertigo in the face of boundless potential also gives rise to a tendency that appears to be the opposite of selfishness, namely the desire to surrender to the other. Kierkegaard's brilliance lies in seeing the egotistical underbelly of this phenomenon. It is no contradiction for Johannes to proclaim: "I am happy like a child who cannot and must not own anything. I own nothing, for I belong only to you. I am not; I have ceased to be in order to be yours" (*EO I* 406). By continuously trying to overcome the moment, Johannes is chasing his own nullity, which is the only consistent thread woven through his ceaseless striving. Only the totality of nothingness is open to him, because every finite experience functions as a limit. The only way that Johannes can belong to another is to cease to be.

Johannes's biggest complaint against the ethical realm, with its repetitious nature, is that it is woefully uninteresting: "The banefulness of an engagement is always the ethical in it. The ethical is just as boring in scholarship as in life. . . . Under the esthetic sky, everything is buoyant, beautiful, transient; when ethics arrives on the scene, everything becomes harsh, angular infinitely *langweiligt*" (*EO I* 367). The aesthetic addiction arises from a brush with the infinite which eventuates in a misplaced love fearful of all boundaries and desperately chases the ephemeral: "What does erotic love love? Infinity—What does erotic love fear? Boundaries" (*EO I* 442). However, even in this respect there is a profound ambiguity. Erotic love seeks the comfort of the "enclosure": "Was not paradise itself an enclosed place, a garden facing east. . . . But it hedges on in too closely, this ring" (*EO I* 442). The tension between the comfort of being enveloped in someone's arms is juxtaposed with the desire to escape the embrace, often epitomized by the tangle of flailing limbs in lovemaking. In his rabid pursuit of the infinite, Johannes tries to shun any hint of the finite. The most important thing is to keep moving and this is probably why he insists that to "poeticize oneself into a girl is an art: to poetize oneself out of her is a masterstroke" (*EO I* 369). The moment can only be relished once it is surrendered, because the aesthete has an addiction to perpetual newness which can only be satiated if each moment is eventually thrust aside.

The apparent intention of Assessor Wilhelm is to demonstrate the priority of the ethical over the aesthetic, and the language he employs to do so is explicitly Hegelian in its rejection of immediacy and its emphasis on the activity of self-choosing: "But what it is to live aesthetically, and what is it to live ethically? What is the aesthetic in a man and what is the ethical? To this I would reply: the aesthetic in a man is that by which he is immediately what he is; the ethical is that by which he becomes what he becomes" (*EO II* 181). Rather than avoiding decision, the ethical individual assumes responsibility for his own self-making, taking himself as his most important project: "What is it then that I distinguish with my either/or? Is it good and evil? No: I wish only to bring you to the point where this choice can acquire meaning for you. This is what everything hinges on. Only when one can get a person to stand in such a way at the crossroads that there is no way out for him except by choosing, then he will choose rightly" (*EO II* 168). Instead of being entranced by the kaleidoscope of possibilities, the ethical human being molds himself into a unified personality: "Can you think of anything more appalling than having it all end with the disintegration of your essence into a multiplicity, so that you actually became several, just as that unhappy demoniac become a legion, and thus you would have lost what is the most inward and holy in a human being, the binding power of the personality" (*EO II* 160). This is very reminiscent of Kant's distaste for heteronomy. Purposive self-creation replaces the dissolute wandering of the aesthete.

Judge Wilhelm also tacitly criticizes Hegelian speculative philosophy which, by suggesting that all mistakes and inadequacies are eventually mediated, detracts from the grave nature of our decisions where we are compelled to choose between alternatives: "As truly therefore as there is a time to come, so truly is there an either/or" (*EO II* 173). He would surely count Hegel amongst those "whose souls are too dissolute to grasp what is implied in such a dilemma, whose personalities lack the energy to say with pathos, either/or" (*EO II* 157).

Furthermore, Assessor Wilhelm notes that by committing himself to an ethical ideal, the individual is expressing the universal selfhood which all human beings participate in: "The task that the ethical individual takes on is the transformation of the self into a universal individuality" (*EO II* 256). He allegedly does this "not by taking off his concretion, for then he becomes a complete non-entity, but by putting it on and interpenetrating it with the universal" (*EO II* 256). The moment of choice for the ethical individual is a time at which the universal mediates the particular, informing the decision we make. The universal bestows the stamp of legitimacy on the particular decision. Furthermore, transparency is an important aspect of universality, and thus the ethical domain must bear the mark of commonality which allows him to disclose himself to others, for it is "every man's duty to become revealed" (*EO II* 327). Universal laws are supposed to be easily comprehended by human beings, and therefore he can speak without hesitation of his actions.

While the aesthete remains suspended between either and or, unwilling to commit himself to either, the ethical man underlines the gravity of making a decision, but wishes to ensure that his choice is the correct one. This is why the ethical realm often eventuates in adherence to custom, which is cloaked in the legitimacy that universality bequeaths.

Judge Wilhelm considers himself the paragon of the exemplary citizen, for whom fulfillment of duty is the principal component of his ethical self-creation. He thus takes the dual responsibilities of work and marriage very seriously: "It is precisely by working that man makes himself free, by working he becomes lord over nature, by working he shows that he is higher than nature" (*EO II* 286–7). This explicitly draws upon the master-slave dialectic in Hegel, whereupon the self alienates himself in the act of objectification and returns to himself by recognizing himself in the outside world. Because Wilhelm attempts to bring the particular and the universal into harmonious accord, he confuses the ideal of universal selfhood far too easily with an acceptance of local customs and traditions, which would earn social approval for him. Participating in a common social and cultural heritage seems to be the highest expression of the ethical. For Wilhelm, to be a responsible adult, one must accept one's embeddedness in a collective setting. Therefore, he chooses by relying upon the bourgeois conventions of the day, and believes that by complying with them, his existence is infused with meaning.

Wilhelm is disdainful of the profound indifference that the aesthete represents: "Marry, you will regret it; don't marry, you will also regret that, marry or don't marry, you will regret both. . . . Laugh at the world's follies or weep over them, you will regret both" (*EO II* 40). Not choosing is itself a kind of choice by which one "goes into a consumptive decline" (*EO II* 163). One cannot escape responsibility simply by avoiding making a decision, because even inaction will set a course of events in motion. However, he does not acknowledge his own fear of choosing. In making a choice, one must affirm one's finitude and limitation, for by choosing I recognize that I will never be all that I could be. This, for Kierkegaard, represents a willingness to repent not only for my own moral errors and sins, but for the legacy of wrongdoing that I inherit within any social order. Therefore, I have a responsibility that extends beyond my own direct sphere of activity. This is why God is necessary to ethics, for as the sermon of the Jylland pastor reminds us that in relation to God, "we are always in the wrong" (*EO II* 353). However, Judge Wilhelm very blatantly refuses to repent, assuming that he is beyond reproach for having taken the responsibilities that are required of him.

When Judge Wilhelm's thoughts and actions are examined, it is apparent that he is no less instrumental than the aesthete, particularly in the treatment of his wife upon whom he relies to find repose and satisfaction in the ethical realm. Undoubtedly, this constitutes a critique of Hegelian *Sittlichkeit*, which Kierkegaard associates with comfort and complacency. Confident that the aesthetic, erotic, and ethical can be fused through marriage, Wilhelm extols the domestic life of bliss as the dutifully wedded Christian, and thus is rather complacent with respect to his own shortcomings. In doing so, he relies heavily on the self-sacrificing work of his wife who, as a woman "in harmony with time" (*EO II* 308), is largely responsible for weaving the domestic tapestry that prevails in the household. He is completely impervious to the self-serving nature of his own arrangement, which he is convinced is sanctified by God: "God is an eyewitness who does not cramp one's style" (*EO II* 56). There is something intensely possessive about his homage to "immediate love" (*EO II* 30). He tries to assure the skeptical aesthetic reader that God would surely choose a "young and beautiful wife" (*EO II* 44). Describing a woman's hair as a "flower's tendrils by which she has grown fixed to the earth" (*EO II* 313), he insists that it is she who saves him from the wandering aesthetic tendencies and provides him with a sense of belonging. She allows an aesthetic concern for beauty to sit comfortably with responsibility, by making duty alluring and appealing. Ever patient, she knows how to deal with his more impetuous moods and ensure that they do not upset the balance of the home. Thus, when he is impatient, she is accommodating. Marriage is presented not as the antithesis of the aesthetic realm, but as a more secure fulfillment of aesthetic demands which, sanctioned by God, provide a comfortable synthesis of the aesthetic, ethical, and religious spheres. According to Judge Wilhelm, God is not a poet "who wishes to torment people with the most horrible conflicts, and if there actually were a conflict between love of God and love of human beings, the love of whom he himself has implanted in our hearts, it would be hard to imagine anything more horrible" (*EO II* 245). Judge Wilhelm is an example of the kind of ethical self-righteousness that the religious dimension is to overcome.

Religion and Ethics

The problem with the ethical dimension from Kierkegaard's perspective is that the pursuit of reconciliation between universal and particular generates a kind of collective egoism, wherein individuals are convinced of the rightness of their actions because they are coterminous with the customs of the social order. Kierkegaard suggests that this merely broadens the scope of the individual's self-centeredness rather than transcending it altogether. This process has a peculiarly bourgeois twist in which the other is evaluated according to the parameters of the self, and the self is dependent on the judgment of the other.

Extremely critical of the impersonal and allegedly "objective" strain in Hegelian philosophy, Kierkegaard encourages the individual to chart a particular course of existence which she can call authentically her own. While upon first glance this may appear to constitute a simple re-orientation of self-centeredness, Kierkegaard remarks that an authentic existence is one which acknowledges the openness of the infinite at the core of one's being as well as that of others. Connected to this is the imperative that the individual be able to respect the particularity of the other, not as an extension of himself or herself, yet as wholly "other" such that our relationships are not predicated on identity but rather on difference. Kierkegaard struggles against a position which attempts to subsume the particular "I" under the universal "I" of the Hegelian spirit. An ethics that transcends a mere extension of the self and dares venture into the terrain of the unfamiliar must be underpinned by religion.

Kierkegaard is contemptuous of an ethics predicated on social convention and conformity, whose primary intention is to elicit public and social approval. Mocking a bourgeois social order which renders actions hollow and meaningless, he maintains that everything "is to be had at such a bargain that it is questionable whether in the end there is anybody who will want to bid" (*FT* 5).[7] Interestingly, he begins his work *Fear and Trembling* by castigating the apparent ease with which we engage in the act of doubting, insisting that this alleged skepticism has noth-

7 Søren Kierkegaard, *Fear and Trembling*, ed. and trans. Howard V. Hong and Edna H. Hong (Princeton: Princeton University Press, 1983).

ing in common with the hard-won skepticism of the ancient Greeks or of Descartes. Due to a pervasive lack of commitment to anything, doubting, which had once been an agonizing and arduous feature of the philosophical journey, has become so commonplace as to be vacuous: "What those ancient Greeks . . . assumed to be a task for a whole lifetime because proficiency in doubting is not acquired in days or weeks. . . . With that everyone begins in our age" (*FT* 7). It becomes easy to doubt, when one shirks the responsibility for a passionate and serious engagement with anything, and operates primarily at the surface of things. Kierkegaard notes that the master of doubt, Descartes himself "did not doubt with respect to faith" (*FT* 5). To doubt is courageous if it represents a willingness to suspend certainty in relation to those things to which one has been wedded or committed. It is why genuine doubt requires faith as its correlate in Kierkegaard's view. Doubting only has value in the context of committed belief.

Kierkegaard uses the Biblical character Abraham to throw conventional ethics into question. Abraham is confronted with a profound ethical dilemma. No amount of reasoning can render the choice that Abraham is forced to make an easy one from an ethical perspective: "In order to perceive the prodigious paradox of faith, a paradox that makes a murder into a holy and God-pleasing act, a paradox that gives Isaac back to Abraham again, which no thought can grasp, because faith begins precisely where thought stops" (*FT* 53). He is equally obligated both to obey his God and also to protect his son: "In ethical terms, Abraham's relation to Isaac is quite simply this: the father shall love the son more than himself" (*FT* 57). Either decision Abraham makes could have dreadful repercussions from a moral point of view. As Edward Mooney points out, such conundrums undermine the position that "if only we could think hard enough, we will stumble upon a rational solution to life's difficulties."[8]

When Kierkegaard recounts the story of Abraham, he is intending to extricate it from the platitudes with which it is associated in Sunday sermons and shock his readers with the dramatic message of the story.

8 Edward Mooney, *Knights of Faith and Resignation: Reading Kierkegaard's Fear and Trembling* (Albany: State University of New York Press, 1991), p. 67.

This is not a tale that he believes should be palatable, or that we should be able to relate to easily. In fact, the narrator remarks repeatedly that he cannot understand Abraham. It is intended to leave one completely confounded. The multiple and confused preludes to the tale in the text are presented in order to encourage doubt and discomfort, and to inspire us to throw our own interpretation of the tale into question. No prescription for a code of action can be reaped from it. It cannot serve as an example of how to act in other situations. In short, in stark contrast to the actions of Judge Wilhelm, it is incommunicable: "The ethical expression for what Abraham did is, that he would murder Isaac; the religious expression is, that he meant to sacrifice Isaac; but precisely in this contradiction is the anxiety that can make a person sleepless, and yet without this anxiety Abraham is not who he is" (*FT* 30).

Abraham complies with God's request despite his deep and abiding love for his son and his unwavering commitment to his people. From a moral perspective, the act is clearly reprehensible and easily invites the judgment that Abraham is obedient when confronted by the authoritarian whims of an insensitive and power-hungry God who will stop at nothing to glorify his own omnipotence. God asks nothing less than for Abraham to abandon these most sacred social duties in order to comply with a draconian wish that does not lend itself to ready justification. Kierkegaard points out that the priest who recounts this story to his congregation without flinching would undoubtedly be horrified if one of his parishioners committed a similar act in the name of faith. Abraham's act cannot be publicly understood. And yet, even though Abraham performs an act that is without question immoral, he is not acting immorally. This is one of the incomprehensible paradoxes at the heart of Kierkegaard's text.

The notion that Kierkegaard is not trying to render the story of Abraham comprehensible is accentuated by the pseudonymous teller of the tale, Johannes de Silentio, who makes bumbling attempts to begin the story several times. In a citation that provides an opening to the text, Kierkegaard quotes: "What Tarquinus Superbus said in the garden by means of the poppies, the son understood but the messenger did not" (*FT* 3). The sender of the message is mistrustful of the messenger, and

Kierkegaard thereby implores the reader to suspect that the narrator is not completely reliable in relaying his story. The whole work is subtitled "a dialectical lyric" suggesting that the response to this story on the part of its narrator is not a speculative, reasoned argument but an impassioned and baffled outpouring of both admiration and terror. Abraham's act is simply incomprehensible and cannot be adopted as a guide for action by anyone. The sacrifice he is called to make cannot be justified on the grounds of achieving some higher good, such as the wellbeing of the nation state.

As a foil to the story of Abraham, Kierkegaard recounts the story of Agamemnon who sacrifices his daughter Iphigenia to placate the goddess Artemis, whose cooperation and aid are needed to wage the war against Troy. Kierkegaard notes that everyone can understand Agamemnon: "There will never be a noble soul in the world without tears of compassion for their agony, of admiration for their deed" (*FT* 58). Conversely, Abraham is the father of a tribe that depends on him for protection. Abraham's sacrifice of his son does not reinforce the social order but rather threatens to subvert it utterly and throws into question his status as progenitor of the nation. Agamemnon had remained within the domain of the ethical and was forced to subordinate his ethical duty to his daughter to his ethical duty as king. While his action elicits the pity and lament of his subjects, it also brings forth their understanding.

The ethical confusion surrounding Abraham's tale is portrayed by presenting four alternative versions of the tale at the beginning, which illustrate different Abrahams who could not have become the fathers of faith. In the first account, Abraham tells Isaac what he is about to do, and receives a response of anguish and incomprehension. Abraham subsequently turns himself into a monster in order to preserve Isaac's faith in God. The story is accompanied by a footnote which describes the painful process of a mother who blackens her breast in order to make the weaning of her child easier. It is significant that the image of the patriarch of faith, Abraham, is juxtaposed with the imagery of motherhood. This reminds us that we are not merely reading a tale of mythical proportions, but that similar dilemmas are addressed in dealing with separation between individuals. Our first experience of love and separation is in relation to the maternal. Not only is this seemingly ordinary experience imbued with a profound spiritual significance, but it tells us that the act of Abraham is in part about the need to separate oneself from those one is closest to, in order to let them come unto their own. Thus, the appendages detail the torment of a mother who must distance herself from her dependent other, and yet rest assured that the child will thrive and be returned to her as an independent being, whom she must love as such rather than as her possession. Abraham's faith inheres in the idea that not only will he sacrifice Isaac, but that Isaac will be returned to him, just as the mother rests assured that the bond between her and her child can never be severed.

Another possible beginning portrayed by Johannes imagines a situation where Isaac loses his faith and Abraham is consequently immersed in a cloud of sorrow. There is another story wherein Abraham begs God's forgiveness for having mistakenly believed that he is called upon to sacrifice his son. In each of these cases, Abraham remains firmly ensconced in the realm of the ethical. In contrast, the real Abraham was resolute in his determination to fulfill God's command: "But he did not doubt, he did not look in anguish to the left and to the right, he did not challenge heaven with his prayers" (*FT* 22).

While it is obvious that the story of Abraham has been held up as an expression of the most profound faith in God, Kierkegaard does not interpret the tale in the classic vein as simply affirming Abraham's obedience to divine command, which necessarily takes precedence over all moral conventions. The story could not work if Abraham did not remain a profoundly ethical person who manifests a stalwart commitment to his people, his family, and his God. It is replete with paradoxes from the very beginning. We are told that Abraham walks resolutely with "sorrow before him and Isaac beside him" (*FT* 9). He must distance himself fully from Isaac while also maintaining the intensity with which he loves him. Although Abraham is called upon to commit an act that ethically constitutes murder, his moral rectitude remains firmly in place throughout his ordeal. He suspends the ethical obligation to his son, "Without moving beyond the teleology of the ethical" (*FT* 57). Within the human realm which Abraham does not abandon, ethical duties are paramount. Abraham acknowledges this and at the same time steps beyond this world into the infinite. The limit situation which Abraham experiences is also intended to make us cognizant of the self-enclosed nature of ethics, to which we would not be attentive without stepping beyond it: "The whole existence of the human race rounds itself off as a perfect, self-enclosed sphere, and then the ethical is that which limits and fills at one and the same time" (*FT* 68). Because the individual is always between the finite and the infinite, without the duty toward God (the infinite), his or her individuality cannot be recognized.

Moral virtue demands an extension of the self that includes the other. Religious faith goes one step further and demands that we relinquish everything that we call our own, including our own families, our country, our possessions—in short, anything that binds us to the temporal world, while being assured that we will get them back in a non-acquisitive way. The ego-self is suspended. Abraham did not renounce the temporal in favor of the eternal. His love of God was *both* beyond this world and in this world: "He did not have faith that he would be blessed in a future life but that he would be blessed here in the world. God could give him a new Isaac, could restore to life the sacrificed. He had faith by virtue of the absurd, for all human calculation ceased long ago" (*FT* 36). Abraham recognizes in a powerful way that there is something beyond human reckoning. The confidence that he will receive Isaac back in no way is intended to lessen the act of renunciation. One is prepared to surrender one's attachments completely. Yet, one receives them anew in such a way that their particularity is appreciated in itself, irrespective of one's relationship to them. The Isaac that is returned to Abraham is both intimately familiar and yet a different person than the one who accompanied him to Mount Moriah.

Abraham must be prepared to recognize the intrinsic worth of Isaac, irrespective of the fact that Isaac is *his* son. While the infinite has generally been regarded as a quantitative and eternal repetition of the same, Kierkegaard suggests that each particular is infinite in and of itself because it cannot be subsumed by another. Infinity is difference. While Kantian morality imputes dignity to human beings because they resemble each other due to their common capacity to reason, Kierkegaard bestows dignity on the individual as a particular that cannot be reduced to another. In order to acknowledge this, one must go beyond ethics. The problem with Kantian morality is that it can become inhumane since the relationship to oneself through the moral law is applied to another only secondarily.

Difference allows us to greet the world not with the distance of indifference, but with the distance of wonder. This distance is also a kind of intimacy, which does not reduce the other to the same. For Kierkegaard, God is both intricately woven into the deepest caverns of the self and undeniably remote. Thus, our relationship to the infinite will never be understood, no matter how many historical transformations it has undergone: "Every individual ought to live in fear and trembling, and so too there is no established order which can do without fear and trembling. . . . And fear and trembling signifies that a God exists—a fact which no man and no established order dare for an instant forget" (*TC* 89).[9]

Kierkegaard remarks that Abraham's faith demands a "teleological suspension of the ethical" (*FT* 54). Ethics is not abandoned, but rather is suspended. Faith marks the paradox that "the single individual is higher than the universal . . . so that after having been in the universal he as the single individual isolates himself as higher than the universal" (*FT* 55). However, faith not only destabilizes ethics but reinforces it by guarding against the unethical potential of a universalism that impels the individual, who is after all the agent and object of ethical behavior, to be relegated to secondary importance. The Kantian love for the moral law could be implemented by an individual who detests human beings. Furthermore, in Kierkegaard's view, ethics cannot incorporate the inconceivable, and therefore cannot be attentive to the paradox that the other is both part of the self and radically distinct from it. The strangeness and familiarity of the other is entangled through the paradox of faith.

Abraham, as a man of faith, answers the call of God from without. This could not be further from Kantian or even Hegelian morality, which always turns the ethical commitment to another into an exten-

---

9 Søren Kierkegaard, *Training in Christianity and the Edifying Discourse Which Accompanied It*, trans. Walter Lowrie (Princeton: Princeton University Press, 1944).

sion of a fundamental commitment to oneself. In contrast, a person of religious faith "determines his relation to the universal by his relation to the absolute, not his relation to the absolute by his relation to the universal" (*FT* 70). Abraham is spoken to directly and immediately, and cannot avail himself of ethical strictures in order to plot his course of action. He cannot take comfort in the knowledge that he has met social obligations and will be recognized by the community. Kierkegaard's God reminds us that no matter where we are, there is always further to go. God serves as a reminder that our morality never goes far enough.

Abraham stands in a private, immediate, and particular relationship to God which cannot be communicated, "for only the individual becomes a knight of faith as the individual, and this is the greatness of this knighthood" (*FT* 82). The story of Abraham cannot be conflated with the story of anybody else. It is his story alone: "Therefore if Abraham would express himself in terms of the universal, he must say that his situation is a temptation, for he has no higher expression for that universal which stands above the universal which he transgresses" (*FT* 71). Temptation is normally associated with a deliberate transgression of an ethical or legal order. From a moral perspective, this is the only language that Abraham could employ, since ethics does not accept being eclipsed by anything higher.

The irony that Kierkegaard depicts is that the man of faith in surrendering everything that he holds dear, and in what seems to be a complete self-surrender to the Absolute affirms his particular self in a way that the ethical realm does not permit. The Absolute cannot be experienced in an abstract sense; it must be savored in all its immediacy by the individual who recognizes his dreadful solitude in the world. His difference from others renders him completely alone. The schism between himself and others is infinite. His authenticity rests in part on the recognition that he is called upon by an "other." Kierkegaard is not trying to subvert the ethical experience. The relationship between ethics and faith reveals two dimensions of our existence, namely that we are like others, and thus part of a larger community and yet also travel through the world alone: "He knows that it is beautiful to be born as the individual who has the universal as his home, his friendly abiding-place, which at once welcomes him with open arms when he would tarry in it. But he knows also that higher than this there winds a solitary path, narrow and steep; he knows that it is terrible to be born outside the universal, to walk without meeting a single traveler" (*FT* 43). Kierkegaard is postulating that in each of us is buried something that can never be conveyed to another human being.

The infinite, in Kierkegaard's view, is not part of a system that unfolds through human consciousness, but rather is both completely other to the self and yet allows for an intimate return to the particular self in a way that only religious faith can offer. In Hegel, paradoxes are always resolved in a higher synthesis; in Kierkegaard, God is both radically other as well as familiar, and neither aspect of this contradiction can be subsumed by the other. It is significant that Abraham responds to God's call with the words "Here am I" (*FT* 21). John Caputo retells the story by translating it into the French "Me voici" because the French uses the accusative, denoting an "addressee of an address." He notes that "Abraham does not try to assume the position of the author, the addressor, the transcendental sender. . . . This command is not Abraham's idea but an intervention upon Abraham, something that shatters his circle of self-interest." [10] This is a call that comes from outside, and therefore is other to Abraham. And yet, it is through the other that one experiences the self. Caputo draws upon the absolute otherness of God that Kierkegaard portrays. For Kierkegaard, there is an "infinite" difference between human beings and God which can never be permanently bridged, and thus God is absolutely other. God is not like me, and thus is out of reach to the tentacles of reason. However, this God returns us to our particular identity and makes possible an authentic and passionately engaged existence that the realm of ethics or aesthetics cannot bring. The other, through God, is radically other, and yet also is brought to a level of intimate closeness that does not constitute an extension of the self. This is closeness without repetition; it is an intimacy that is not predicated on resemblance. The art of loving the other as one's self, but not as an extension of the self, is a phenomenon which leaves reason stuttering and confused.

10 John Caputo, *Against Ethics: Contributions to a Poetics of Obligation with Constant Reference to Deconstruction* (Bloomington: Indiana University Press, 1993), pp. 10–1.

Thus, Kierkegaard is not demanding that the man of faith let go of his appreciation and love for the particular. He must love it with an intensity that is seldom understood in the world of market economics, where everything is a passing fad: "If a person lacks this concentration, this focus, his soul is dissipated in multiplicity from the beginning and then he never manages to make the movement; he acts as shrewdly in life as the financiers who put their resources into widely diversified investments in order to gain on one if they lose on another" (*FT* 43). In order to emphasize the importance of the particular, Kierkegaard differentiates between the knight of resignation and the knight of faith. The former experiences the agony of losing the particular but finds solace in the light of the eternal. According to Kierkegaard, this is only a preliminary step on the road to faith, because the infinite replaces the lost finite. The example he cites is that of the young swain who is in love with the princess: "He is not cowardly, he is not afraid to let it steal into this most secret, his most remote thoughts, to let it twist and entwine itself intricately around every ligament of his consciousness—if his love comes to grief, he will never be able to wrench himself out of it. He feels blissful delight in letting love palpitate in every nerve" (*FT* 42). The knight of resignation is no speculator but takes love as the pinnacle of experience. He is completely unmoved by the opinion and derogatory attacks of others which make light of the intensity of his experience. Only after this love has engulfed his whole being is he prepared to "make trial of everything" (*FT* 44). Eventually, the earthly love for his princess is transmogrified into an eternal love which persists even when subjected to all sorts of tribulations. By renouncing the princess, he discovers a new love which is beyond the temporal realm. His faith is a shirt "spun in tears" (*FT* 45) because it is based on a dreadful loss; but through this, he is able to see the eternal in the midst of everything.

The knight of resignation, admirable though he is, represents the preliminary step to faith. When we return to the familiar and temporal with a renewed sense of wonder, this constitutes recognition of the infinite in the finite. The knight of faith gains eternal love, but receives temporal love again even after having relinquished it. Kierkegaard does not wish the finite to be a mere pawn in a universal structure that launches us on a sullen path, where we delight only in concepts and not in the multiplicity of experience. The knight of faith is joyous in the midst of the world. In order to accentuate this point, Kierkegaard portrays an ordinary tax collector who is indeed a knight of faith. His ordinary appearance belies that greatness that he incarnates (*FT* 39). His religious fortitude is exemplified by a seemingly banal event. He anticipates with relish the meal that his wife is to prepare for him but when she has not, "it is quite the same to him" (*FT* 40). He cannot be tormented by the vicissitudes of life although he fully appreciates and savors them. He greets the finite world with both the distance of serenity and the intensity of wonder.

Kierkegaard points out that there are various degrees of greatness which are all measured in terms of what we love: "For he who loved himself became great by himself, and he who loved other men became great by his selfless devotion, but he who loved God became greater than all. . . . But Abraham was greater than all, great by reason of his power whose strength is impotence, great by reason of his wisdom whose secret is foolishness, great by reason of his hope whose form is madness, great by reason of the love which is hatred of oneself" (*FT* 6). Love of God becomes self-hatred only because the ego-self is relinquished. Wisdom becomes foolishness in the willingness to let go of all that is familiar. The power of impotence inheres in the remarkable ability to acknowledge one's dependence on God, which is also an empowering recognition of the infinite within oneself.

Abraham experienced the anguish of having to surrender Isaac, while remaining confident that he would get his son back: "During all this time he had faith, he had faith that God would not demand Isaac of him, and yet he was willing to sacrifice him if it was demanded. He had faith by virtue of the absurd, for human calculation was out of the question, and it certainly was absurd that God, who required of him, should in the next moment rescind the requirement" (*FT* 36). If Abraham had complied with God's wishes only reluctantly and hesitated mournfully, he would not have become the father of faith. Faith represents a confidence in something that we do not know, and a willingness to go beyond the ken. It relishes the boundaryless. Johannes muses about how he may have acted in Abraham's place, contrasting his posture with that of Abraham:

> I would not have been cowardly enough to stay at home, nor would I have dragged and drifted along the road or forgotten the knife in order to cause a delay. I am quite sure that I would have been punctual and all prepared—more than likely, I would have arrived too early in order to get it over sooner. But I also know what else I would have done. The moment I mounted the horse I would have said to myself, "Now all is lost. God demands Isaac, I sacrifice him, and along with him all my joy—yet God is love and continues to be that for me; for in the world of time God and I cannot talk with each other, we have no language in common." Perhaps someone in our time would be so foolish, so envious of the great, as to want to delude himself and me into believing that if I had actually done this I would have done something even greater than what Abraham did, for my immense resignation would be far more ideal and poetic than Abraham's small-mindedness. But this is utterly false, for my immense resignation would be a substitute for faith.
>
> (*FT* 34)

Faith in Kierkegaard's thought represents the wondrous strangeness of the seemingly banal and familiar. It is therefore both a contravention of ethics, which remains firmly embedded in the realm of familiarity, and a transgression that is necessary to the survival of ethics because it celebrates respect for the particular which cannot be reduced to the same. Faith exposes the dark and sometimes pernicious underbelly of our ethical security. Yet, Kierkegaard is not demanding that we surrender the realm of the familiar in favor of the incomprehensible and float perpetually in an ocean of uncertainty and bewilderment. Abraham's situation is a limit situation which casts light on the restrictiveness of the ethical and can help to rejuvenate it. By recognizing that there is something beyond ethics, we can also protect it from its own evils.

Works of Love

The link between ethics and faith becomes more obvious when examining Kierkegaard's *Works of Love* because it is in this work that he deals most directly with the theme of how to interact with the other. While, in *Fear and Trembling*, Abraham was forced to relinquish his attachment to his son Isaac so that he could renew his relationship with him upon his return, *Works of Love* examines the ethical obligation we have toward our neighbor whom we may encounter by chance and toward whom we have an obligation, even though there may be no direct ties that bind us to him or her. The former tells the story of the limit situation, while the latter brings the infinite respect for the particular into daily life.

Kierkegaard has perhaps unfairly been accused of privileging the individual's personal relationship with God to the exclusion of ethics, and therefore is often assumed to have no genuine ethical philosophy. Religion in Kierkegaard does not trump ethics, but rather places more stringent demands upon ethics that go far beyond Hegelian *Sittlichkeit* wherein ethics can easily be reconciled with the desire for belonging and public approval. Hegelian ethics is comfortable, while Kierkegaardian ethics can be uncomfortable. The former demands an extension of the self which moderates but does not eliminate selfishness, while for Kierkegaard, true ethics is entirely bereft of selfishness: "The distinction which the world makes is namely this: if a person wants to be all by himself in being selfish—which after all is rarely seen—the world calls it selfishness, but if in selfishness he wants to form a group with several other selfish people, especially with many other selfish people, the world calls it love. . . . It demands that he shall sacrifice a portion of his own selfishness in order to maintain the united group-selfishness" (*WL* 123).[11]

The ethics that Kierkegaard proposes takes the individual far beyond the comfortable confines of the familiar, and indeed demands that she also become a stranger to herself, recognizing that the ethical demands upon her are infinite, and that she will never be able to satisfy them. Religious ethics rattles the individual to her foundation; it is extremely unsettling. It calls upon the individual to affirm and recognize the infinite within herself.

In *Works of Love*, Kierkegaard focuses largely on the divine command to love one's neighbor as oneself, emphasizing repeatedly that "to love is duty" (*WL* 40). Kierkegaard is fully cognizant of the irony underlying the juxtaposition of love and duty because love is most commonly associated with eros and friendship, which are not forced upon the individual

11 Søren Kierkegaard, *Works of Love*, trans. Howard V. Hong and Edna H. Hong (Princeton: Princeton University Press, 1998).

but appear to erupt spontaneously from the very fiber of her being. But such love is volatile and can easily become hatred when it is unrequited or when the beloved no longer acts in accordance with our expectations: "Spontaneous love can be changed within itself; it can be changed to its opposite, to *hate*. Hate is a love which has become its opposite, a ruined love. Deep down love is continually aflame but it is the fallen of hate" (*WL* 49). In contrast, love which is commanded has become "eternal by becoming duty," and therefore inured to the vicissitudes of fortune or desire and "never changed. . . . It loves—and never hates" (*WL* 49).

Love which is commanded is thrust upon us from the outside, irrespective of our individual desires. Its purpose is to "wrest self-love away from us human beings" (*WL* 34). We are commanded to love our neighbor as ourselves. This movement away from egoism is extremely difficult and the "little phrase *as yourself* . . . critically penetrates to the innermost hiding place where a man loves himself; it does not leave self-love the slightest excuse or the tiniest escape-hatch" (*WL* 34–5). In fact, the summons to love our neighbor as ourselves is replete with irony. We love ourselves often to the exclusion of the other, because we qua individuals want to be all. Self-love is *not* an acceptance of ourselves but rather masks the anxiety at the core of our being, which wants to be infinite while recognizing that it cannot be. If we love the other as ourselves, then self-love must necessarily disappear for when we truly love the other as ourselves, we rend the very pillars that sustain egoism.

Love of our neighbor comes to us in the form of a command precisely, because it intrudes so powerfully upon a territorial self-love or love of one's own. When we are wrapped in the sheath of egoism, the call of the other can jolt us out of our complacency. Furthermore, the fact that Kierkegaard chooses to focus on the neighbor in a world infused with the bourgeois obsession around property is significant. The neighbor circumscribes our space and reminds us that our property has limits. We often do not know our neighbors and pretend they do not exist by setting up higher fences, so that we can live comfortably with the illusion that we are a world unto ourselves. Yet, the very boundaries we are so keen on erecting also remind us that in trying to shut out the neighbor, we constrict ourselves even further, depriving ourselves of open spaces.

The neighbor also represents a distant nearness. Our neighbors may be like us, or inhabit a contiguous area, but we do not seek them out. Most of the time, our encounters with the neighbor are fortuitous and Kierkegaard emphasizes that is unlike friendship which "is determined by the object," and "love to one's neighbour is determined by love" (*WL* 77). The neighbor stumbles across our path often unwittingly, and may call upon us without waiting for a prior invitation: "The task is not: to find—the lovable object; but the task is: to find the object already given or chosen—lovable, and to be able to continue finding him lovable, no matter how changed" (*WL* 158). Loving our neighbor takes the form of an imperative because it does not come easily: "He toward whom I have a duty is my neighbour, and when I fulfil my duty I prove that I am a neighbour" (*WL* 38). According to Kierkegaard, the neighbor is the other *par excellence*, for he is a symbol of distant closeness or close distance. In a solipsistic world, what frightens us about the other is the juxtaposition of the familiar and unfamiliar. We cannot easily bring neighbors into our fold, as we can a lover or friend: "The beloved and the friend are therefore called, remarkably and significantly enough, the *other-self*, the *other-I*—for one's neighbour is the *other-you*" (*WL* 66). The command to love one's neighbor demands a kind of openness that is not linked to possession: "*Neighbour* is what philosophers would call the *other*, that by which the selfishness in self-love is to be tested. . . . To be sure, *neighbour* in itself is manifold, for *neighbour* means *all men*" (*WL* 37). Because love of our neighbor is a radical openness, it becomes love of everyone: "Since one's neighbour is every man, all distinctions are indeed removed from the object" (*WL* 77).

Loving all human beings is an impossible task and would demand an unencumbered openness on the part of a finite individual. This is why Kierkegaard insists we remain indebted in love in perpetuity: "If the duty is to be fulfilled, love must be limitless" (*WL* 164). Our indebtedness bears witness to the infinite potential we harbor within us in the presence of God, who allows us to always become greater than what we are. The fact that we always have further to go marks not only our finitude but our infinity. The kind of indebtedness Kierkegaard alludes to provides a deliberate contrast to any debt we may incur in contractual relations, which can eventually be repaid. Love constantly makes claims upon us, and thus the "essential characteristic of love" is that "the lover by giving infinitely comes into—infinite debt" (*WL* 172). Kierkegaard is not trying to burden us with inexorable feelings of ineptitude, but rather reminds us that there is always more we can do for another. The other's call upon us never ceases. Kierkegaard is imploring us to engage in unceasing self-examination, and be weary of selfish motives that may cloud our love or lead us down the path of undeserved self-satisfaction.

Selflessness in Kierkegaard is a kind of radical openness and can only be cultivated with God as an intermediary: "The love relationship is a triangular relationship of the lover, the beloved, love—but love is God. Therefore to love another person means to help him to love God and to be loved means to be helped" (*WL* 124). God is infinite and by loving the unbounded, one is able to accept the particular individual as she is, without trying to bring her into my fold. The neighbor is no longer one who delimits my own territory, but rather someone with whom one shares in the infinite.

Such love sensitizes us to the suffering of others: "When you walk in God's company, you need only see one single person in misery, and you will not be able to escape what Christianity will have you understand, human likeness" (*WL* 87). All human beings have the infinite within them and yet are tormented by their finitude. In the presence of God, we are all equal because the difference between each one of us and God is infinite, and cannot be measured in human terms. One can neither be more or less *not* infinite, nor more or less infinite: "Christianity lets all the distinctions of earthly existence stand, but in the command of love, in loving one's neighbour, this equality of lifting oneself above the distinctions of earthly existence is implicit" (*WL* 83). Without the divine, Kierkegaard fears that love may quickly be infused with selfishness:

> Love is a relationship to another human being or to other human beings, and by no means dares to be a marital, a merely human accord, a relationship (no matter how faithful and tender it is just, between man and man). Everyone as an individual, before he relates himself in love to a beloved, to a friend, to lovers, to contemporaries, must first relate himself to God and the God-demand. . . . When, however, the God-relationship determines what constitutes love

> between man and man, then love is prevented from stopping in some illusion or self-deception and simultaneously the demand for self-denial and sacrifice is again made infinite.
>
> (*WL* 118)

God is the intermediary that makes it possible to love another without being shackled by self-interest. We must first be freed from ourselves by God in order to relate to another unselfishly: "Worldly wisdom thinks that love is a relationship between one person and another; Christianity teaches that love is a relationship between a person–God–a person: that is God is the middle term" (*WL* 106). If the "I" does not become "you," then our love is meaningless from a religious perspective: "It is characteristic of childhood to say: '*Me want—me—me.*' It is characteristic of youth to say 'I—and I—and I.' The mark of maturity and the dedication of the eternal is to will to understand that this I has no significance if it does not become the *you*, the *thou* to whom the eternal incessantly speaks and says: '*You shall*, *you* shall, *you* shall.' It is youthful to want to be the only I in the whole world" (*WL* 98). Because God can neither be represented nor conceived, our love for God cannot be a mere extension of self-love. This allows us to accept the other as is, rather than as a means of returning into the solipsistic fold of the self: "Love seeks not its own; for in love there is no mine and yours. But mine and yours are only relational qualifications of one's own consequently if there is no 'mine' nor 'yours' there is no 'one's own' either, but if there is no 'one's own,' it is indeed impossible to seek one's own" (*WL* 248). We do not augment our range of concern to include another in the way that Mencius's king is asked to extend his sphere of compassion to include his own subjects. Kierkegaard would argue this merely constitutes an extension of particular love, and not a participation in infinite love. This kind of love transcends the self:

> We discern, therefore, that friendship and erotic love, as such, are only augmented and refined self-love. . . . Indeed, the exchange of rings between the lovers is regarded as a very fitting symbol of erotic love; and in truth it is an absolutely fitting symbol, this exchanging, but it is a poor symbol of love. An exchange does not really mean a cessation of the distinction between mine and yours, because that for which I exchange myself becomes mine again.
>
> (*WL* 249)

The religious awareness that Kierkegaard hopes to cultivate is a far cry from the self-confident complacency of Judge Wilhelm. He warns that ethical commitments can never be fulfilled, because we must continuously open ourselves up to the other, while not trying to bring him or her into the fold of the self. Conventional ethics broaden the sphere of self-interest rather than going beyond it altogether. It operates within the realm of the bounded. Religious ethics allows us to love the other through the radical openness of the infinite, which enables us to accept their particularity on its own terms, rather than accommodating the other to oneself, or vice versa.

Daoist Formlessness

Upon first glance, the serenity of the Daoist sage does not appear to have much in common with the fear and trembling that is precipitated by an encounter with God in Kierkegaard. Nobody seems to stray further from Kierkegaardian *Angst* than the sage, who not only fails to resolutely choose him- or herself, but is devoid of the inflamed passion that Kierkegaard extols. Nevertheless, Daoist philosophy invokes the formless *Dao* 道 to question prevailing moral systems and advocates a release from the ego-self allowing for the respect of particularity. It not only rejects the ritual and deference enshrined in Confucian thought, but is suspicious of moral prescriptions of any kind. However, this is not to claim that a text such as the *Daodejing* spurns the *activity* of morality, but rather that it objects to a morality which becomes closely wedded to convention. This becomes inevitable from a Daoist perspective at the very moment when moral labels are applied, which all too easily turn morality from a process of harmonizing to a possession that is sought after in order to be able to garner the title of "moral person." The activity is no longer engaged in for its own sake, but rather with a view to the label. Moral acts are reified, and acquiring the "form" of morality begins to trump the process of morality. As soon as moral activities are eclipsed by the acquisition of moral attributes, morality inadvertently functions, from a Daoist perspective, by harmonizing the behavior of *separate* individuals.

Confucian thinkers were not unaware of this issue, which is why

Confucius repeatedly pointed out that he had not arrived at sagehood. However, the *Daodejing* goes beyond Confucian humility in the face of the highest virtues and resists the positing of moral labels altogether. Morality is not a goal that one can reach from a Daoist perspective, but rather a process that one must always participate in, without lending a thought to *who* engages in the activity or *what* one is trying to attain. The *form*ation of morality must be resisted at all costs, and this is why Daoism places such a high premium on formlessness, as a kind of antidote to the reification of moral processes.

Formlessness in Daoism is radical, and throws into question the permanence of all forms, including that of the individual. It affirms the non-separateness of things which collapses the very distinction between self and other that Kierkegaard continues to uphold. Thus, self-cultivation must also constitute the cultivation of the cosmos: "A boat can be hidden in a gorge, and a fishing net in a pool and you may think they are therefore safe. However, in the middle of the night a strong man comes and carries them off. Small-minded people just cannot see that hiding smaller things in larger things does not mean they will not be stolen. If you take everything under heaven and try to store it under heaven, there is no space left to be lost in" (*Zh* 6:50). When the boat is enclosed and hidden away, it becomes the object of desire and someone will carry it off while I am not looking. But if there is no difference between the boat and the world, there would be nothing to hide and therefore nothing worth stealing. Thus, one must comport oneself in such a way that there is no difference between self and cosmos, or self and other, and then conflict will have no occasion to arise and I will not be tempted to harm anyone. People are drawn to the Daoist sage, not because they look up to her as a role model to be emulated, but because she makes them feel as though they were the cosmos within the cosmos, and as though in being with her, they are just being themselves. This is a radical challenge to Confucian hierarchy.

It is important to recognize that there are key differences between various Daoist texts with respect to positions on morality. The *Daodejing* is a text that spurns conventional Confucian ethics; at the same time, its avowed intent is political, social, and moral reform. The text is written with the sage-ruler in mind, whose own formlessness is to help cultivate harmony in his populace. The *Zhuangzi* is a text that more often than not rejects politics and addresses those at the fringes of the social order, promoting the kind of self-cultivation that furthers open relationships with others. The kinds of prescriptions for rulers that the *Daodejing* espouses are notably absent because of a profound pessimism with respect to the possible reformation of any political elite.

Despite these differences, I would argue that the texts share similar understandings of formlessness and nothingness, which are key to understanding the Daoist approach to ethics. *Dao*, meaning way or path, represents the process of the cosmos; it is transcendent and immanent because it runs through all things and beyond each particular thing. We cannot provide a definition of *Dao* because it is neither substance nor being, but rather a process in which all things participate. This is why it resists all labels. Like Kierkegaard's God, it is both near and far. However, Kierkegaard's God is perceived as an infinite *being* and our finite nature imbues us with a profound sense of guilt in relation to the infinite. Conversely, *Dao*'s distance from us is not due to its vast superiority, nor to the fact that it is infinite while we are not. It makes no sense whatsoever to feel guilt for *not* being an entire process, for processes necessitate the interaction between many things. There is therefore no radical schism, as in Kierkegaard, between the finite and the infinite because there is no sense that one is *not* the other. In fact, the idea of *Dao* throws into question the whole notion of the distinction between finite and infinite.

While in Kierkegaard the paradoxical relationship to God provokes fear and trembling, such anxiety is almost completely absent from Daoist texts because there is no notion of an authentic self that must be *had*, which recognizes its limitations in the face of an infinite God. Livia Kohn points out that Chinese mysticism differs markedly from its Western counterpart in that the divine force is so "immanent that it is even in the soil and tiles, so much part of the world, that it cannot be separated from it."[12] Conversely, she notes that the Christian tradition posits a God

12 Livia Kohn, *Early Chinese Mysticism: Philosophy and Soteriology in the Taoist Tradition* (Princeton: Princeton University Press, 1992), pp. 12–3.

that is "totally other" and therefore "concentrates on rare versions of the deity, granted through his mercy, that are overwhelming, ineffable and entirely out of this world."[13] The story of Abraham is an example of this, because it recalls the extraordinary situation into which Abraham is thrust. Daoist philosophy does not focus so much on the anomalous but rather features the extraordinary element of ordinary existence.

Dao is the movement of all things, and because of this it is also no particular thing, or no-thing. Rather than encompassing all things, it propels all motion. Isabelle Robinet points out that *Dao* is comprised of a foundation which is "immobile, silent, unknown and unknowable" and the productive *Dao* which is manifested in action.[14] However, this does not imply that *Dao* is infused with dualism. Because *Dao* both constitutes and propels all motion, it cannot be known, and thus appears mysterious and withdrawn. At the same time, it is manifested in each and every action, and thus is always available to us. It is both ubiquitously present and perpetually absent.

Dao is an endless and formless openness which allows a multitude of particulars to flourish. In Kierkegaard, such openness juxtaposed with necessity gives rise to anxiety and dread because it attests to the fluid nature of one's identity. The awareness of continuously being something other than one is is disorienting, and is the source of intellectual and emotional distress because there is a notion that one must *have* an identity in order to be an individual. However, the language of anxiety does not creep into Daoist texts, because there is no prior preoccupation with self-identity to begin with. According to Kierkegaard, we oscillate between the desire for boundaries and the longing for boundarylessness. In Daoism, there is no equivalent longing to make the self, but rather a constant openness. The Daoist sage is always at home because he establishes harmonious connections wherever he goes. Instead of asking

---

13 Ibid.

14 Livia Kohn, *Taoist Mystical Philosophy: The Scripture of Western Ascension* (Albany: State University of New York Press, 1991), p. 134; also see Isabelle Robinet, "The Diverse Interpretations of the *Laozi*," in *Religious and Philosophical Aspects of the Laozi*, ed. Mark Csikszentmihalyi and Philip J. Ivanhoe (Albany: State University of New York Press, 1991).

himself "who am I," he would ask "where am I," because his location helps shape whatever form he assumes at the moment.

The *Daodejing* is replete with metaphors portraying the formless. *Dao* is likened to a great opening symbolized by the valley and the womb, as well as muddy water and uncarved wood. These fluid and featureless landscapes are all devoid of distinct forms and engender flourishing. The emptiness itself is not extolled but rather the potential that it represents. Furthermore, the shapelessness of the valley contrasts with the forms of the mountains that tower over it. Because the valley is empty, it is also inexhaustible and fertile. This is why the sage hopes to emulate such formlessness in his own being:

> The spirit of the valley never dies.
> This is called the mysterious female.
> The gateway of the mysterious female
> Is called the root of heaven and earth.
> Dimly visible, it seems as if it were there,
> Yet use will never drain it.
>
> (*DDJ* 6)[15]

The female is associated with the formless, and "possessing the mother" is important in order to participate in this formlessness:

> When he possess the mother of the country
> he can then endure.
> This is called the way of deep roots and firm stems
> by which one lives to see many days.
>
> (*DDJ* 59)

Men are encouraged to cultivate the female side of their being. However, this association of the female with the formless may be problematic for women, who do not "return" to formlessness in the same manner as men, because they are so closely identified with it. They, like *Dao*, remain the formless backdrop of the male journey to wisdom.[16]

---

15 *Tao Te Ching*, trans. D. C. Lau (London: Penguin Books, 1963).

16 I have discussed the implications of this in greater length in Chapter Five of my book *Nietzsche, Heidegger and Daoist Thought: Crossing Paths In-Between* (Albany: State University of New York Press, 2006).

According to Kierkegaard, the relationship to God is defined in part by commands that are thrust upon the individual from the outside, while *Dao* neither imposes nor issues orders of any kind. Kierkegaard's God is seen as the absolute other, while *Dao* is like water, which always flows into the midst of things and is part and parcel of our very being. It trickles into the deepest crevices that others are likely to spurn, and as such is hardly noticed: "Highest good is like water. Because water excels in benefitting the myriad creatures without contending with them and settles where none would like to be, it comes close to the way" (*DDJ* 8). Water also assumes the shape of its environment and undergoes different transformations depending on the season, but can also spill over the boundaries in which it is contained. In the *Huainanzi* 淮南子, the pliancy and weakness of water is extolled. Water appears to be weak, but is the source of all life:

> In the world there is nothing more pliant and weak than water
> And yet is great beyond reckoning
> And deep beyond fathoming
> In length it ends only in the interminable
> And in distance it merges into the boundless;
> Waxing and waning, increasing and decreasing,
> It runs into the incalculable.
> Going up to the heavens it becomes rain and dew;
> Going down to the earth it becomes moisture.
> The myriad things cannot be produced without it,
> And the events of the world cannot culminate without it.
>
> (*YD* 14)[17]

Water reflects the Daoist understanding that nothing exists for itself, and therefore there is no return to the self spurred by one's encounter with another. Instead, everything opens itself to another and becomes another: "Heaven and earth are enduring. The reason why heaven and earth can be enduring is that they do not give themselves life" (*DDJ* 7). Infinity is seen in terms of interconnection rather than completeness, because completeness depends upon boundaries and can hinder growth.

---

17 Huainanzi, *Yuan Dao: Tracing Dao to its Source*, trans. Roger Ames and D. C. Lau (New York: Ballantine Books, 1998).

Movement and transformation, rather than fullness, are extolled. Fullness suggests that a form can be filled, while movement implies that it is always being transformed into another form. Fullness has limits while movement does not:

> He who holds fast to this way
> Desires not to be full.
> It is because he is not full
> That he can be worn and yet newly made.
>
> (*DDJ* 15)

The idea of formlessness can also be used to elucidate the controversial passage in the *Daodejing* which refers to the straw dogs that are destined for sacrifice: "Heaven and Earth are not benevolent; they treat the myriad creatures as straw dogs. Sages are not benevolent; they treat the people as straw dogs" (*DDJ* 5). This appears to describe a shocking indifference towards human life. The straw dogs are representative symbols. If their form is retained, then we cling to the symbol, forgetting the ritual process which gives the symbol of the straw dog its meaning. Destroying them constitutes a recognition that the symbol itself is only a metaphor for a process and can never become its substitute. The danger in not burning the straw dogs is that objects begin to assume a greater importance than the actions that they only represent or allude to. Similarly, when the sage treats human beings as straw dogs, she is not participating in their wanton destruction. Instead, she refuses to treat them as objects, and thus is symbolically destroying their objectified existence.

Because everything is interconnected and no person owns her or his identity, *Dao*, unlike Kierkegaard's God, cannot be radically other. God wrests one from one's self-interest in such dramatic fashion in Kierkegaard's writings, because a self that presumes to be all is rattled by the realization that there is something infinite beyond it. There is a huge schism between the infinite and finite; like the aesthete, we cannot resist attempts to become the infinite or appropriate it for ourselves. We are perpetually tormented by the knowledge that the infinite is out of reach only because we are plagued by the desire to *have* it. In Daoist thought, there is no anxiety over the fact that one is not the infinite, because *Dao* is not something one dreams of becoming but rather a process one participates in and harmonizes with. Rather than reminding us of radical alterity in a painful manner, *Dao* fosters an immediate connection between things without the reduction of one thing to another. Radical alterity can only exist in relation to defined identity.

The *Daodejing* notes that there is a thing that is "confusedly formed" (*DDJ* 25). The Chinese text reads 有物混成 (*you wu hun cheng*; *DDJ* Ch 25). *Hun* refers to a kind of hodgepodge, while *cheng* connotes a process of constant becoming. Indeed, one could argue that *Dao* is never complete. There appears to be a deliberate irony in this passage, for *you wu* 有物 is a term that juxtaposes "thingness and having," while the next part of the sentence challenges this thingness by insisting that it is chaotically becoming.

Dao, like Kierkegaard's God, is imbued with paradox. It is a process of appearance and withdrawal. It stands still and yet moves continuously. However, its withdrawal is part of its appearance, and its movement is part of its motionlessness. Just as dissonant notes in a piece of music can accentuate the underlying harmony, the withdrawal of *Dao* draws us towards it. But, if it were not also deeply embedded in us, we would not notice its absence. It is close and far at the same time because it is beyond all things, and yet is in each particular thing. This relationship between presence and absence fuels the process of becoming. *Dao* is still in its motion because the experience of movement pertains to finite beings, who are dependent upon other things for their becoming. All finite beings come into existence and pass away, and since *Dao* never passes away, it does not move. Each step toward *Dao* is also a movement away from it:

> There is a thing confusedly formed,
> Born before heaven and earth.
> Silent and void
> It stands alone and does not change,
> Goes round and does not weary,
> It is capable of being the mother of the world.
> I know not its name
> So I style it "the way."
>
> (*DDJ* 25)

The *Daodejing* maintains the mystical and indescribable nature of the formless *Dao*. Later Daoist texts, such as the *Zhuangzi*, uphold the notion of formlessness, but transform its meaning slightly. In the *Zhuangzi*, there is a much closer relationship between formlessness and the transformation into a multitude of forms. Formlessness and form are not only related; each is an inextricable aspect of the other. The Daoist canon is replete with stories of wandering and travel, where formlessness has much to do with the transformation of forms and the encounter with the unfamiliar. Travel is a symbolic way of participating in the formlessness of the cosmos and ensuring that one is not riveted to a singular identity. In one story depicted in the *Zhuangzi*, the Yellow Emperor went to see the Great Clod at Chuzi mountain. He and his six sages were befuddled and unable to find the way. Finally, they found a cowherd who conveyed his words of wisdom: "When I was younger, I liked to wander within the confines of the six directions but my eyesight began to fail. A wise elderly gentleman told me, 'Climb up and ride in the carriage of the sun and explore the wild region of Xiangcheng. Now my eyesight is better and I am able to wander beyond the borders of the six directions. Ruling everything under heaven is just like this. So what's the big problem?" (*Zh* 24:213). This is a poignant statement conveying the need to venture beyond the realm of the familiar. From this perspective, Daoist philosophy reminds us of the Kierkegaardian admonition that the domain of ethics easily becomes too comfortable. Furthermore, encounters with the forms of other things remind me of the formlessness that is at the root of what I am. The formlessness of one individual allows her to be open to the forms of others.

The *Zhuangzi* refuses to come to any cosmological conclusions based on the formlessness of *Dao*, and indeed pokes fun at such attempts: "There is the beginning; there is not yet any beginning of the beginning; there is not as yet beginning not to be a beginning of the beginning. There is what is, and there is what is not, and it is not easy to say whether what is not, is not; or whether what is, is. I have just made a statement, yet I do not know whether what I said has been real in what I said or not really said" (*Zh* 2:15). In this case, Zhuangzi mocks the attempts to identify the beginning, since each beginning is preceded by other beginnings, ad infinitum. There is no relationship of cause and effect wherein *Dao* is the ancestral creator responsible for all life, since there is no temporal point of origin in Chinese cosmogony. The *Huainanzi* appropriates part of this passage from the *Zhuangzi* and uses it to posit a kind of Daoist cosmology: "There was a beginning. There was a time before that beginning. There was a time before the time which was before the beginning. There was being. There was non-being. There was a time before that non-being. There was a time before the time which was before that non-being" (HN Chan 306).[18] The Chinese text begins 有始者，有未始有有始者，有未始有未未始有有始者 (*you shi zhe, you wei shi you you shi zhe, you wei shi you wei wei shi you you shi zhe*; HN 44).[19] *Wei* 未 can mean both "not yet" and "not." Zhuangzi's text seems to maintain the ambiguity of *wei*, while the *Huainanzi* stresses the meaning of "not yet" which becomes the formless origin of form:

> What is meant by "there was a beginning" is that there was accumulation which has not sprung unto activity. There were signs of sprouts and shoots but no physical form. Like insects moving, they are about to spring into life but their species have not yet been formed. At the time before that beginning, the material force of Heaven began to descend and that of earth began to ascend. Yin and Yang interacted and united, competing leisurely to expand in the universe. Embracing genuine character and containing harmony, they were interfused and stayed together. They wanted to come in contact with other things but they had not yet had physical form.
>
> (HN Chan 306)

It is clear in this passage that formlessness precedes form while Zhuangzi does not intend to make such a case. In his rendition, form and formlessness are related, since each thing that is, also is not. This interplay between form and formlessness makes the ongoing process of creation possible. Formlessness in the *Huainanzi* is the potential leading to form, while in the *Zhuangzi*, formlessness and form are indistinguishable, and therefore impossible to disentangle.

Adapting one's body to the formlessness of *Dao* is an important

---

18 Huainanzi, "The Taoism of *Huai-nan Tzu*," in *A Sourcebook in Chinese Philosophy*, trans. Wing-Tsit Chan (Princeton: Princeton University Press, 1963).

19 Huainanzi, *Huainan honglie jijie* (Beijing: Zhonghua shuju chubanshe, 1989).

aspect of maintaining harmony. The *Zhuangzi* presents a host of characters who do not hold the proper form and yet act in sagely ways: "The Crooked Man with No Lips offered advice to Duke Ling of Wei who greatly appreciated his words of advice, so much so that he thought ordinary people had backs too straight and lips too big. The man with a Jug-sized Goitre offered advice to Duke Huan of Chi. Duke Huan appreciated his counsel so much so that he thought ordinary people had necks which were too thin and short" (*Zh* 5:43). This passage is found in a chapter entitled "Signs of Real Virtue" (*de chong fu* 德充符; *Zh* Ch 5:65)[20] which abounds with mangled and crippled characters. *Fu* is a word that is often associated with an official seal, so the title is doubly ironic since the chapter describes characters who by no means would be granted such official recognition and are more likely to have elicited official scorn. Wang Tai had lost a foot yet had as many followers as Confucius. The hideous man draws in crowds, including beautiful women eager to be his concubines rather than more proper men's wives (*Zh* 5:41). His ugliness was enough to "frighten the whole world" but because he was freed from conventional forms, people were not threatened in his presence, and he "agreed with whatever was suggested" (*Zh* 5:42). These people are deformed and, as a result of this, are able to draw a variegated audience in which the forms of all are appreciated. Their deformity also functions as a kind of antiform, which throws into question the evaluative standards of the elite. Zhuangzi's ethics here is deliberately counterposed against conventional ethics, and it is this refusal to bend to the form of convention that allows others to openly come together in the presence of these deformed men.

Nothingness

The notion of formlessness is intimately connected to the idea of nothingness which becomes a central pillar of Wang Bi's interpretation of the *Daodejing*, wherein *wu* 無 is the definitive concept. His analysis is based in large part on the following passage: "'Non-existence' I call the beginning

20 Zhuangzi, *Zhuangzi duben* (Taipei: Sanmin shuju, 1998).

of Heaven and Earth. 'Existence' I call the mother of individual beings. Therefore does the direction towards non-existence lead to the sight of the miraculous essence, the direction towards existence to the sight of spatial limitations" (*DDJ* 1). In his interpretation of the opening lines of the text, Wang Bi maintains that non-being is a point of origin:

> All being originated from non-being. The time before physical forms and names appeared was the beginning of the myriad things. After forms and names appear, "dao" develops them, nourishes them, provides their formal shape and completes their formal substance, that is, becomes their Mother. This means that the Tao produces and completes things with the formless and nameless.[21]

Wang Bi's analysis suggests that *wu* is not simply the negation of being, but rather has a kind of mysterious presence as the underlying unity of all things. However, unlike the kind of nothingness which implies an absence of something, its connotation here is positive and implies an absence of determination or the empty space that allows things to make their appearance. While Wang Bi suggests that nothingness is a point of origin, one could also interpret its centrality as a rejection of temporal origins. Just as the finite is not the absence of the infinite but rather is part of the manifold through which *Dao* moves, nothingness is not the negation of being, nor does it connote a suggestion that before being, there was nothingness from which being emerged *ex nihilo*. Instead, nothingness is akin to a kind of radical openness that makes becoming possible because it represents formlessness, and therefore endless potential that is at the root of everything. If priority is imputed to nothingness, it is because its openness underscores the transience of all boundaries.

The identification of *Dao* with metaphysical nothingness that becomes the root of all things is perhaps more closely linked to the *Daodejing* than to the *Zhuangzi*. Following Charles Wei-hsun Fu, Geling Shang points out that the language of the *Daodejing* is much more closely tied to the language of origins and roots than the *Zhuangzi*: "However, Laozi couldn't help talking about *Dao* metaphysically. The whole work he

---

21 Bi Wang, *Commentary on the Lao-Tzu*, trans. Ariane Rump and Wing-tsit Chan (Honolulu: University Press of Hawaii, 1981), p. 3.

wrote rested on the foundation of *Dao* as metaphysical reality, universal principle and cosmological origin of all things."[22] On the one hand, the language of the text does resonate with notions of metaphysical origins and foundations; on the other hand, nothingness is in itself a foundationless foundation. Just as we cannot stop speaking about *Dao*, while recognizing that our efforts always fall short, it is difficult to dispense with the language of origins. When *Dao* is likened to the womb, its opening is described as endless. Something which is endless not only has no end, but also has no beginning.

You 有 and *wu* 無 are related to each other, since the emptiness of *wu* allows things not only to emerge but also to disappear. Its emptiness is its fullness. When *you* and *wu* are juxtaposed, the notion of form is re-presented. *You* is a temporary constellation of processes but it is not an object. *Wu* is needed to remind us of what *you* "is or is not." All boundaries are fluid. Heaven is unbounded and formless and this, in interaction with the bounded earth, gives rise to the many processes that constitute the rhythms of the cosmos. Even the earth represents a complex web of processes rather than a single entity, so it is form in relation to the formless heaven, but is formless in relation to the varieties of life that inhabit it. Nothingness is the openness within each thing that enables it to connect to other things, and the space between things that allows them to interact. The space between them endows them their form while also reminding them that the temporary "boundary" of the form only exists against a backdrop of formlessness. The formless is therefore at the heart of form.

The centrality of nothingness has ethical implications, counterintuitive though this may seem. It demands a receptivity and openness to others that allows their particularity to flourish. One must not only know when to speak, but also when to withdraw. Interaction between people and between beings requires a delicate balance. Just as the specific form of a flower may best be viewed against a formless sky, we need to become formless so that the specific virtues of others can be enhanced.

---

22 Geling Shang, *Liberation as Affirmation: The Religiosity of Zhuangzi and Nietzsche* (Albany: State University of New York Press, 2006), p. 18.

At the same time, we gain a different perspective on the flower by noticing it in the midst of a meadow where it is surrounded by *different* flowers. Formlessness is not simply an absence of form, but also refers to the multiplicity of forms. Daoists maintain that codes of ethics interfere with the constant search for equilibrium, because it inhibits the response to the particular exigencies and plural potential of the moment. The wheelwright remarks: "When I work on a wheel, if I hit too softly, pleasant as this is, it doesn't make for a good wheel. If I hit furiously, I get tired and the thing doesn't work! So not too soft, not too vigorous, I grasp it in my hand and hold it in my heart. I cannot express this by word of mouth, I just know it" (*Zh* 13:115). Formlessness does not mean that one simply vanishes into an abyss. In order to be formless, one must know which actions will enhance the virtues of others, just as the artist knows which colors will help to complement and highlight others, or the musician knows which notes will help to accentuate the timbre of other tones. Formlessness is thus not merely an *absolute* empty space, but a responsive one that knows how to harmonize within the situation at hand. Nothingness is the opening within ourselves that allows us to respond to another, just as the wheelwright does not simply hammer with abandon to make the wheel, but rather reacts to the material he is working with. If one attempts to fill in the empty spaces of nothingness, one undermines the flourishing of life, just as our overcrowded cities eventually begin to exhibit a kind of lifelessness:

> Rather than fill it to the brim by keeping it upright
> Better to have stopped in time;
> Hammer it to a point
> And the sharpness cannot be preserved forever;
> There may be gold and jade to fill a hall
> But there is none who can keep them.
> To be overbearing when one has wealth and position
> Is to bring calamity upon oneself.
> To retire when the task is accomplished
> Is the way of heaven.
>
> (*DDJ* 9)

In Kierkegaard, nothingness takes the form of renunciation and sacrifice. This has markedly different connotations from the idea of withdrawal because it is associated with the anguish of loss that accompanies the struggle with egoism. One must be prepared to surrender something that is irrevocably tied to one's identity in order for the finite to be returned in such a way that one is able to savor it on its own terms, stripped of the trappings of one's own ego. The self must stand naked before God so as to be ready to receive gifts anew. For the man of faith, the finite "tastes just as good to him as one who never knew anything higher" (*FT* 40). Withdrawal, on the other hand, does not demand such heady sacrifices but rather represents a retreat that draws the other forward. The sage who is practiced in this art is never lonely because all beings come to her. She does not sacrifice herself in the act of withdrawal since she merely allows for the interaction that precipitates the process of becoming, which endows all things with their specific character (*xing* 性). It is important to note that this character consists of the radicals for heart and for the process of growth (*sheng* 生). One's identity is not defined by fixed essence but rather by the process of flourishing and growth.

Abraham's readiness to sacrifice Isaac signifies the relinquishment of his most precious attachment. Isaac is returned to him as a being in his own right, whose particularity is not diminished by Abraham's ego. However, the extreme nature of the act that Abraham is asked to undertake and can only perform because of his faith in God, also attests to the dramatic gestures that, in Kierkegaard's view, are necessary to provide a release from the ego-self. A Daoist sage would not be asked to sacrifice his son, although he would view his son's death with equanimity as part of the unceasing transformation of things. The hold of the ego in Kierkegaard's universe is much stronger, and Abraham must let go of the one individual in the world who means most to him. Nevertheless, the abandonment of the ego by the man of faith opens up an entirely new vista of an enchanted world which is similar to the joyousness of the sage: "He enjoys everything he sees, the swarms of people, the new omnibuses, the Sound" (*FT* 39).

While in Kierkegaard, the language of renunciation and sacrifice plays a prominent part in the journey toward faith, the phenomenon does not even arise in Daoism. The sage has no ego-self to jettison. Difference is not "other" to him—it is simply difference. The Daoist sage is at once behind others *and* in front of them. His individual identity neither assumes priority nor a backseat to that of others. Where he stands in relation to others is irrelevant. Instead, it is the interaction between particulars that generates the unity of *Dao* and also fosters individuated uniqueness. Others do not precipitate a return to the self nor do they constitute the self's extension. The sage must neither sacrifice nor extend herself in order to enter into a relationship with them. Rather, she transforms with the other. It is almost impossible to express such a relationship in language: "Therefore the sage put his person last and it comes first, treats it as extraneous to himself and it is preserved" (*DDJ* 7). Daoist sages simply are, and in so doing allow others to be. They become without striving, and are neither altruistic nor egoistic.

Silence

Closely connected to the understanding of nothingness is the importance attributed to silence in the Daoist tradition. Conventional ethics is predicated on the use of language, which often serves as a paltry substitute for harmony. Attentiveness to the use of language is not simply an intellectual exercise, but has profound effects on our way of being in the world. As indicated above, language makes possible a dynamic of possession. Ironically, the *Daodejing* begins on a cautionary note, expressing the difficulty of something that cannot be spoken. The limits of human understanding are revealed: "The Dao that can be spoken is not the constant Dao" (*DDJ* 1). This can also be read as: "The *Dao* that can be *dao*'d is not the constant *Dao*." The words for "*Dao*" and "speaking" are identical in this passage: 道可道，非常道 (*dao ke dao, fei chang dao*; *DDJ* Ch 1), suggesting that speech is an imitation of the movement of *Dao* that always falls short. As Zhang Longxi notes, an "intimate relationship" between thinking and speaking is adumbrated here, which he compares to the use of the word *logos* in the West.[23] Because *Dao* cannot be captured in words,

---

23 Longxi Zhang, "Qian Zhongshu on Philosophical and Mystical Paradoxes in the *Laozi*,"

which are always finite attributions, no word can adequately portray its infinitely transforming nature. We have a tendency to think of language as a way of knowing the world, and here *Dao* is being used to repeatedly remind us that we *cannot* know. Paradoxically, a word that also means language is used to encourage us to use words hesitantly, recognizing that they always fall short of that which they are intended to portray. Furthermore, it is interesting that *Dao* has the connotation of both path and language. This suggests that language is similar to a kind of path that allows one to journey through life. It should point the way rather than leading us to grasp. Because choosing one path implies that we have abandoned another, *Dao* inevitably conceals as much as it reveals.

The above passage can also be reversed in its meaning. *Dao*'ing language can also undo the linguistic effects of objectification. Language which is *Dao*'d is not the constant *Dao* because it is not objectified and is always transforming. The multivalent meanings of this passage are quite deliberate. This admonition that we use language carefully is not an injunction to stop speaking about *Dao*.[24] Instead, language becomes a way of participating in the game of appearance and withdrawal that is part of *Dao*'s movement. The metaphorical nature of language must be celebrated. Because language is a marker of both proximity and distance, we must engage in an unceasing process of naming and unnaming. Zhang

---

in *Religious and Philosophical Aspects of the Laozi*, ed. Mark Csikszentmihalyi and Philip J. Ivanhoe (Albany: State University of New York Press, 1999), p. 104.

24 Karen Carr and Philip J. Ivanhoe point out that Kierkegaard and Zhuangzi share an antirationalist posture, which they are careful to distinguish from an irrational one. They astutely point out that the antirationalism embraced by both does not reject reason outright, but rather recognizes that "reason alone will never enable one to attain their respective spiritual ideals." See Carr and Ivanhoe, *Senses of Anti-Rationalism: Religious Thought of Zhuangzi and Kierkegaard* (New York: Seven Bridges Press, 1999), p. 54. However, it is important to recognize that the sense in which Kierkegaard uses rationalism and the manner in which it can be applied to Zhuangzi's thought differs. Kierkegaardian rationalism is specifically anti-Hegelian. Reason in Hegel's philosophy refers to the tendency to continuously find a way of reconciling the universal and particular. This kind of reconciliation is not always possible according to Kierkegaard, nor is it desirable and reflects a desire to reduce everything to fit within the parameters of the self-conscious subject. The manner in which "reason" operates in the *Zhuangzi* differs in important ways. The reductionist thinking that Zhuangzi describes is deeply rooted in convention and does not impute to itself the same kind of universalism represented by Hegel.

Longxi points out that Qian Zhongshu identifies this as an attempt to use words to get rid of words in a "constant process of constructing and deconstructing."[25] In this way, language becomes part of the dynamism of life and shields our words from the intention to grasp. Instead, they alert us to the presence and absence of *Dao*.

It is significant that both Kierkegaard's *Fear and Trembling* and the *Daodejing* open with the problem of naming or speaking. Both assume that conventional ethics is very much dependent upon names. Judge Wilhelm is very verbose, while Johannes *de Silentio* is silent. The Confucian tradition places a high premium upon living up to the name, which establishes a structure whereby people are clearly aware of their roles. There is an epistemological focus to conventional ethics which, Kierkegaard and the Daoist philosophers worry, can run roughshod over the particular. The realm of silence alerts us to the boundaries of ethics and its unethical possibilities.

The paradox of language is cleverly portrayed in the *Xishengjing* 西昇經, a later Daoist text drawing from the *Daodejing*: "Who hears can speak. Who knows does not speak; who speaks does not know. Language is formed when sounds are exchanged thus in conversations, words make sense. When one does not know the Tao, words create confusion."[26] This passage underscores the arbitrary nature of words, which require something beyond them in order to make sense. Words do not make sense standing on their own; they make sense only in the context of a sentence. The spoken language would have no meaning without the unspoken. Stripped of this, they are empty sounds. Furthermore, when words are known, they are captured, and capturing words interferes with the *activity* of speaking. Words can never bring knowledge in and of themselves—they are always relational. Speaking is responsive, since only the person who hears can speak. Silence, as a symbol of *Dao*, can only have meaning in an environment shaped by words. Without words, silence would also be meaningless. Silence is a metaphor for nothingness and *Dao* is itself a kind of wordless word.

---

25 Zhang, "Philosophical and Mystical Paradoxes," p. 107.

26 Kohn, *Taoist Mystical Philosophy*, pp. 223–4.

Thus, Daoist texts do not exhort us to remain silent forever. Instead, the spoken word must be punctuated with silences which enable one to preserve the paradox of language. Kierkegaard expresses a similar paradox, when he names the narrator of a tale Johannes de Silentio and has him tell a story that can never be adequately relayed by letting him fumble through language. His alternative versions of Abraham's story attest to the necessarily tentative nature of language. The paradoxical nature of language is also implied in the *Zhuangzi*:

> Our words are not just hot air. Words work because they say something, but the problem is, that if we cannot define a word's meaning, it doesn't really say anything. Is it possible that there is really something here? Or does it really mean nothing? Is it possible to make a proper case for it being any different from the chirruping of chicks? What has clouded our words so that we can have both what is and what is not? How can it be that the Tao goes off and is no longer? How can it be that words are found but are not understood? When the Tao is obscured by pettiness and the words are obscured by elaboration then we end up having the "this is, this is not" of the Confucians and Mohists, with what one of them calls reality being denied by the other, and what the other calls real disputed by the first. If we want to confound what they call right and confirm what they call wrong, we need to shed light on both of them. (*Zh* 2:12)

Because *Dao* impels us to speak, just like the chicks chirrup, we cannot understand the true portent of the words that we are using. We use words precisely because of our relationship to the infinite which is both familiar and foreign to us. Words are not just conveyors of definitions, but rather are akin to musical sounds that constitute a spontaneous response to the world. The section, translated in the English version as "if we cannot define a word's meaning," is closer to "therefore his words are not certain" in Chinese. When we try to pin down the meanings of words, we end up embroiled in a process of affirmation and negation because the word always leaves something out. This provides endless fodder for philosophers, represented here by the Confucians and Mohists who become entangled in a web of affirmations and negations, not realizing that the words themselves are not what matter. We must recognize that words signify a relation to *Dao* rather than capturing it. This is why the chirruping of chicks symbolizes both nonsense and a form of language that is in concord with *Dao*, precisely because it does not lay claim to any ultimate meaning.

The *Zhuangzi* alludes to the danger of reifying language: "A fish trap is used to catch fish, but once the fish have been taken, the trap is forgotten. The rabbit trap is used to snare rabbits, but once the rabbit is captured, the trap is ignored. Words are used to express concepts, but once you have grasped the concepts, the words are forgotten. I would like to find someone who has forgotten the words so I could debate with such a person" (*Zh* 26:242). However, words easily become ossified empty shells and we cling to them, forgetting what they point to. From this perspective, the chirruping of chicks is more significant because it is an immediate and spontaneous outburst that has no underlying reason. When we become attached to the words, losing sight of the nebulous *Dao* from which they emerge, they are often used to pin down meaning, and we create opposition that tries to obliterate paradox by categorizing it into assertions of truth and falsehood.

The Daoist interest in language does not just stem from a delight in semantics and playful humor, for there is a serious ethical message that underlies it. A failure to appreciate paradox eventuates in rigid postures that foster dogmatism and opposition. The interplay between silence and language constitutes a reminder of *Dao*, which is both present and absent at the same time. It also reminds us that there is always something in the particular beyond the word. This is why Johannes de Silentio must talk about not speaking and must be silent with his words. The extreme discomfort with silence in some Western cultures points to an unwillingness to acknowledge truths that cannot be possessed. Silence alerts us to the limits of the understanding, and the limitlessness of *Dao*. This is in part why Zhuangzi looks for a man who is silent so that he can have a conversation with him. Only when one recognizes the value of silence can one use words that recognize the nature of the limitless. In order to be able to speak, one must know how to be silent.

Conventional Ethics

As I have mentioned above, the spurning of Confucian values in Daoist texts does not constitute an objection to many of the processes that characterize Confucian morality. Instead, they take issue with the process of labeling that leads to a kind of reverence for tradition and a preoccupation with *having* these virtues. I have pointed out in Chapter One that Confucius demonstrates an incredible flexibility with respect to *li*, but at the same time is disturbed when mats are not aligned in the proper rows. To Daoist thinkers, this would come as no surprise because the word in itself gives rise to the desire to define. We are wedded to the word, while forgetting that the word is like the straw dog, which symbolizes but does not capture. If words are invoked too reverently, they attempt to contain, and thus are akin to amassment. From a Daoist perspective, too much acquisitiveness leads to loss, because it impedes the flowing interactions between things that propel the process of *Dao*.

We must use the name cautiously, just as we must learn when to cease amassment. Ethical codes can act as divisive barriers that impede the responsiveness on the part of one individual to another. Silence is intended to remind us of the limits of knowledge. The relationship between good and evil posited in the *Daodejing* reveals the role that labeling and knowledge play, not just in identifying bad but also in fomenting it. Good only has meaning in relation to the bad, and therefore it must covertly cultivate it. The *Daodejing* suggests that by drawing boundaries, we invite transgression. Because of goodness, there is badness. Any restriction invites its opposite. Even in Kierkegaard, there are faint echoes of this sentiment. Cloaked in the language of ethics, the only way to make sense of Abraham's actions is via the language of *temptation*. This implies that the foray into the non-ethical is not just due to an error of judgment, but rather that it can be described as alluring. The Daoist understanding raises the possibility that a latent longing for openness may underlie morally bad acts. Our fascination with evil is ignited not in spite of our desire for goodness but because of it. We derive pleasure from jettisoning the restrictions of morality. In *The Concept of Anxiety*, Kierkegaard describes this phenomenon as particularly pertinent to children and adolescents who are tempted by prohibitions. By laying down the rules of behavior, one actively encourages the transgression of boundaries and in so doing precipitates the very acts that make the rules necessary. Goodness does not just avoid evil; it also shapes it.

Thus, Daoist philosophy teasingly suggests that in order to avoid evil, one must also avoid good, interacting with others in a mutual process of becoming. Principles of goodness are also markers of exclusion. In order for goodness to be recognized, it needs its outcasts who help to congeal it. Immorality undergirds the moral system which depends upon the evil it can act against. The connection between the good and the bad is symbolically represented by the symbiotic relationship between Liuxia Ji, a friend of Confucius who was deemed morally upright, and his brother, the infamous Robber Zhi. Significantly, both are members of the same family. It is Robber Zhi who berates Confucius for the hypocrisy of the value system he extols, outlining the acquisitive nature of the sage-kings of yesteryear:

> There is no walled city as big as the whole world which was ruled by Yao and Shun, yet their descendents own so little land that they can hardly stick the points of an awl into it! . . . Dressed in your distinctive garb and wearing a narrow belt, armed with false speeches and hypocritical behaviour, you fool the many lords and princes of diverse countries and prowl around looking for riches and fame. There is no greater robber than you, Sir. Why doesn't the whole world which calls me Robber Zhi, call you Robber Confucius?
>
> (*Zh* 29:265)

While Robber Zhi steals in order to acquire material goods, Confucius tries to steal attention for himself in order to be recognized as a man of knowledge and virtue. In this chapter, a connection is drawn between morality and acquisitiveness. Boundaries are established, but like the desperate attempt to acquire riches, this only entices the robbers and thieves: "They heap up their wealth beyond anything they could ever use, but cling to it frantically. Even when they know the distress it causes, they want yet more and more. This state is called pathetic. Behind doors they fear robbers and thieves. Out of doors, they are afraid of being mugged" (*Zh* 29:273).

According to Daoist thinkers, conventional morality is a kind of walled city that invites the very transgressors it purports to spurn:

> The whole world recognizes the beautiful as the beautiful, yet this is only the ugly; the whole world recognizes the good as good, yet this is only the bad.
> The Something and Nothing produce each other;
> The difficult and easy complement each other;
> The long and short offset each other;
> The high and the low incline towards each other;
> Note and sound harmonize with each other;
> Before and after follow each other.
>
> (*DDJ* 2)

It is interesting to note that in this passage, *knowing* goodness results in badness and knowing beauty gives rise to ugliness. Rousseau has drawn attention to the fact that prior to the advent of reason, there was no evil and no desire to do harm to others. Knowing something is akin to capturing it. From a Daoist perspective, the more pervasive the prohibitions and taboos, the more likely it is that evil will ensue. This is why the sage revels in muddleheadedness:

> The multitude all have more than enough
> I alone seem to be in want.
> My mind is that of a fool—how blank!
> Vulgar people are clear.
> I alone am drowsy.
> Vulgar people are alert.
> I alone am muddled.
> Calm like the sea;
> Like a high wind that never ceases.
> The multitude all have a purpose.
> I alone am foolish and uncouth.
> I alone am different from others.
> And value being fed by the mother.
>
> (*DDJ* 20)

Certainty is not laudable according to this passage. The sage drifts aimlessly because he accepts paradox as well as the multifaceted nature of being. He does not own himself and thus appears confused. Evil does not tempt him, because he does not allow himself to be hemmed in by moral prescriptions, so there is no desire to rebel by inflicting harm.

In the Daoist tradition, Confucian virtues are often ridiculed and presented as a constraint imposed upon natural dispositions of human beings. Because conventional morality is associated with a process of labeling, it invites hypocrisy and flattery. Kierkegaard also points to this danger through the figure of Judge Wilhelm, who can extol the virtues of marriage, religion, and work while taking advantage of the labors and accommodating behavior of his wife, for whom he appears to have little respect. His accomplishments become his possessions that he bandies about for all in order to receive social acceptance. Norms provide bait for sycophants and are invoked, when *Dao* has already been abandoned and people have forgotten how to communicate with each other. According to Daoist thinkers, one cannot prescribe ritual and avoid hollow mimicry. Therefore, Daoism recommends doing away with such standards for ethical reasons:

> Exterminate the sage, discard the wise,
> And the people will benefit a hundredfold;
> Exterminate benevolence, discard rectitude,
> And the people will again be filial;
> Exterminate ingenuity, discard profit,
> And there will be no more thieves and bandits.
>
> (*DDJ* 19)

Spontaneity and Wandering

The distrust of traditional ethics does not mean that there is no ethical dimension to Daoism. In both Kierkegaard's and Daoist writings, there is an ethical imperative to be an authentic individual who is perpetually engaged in the process of becoming. Rather than uncovering an inner core to which one is wedded, it signifies the process of self-making in an ever-changing world. But for Daoist thinkers, the process of becoming is part of the harmonious interaction with others and with the cosmos. Only the individual who roams spontaneously can adapt to the rhythm of the cosmos and let others be. Roaming and travel are not seen as ways of expanding the horizons of the self, but rather as a way of cultivating the openness that allows others to thrive. Upon first reading, the emphasis on non-action and personal contentment seems to imply that Daoism is a fundamentally self-centered mode of living. However, because the sage has no awareness of lack, she can encourage the flourishing of others rather than use them as instruments for her own self-completion. The sage is self-sufficient at all times because she is not concerned with her own completeness. Rather, she participates in rhythm of the world, and hence she is no impediment to the development of others. Their flourishing is concomitant with her own.

The Daoist sage is not wedded to any particular place. This provides a stark contrast to the ethical individual, both in traditional Confucianism and European bourgeois *Sittlichkeit*: "From the empty comes stillness; in stillness they can travel; in travelling they achieve. In stillness they take actionless action, through actionless action they are happy, very happy; being so happy they are not afflicted by cares and worries, for these have no place" (*Zh* 13:106–7). Confucian morality depends upon attachment to a particular locale, as does the Hegelian *Sittlichkeit* that Kierkegaard scorns. Even the importance placed on traditional familial roles in Confucian thought indicates that ethics must arise from a stable place. The frenetic striving which Kierkegaard describes is associated with willed action and often signifies an attempt to harness everything for the self, rather than opening oneself up to the world. "Having" rather than "being" instigates this kind of motion. The rapacious hankering for infinity, which drives a figure such as Johannes the Seducer, manifests a deep resentment against kinesis because he longs for a condition where there is nothing outside the self, and this would put an end to his motion. This is why his striving is also expressed as a longing for death. Ironically, we strive in the hope of putting a stop to movement when we possess everything. Contempt for movement fuels our hyperactivity.

The wandering that propels the Daoist sage cannot be equated with the constant becoming that is portrayed in Kierkegaard's writing, for they have very different types of impetus. According to Kierkegaard, the space we straddle between the finite and infinite results in perpetual dissatisfaction with the present, and leads to agony and despair. Anxiety has its roots in childhood, and is reflected in the relationship between actuality and possibility. Unknown possibility leads to the anxiety at the root of our being which has no name, because we are tormented by the knowledge that we are not all: "He has no idea of what it is he can do for that would mean presupposing what indeed mostly happens but which comes later, the difference between good and evil. There is only the possibility of being able as a higher form of not-knowing as a higher expression of anxiety, because in a higher sense, it both is and is not, because in a higher sense, he both loves and flees it" (*CA* 44–5).[27] Pursuit of something higher than the self painfully awakens one to one's finitude. Passion is the hallmark of a being that is drawn to something greater than itself: "Ethically the highest pathos is the pathos of interestedness (which is expressed in this way, that I, acting, transform my whole existence in relation to the object of interest)" (*CUP* 390).[28] While Daoist thinkers would view passion as a form of attachment that ultimately has its roots in egoism, Kierkegaard's writings suggest that it is merely the voice of a being that is pulled beyond itself, because it straddles the position between the finite and the infinite. This not only plunges one into the dark caverns of despair, but also allows for a joyous participation in life: "The pathos that corresponds to and is adequate to an eternal happiness is the transformation by which the existing person in existing changes everything in his existence in relation to the highest good" (*CUP* 389).

The Daoist sage is not preoccupied with his own becoming, and travels in such a way that he appears to stand still, thereby adapting to the motionless movement of *Dao*. Each moment for him is complete, for he is not striving to become other than he is. His journeying is motionless because he does not aim to transform himself. The Daoist sage becomes without being burdened by the will. This kind of levity explains why Liezi, a popular Daoist figure, could allegedly fly in the air, traveling freely. In fact, the *Liezi* 列子 encourages us to "wander and not know where we are going, settle and now know what keep us, and eat and not know how we are fed" (*Lie* 24).[29]

27 Søren Kierkegaard, *The Concept of Anxiety: A Simple Psychologically Orienting Deliberation on the Dogmatic Issue of Hereditary Sin*, trans. Reidar Thomte (Princeton: Princeton University Press, 1981).

28 Søren Kierkegaard, *Concluding Unscientific Postscript to Philosophical Fragments*, ed. and trans. Howard V. Hong and Edna H. Hong (Princeton: Princeton University Press, 1992).

29 Liezi, *The Book of Lieh-tzu: A Classic of Tao*, trans. A. C. Graham (New York: Columbia University Press, 1990).

Kierkegaard's attitude toward becoming is more ambivalent. It is born out of a sense of anxiety which recognizes that we are always "in the wrong before God," but he also maintains that this "thought puts an end to doubt and calms the cares; it animates and inspires to action" (*EO II* 353). The sense of serenity may herald from the profound sense of relief that we derive from acknowledging we are not perfect and cannot expect to be. At the same time, because we are drawn to the limitless, we always have somewhere to go, and this awareness constantly pushes us, disrupting whatever momentary unity we may have crafted for ourselves. Anxiety and serenity are juxtaposed in Kierkegaard's conception of becoming. Knowing that one is always in the wrong before God is both agonizing and liberating, because it means that one's identity is not limited by any decision, opening up the possibility of redemption. Freely acknowledging one's errors may be the closest Kierkegaard can come to non-attachment.

Having said this, the pain of finitude is not completely alien to Daoist ways of thinking, but it does not take the form of existential anguish. Instead, it reflects the day-to-day hardships of bodily existence: "The cosmos gives me the burden of a physical form, makes life a struggle, gives me rest in old age and peace in death. What makes life good, also makes death good" (*Zh* 6:50). In the same chapter, Zhuangzi exclaims, "To have a human form is a joyful thing. But in the universe of possible forms, there are others just as good. Isn't it a blessing to have these uncountable possibilities!" (*Zh* 6:50). The key to experiencing joyousness within the confines of one's finite existence is not to be attached to any particular aspect of one's identity; this includes an attachment to others. The *Liezi* remarks that a man whose son died suddenly seemed unperturbed by the loss. When asked why he was not heartbroken, he responded: "Before my son came, I had no son. I was certainly not heartbroken back then. Now I have no son. Why should I be heartbroken now?" (*Lie* 71:183). Although the above response smacks of an almost inhuman indifference, its intention is to reveal a posture which does not view all beings as existing for the self.

In Kierkegaard, the authentic individual has no definitive direction, but she always directs herself. The sage, on the other hand, travels freely because she has nowhere to go. She is not attached to any aspect of her being and so cannot be plagued by thoughts of limitations. She is complete at every moment. There is no gripping awareness on her part that something is missing. She simply is.

The continuous journeys of the Daoist sage may, on first glance, appear to resemble the activity of Kierkegaard's aesthete. However, even though the aesthete disavows the notion of a fixed entity, he views all beings as existing for an other: "Plant life, for example, in all naïveté unfolds its hidden charms and is only for-other. Likewise, an enigma, a charade, a secret, a vowel, etc. are merely being-for-other" (*EO I* 430). While Johannes tries to amass experiences, only in thought can he distill his experiences into something for himself and bring them into his fold. Yet, when everything is reduced to thought or a clever fantasy, as is Johannes's Cordelia, we are eventually left with an empty shell. Thought cannot completely incorporate the particular without destroying it. Our enjoyment ceases precisely because we attempt to trap it within the prison house of the self. The intellect devours and consumes. Daoist thinkers are well aware of the link between knowledge and consumption, and this is why they insist that our language and reasoning must be used cautiously.

The Daoist does not seek to possess or make anything his own, but Kierkegaard does consider "en-owning" (*das Ereignis*), to use Heideggerian language, a crucial component of authenticity. An authentic act, in Kierkegaard's view, forces one to take responsibility for one's decision and this necessitates an element of attachment to it by making a choice. Choice is not even part of Daoist vocabulary. Authenticity is instead more closely associated with *ziran* 自然, which is often translated as spontaneity, "self-so-ing" or naturalness: "The Dao takes what is natural as its model" (*DDJ* 25). Authentic existence is not a life lived by and for the self, but one which is attuned to the harmony of *Dao* and to nature. *Ziran* also implies that no external agent is necessary for the arising of the world and its beings. It is action that takes place without one specific agent acting as its motor. Self-so-ing is also the process of allowing others to shape who one is, without attempting to direct or control things. Rather than reducing the world to objects under our control, we recognize that we are part of nature. Nature is not *other* to us.

Liu Xiaogan identifies *ziran* as the core value of Daoism and argues that the term has its origins in the *Laozi*. He cites the following passage from the *Daodejing*:

> Hence the way is great; heaven is great; earth is great; and the king is also great. Within the realm there are four things that are great, and the king counts as one.
>
> Man models himself on earth,
> Earth on heaven,
> Heaven on the way,
> And the way on that which is naturally so.
>
> (*DDJ* 25)

According to Liu, this progression, which culminates in *Dao* modeling itself on the natural or *ziran*, suggests that naturalness is the highest value that reality embodies.[30] This last line in Chinese is 道法自然 (*daofa ziran*; *DDJ* Ch 25). Since *ziran* represents a kind of spontaneity that does not depend on models, *Dao* is using the model-less as its pattern. Human beings take earth as their model because we inhabit it and yet its scope is much greater than ours. Earth takes heaven as its model because it touches upon that which extends beyond it. There is nothing beyond *Dao*, so it embodies the process of spontaneous becoming within itself. What is more expansive than the self enables one to open oneself up to a whole panoply of experiences generating joy rather than anxiety. Yet, in moving away from the self in this manner, one also returns to *Dao* which is complete in and of itself.

The anxiety that Kierkegaard believes necessarily accompanies authentic subjectivity is not part of the Daoist understanding. There is no oppositional relationship between the finite and the infinite in Daoist philosophy, because there is no underlying desire that the self be either self-sufficient, infinite, or singular. The uniqueness of each being is produced out of the interaction with others, and therefore even that which differentiates one thing from another, namely its *xing* 性, is continuously

---

30 Xiaogan Liu, "An Inquiry into the Core Value of Laozi's Philosophy," in *Religious and Philosophical Aspects of the Laozi*, ed. Mark Csikszentmihalyi and Philip J. Ivanhoe (Albany: State University of New York Press, 1999), p. 220.

arising in conjunction with beings. The self can only be gripped by the sentiments of lack, absence, and anxiety, if it is plagued by the notion that it should be more than it presently is and somehow tries to become infinite. Kierkegaard's notion of always being in the wrong before God and his acute awareness of guilt implies that our actions are always incomplete in contrast to God, who is the only complete Being. In Daoism, each moment is what it is, and is neither complete nor incomplete. It would make no sense to speak of that which has been left out, or the call which has not yet been answered. Completion is not in a being such as God. The Daoist sage can be responsive to others without the sense of indebtedness that Kierkegaard describes. She can heed the call of the other without feeling her own inadequacy. Because everything is interconnected, each moment is an instance of the whole, and one need not worry about all the avenues one might have closed off in choosing this particular moment over another. In fact, doing so would encourage the kind of frenetic striving that Daoism spurns. There is no anxiety in the Daoist sage over lost opportunities.

Ziran is also closely associated with the activity of wandering: "The sage sees his role as that of a wanderer, sees knowledge as a curse, convention as a glue, virtue as just a means and effort as common trade. The sage has no great plans, so what use has he for knowledge? He makes no divisions so what use has he for glue" (*Zh* 5:44). Indeed, he seems to be characterized by his refusal to make choices, because he responds to the situation at hand, like a mirror and goes wherever the wind carries him: "The perfect man has no self" (*Zh* 1:3). His freedom inheres in his perpetual responsiveness. However, unlike Kierkegaard's authentic individual, he is completely free from the agony of sin or guilt at having chosen one path rather than another: "He never regretted any failure, nor exulted in success" (*Zh* 6:47). *Ziran* is often translated as freedom, but it is important to recognize that it is not a freedom *from* other things and beings, but rather a freedom *with* others. One allows oneself to float with the world, rather than strenuously working against it.

Openness to *Dao* does not demand self-surrender but allows us to be ourselves without self-attachment. This is why the identity of the self is completely irrelevant: "I continued to teach him for nine days, whereupon he could observe his own being as irrelevant. Having discerned his own self as irrelevant, he saw with true clarity" (*Zh* 6:52). In order to be free to be ourselves, we must be free from ourselves. Zhuangzi learns not to mourn his wife's passing, because he no longer views her as a belonging but rather as part of the transformation of things:

> When she first died, I certainly mourned like everyone else! However, I then thought back to her birth and to the very roots of her being, before she was born. Indeed, not just before she was born but before the time when her body was created. Not just before her body was created but before the very origin of her life's breath. Out of this, through the wonderful mystery of change she was given her life's breath. Her life's breath wrought a transformation and she had a body. Her body wrought a transformation and she was born.
>
> (*Zh* 18:151)

In both Kierkegaard and Zhuangzi, there is a sense in which the authentic individual is engaged in a constant process of becoming, manifesting a resistance to the notion of a fixed identity. However, in Kierkegaard, the self is continuously relating itself to itself, and its activity emerges out of the tension between the finite and the infinite within the self. The "self" is kinetic, and is a verb rather than a noun. Yet, the fact that we resolutely choose ourselves and then experience guilt, because of the avenues we have neglected while moving in certain directions, means that Kierkegaard's perception of motion is still tinged with the notion of having. We will only feel guilt at not being infinite if, at some level, we assume the infinite is something we can grasp. Because we straddle the domain of finitude and infinity, human freedom is always a blessing and a curse.

The Daoist sage also engages in a constant process of becoming, but there is no malaise ensuing from her condition. She does not have to choose herself, which constitutes a territorial marking out of one's terrain; she simply is. When a willow tree suddenly shot up out of Uncle Cripple's left elbow, he remains unperturbed: "What should I dislike? Life exists through scrounging; if life comes through scrounging, then life is like a dump. Death and birth are like the morning and the night. You and I, Sir, observe the ways of the transformation and now I am being transformed. So how could I dislike this?" (*Zh* 18:151).

Compared to the Daoist sage, the Kierkegaardian individual is thrust on an endless treadmill of self-reflection. Kierkegaard implies that we are in a state of perpetual agitation because our identity eludes us. We yearn to define ourselves and then overcome this definition. Because we are always branded by our boundaries, God is necessary as the infinite intermediary between subjects. We need the boundless God to open ourselves to another. We must be continually wrenched from the self because of our tendency toward self-enclosure. The call of the other intrudes upon one's self from the outside. Thus, while Kierkegaard demands a respect for the particularity of the other, his thought is necessarily infused with the traditional presupposition that the other is a problem. This in itself is indicative of the centrality that the self assumes in Western thought.

According to Daoist thought, if the spontaneity of *ziran* prevails, then it does not make sense to conceive of the other as a problem. The difference between the two approaches can be highlighted by examining *ziran* in light of Kierkegaard's notion of love. Kierkegaard reminds us repeatedly of the "command" to love the other as oneself. This is a stark reminder at how deeply the attachment to the self is rooted in our consciousness. *Ziran*, on the other hand, manifests a spontaneous openness to the other where no strong distinction between self and other is made. There is neither altruistic self-denial nor possessiveness that often fuels the passion of love. No intermediary is needed for *ziran*, which attests to the ineradicable interconnectedness of human beings. Kierkegaard's love necessitates an intermediary because we must first relinquish our self-attachment. The sage must not surrender anything in order to be open to the other. He can be himself in the presence of the other, because he is not infected by the desire to be all. In fact, the confusion regarding identity in Zhuangzi's famous butterfly dream can be seen as an allegory for the relationship with the other. Zhuangzi does not know whether he is a butterfly dreaming he is a man, or a man dreaming he is a butterfly. His identity is so fluid that he assumes various forms of being in a single night: "Once upon a time, I, Zhuangzi dreamt that I was a butterfly, flitting around and enjoying myself. I had no idea I was Zhuangzi. Then suddenly I woke up and was Zhuangzi again. But I could not tell.

Had I been Zhuangzi dreaming I was a butterfly, or a butterfly dreaming I was now Zhuangzi? However, there must be some sort of difference between Zhuangzi and a butterfly! We call this the transformation of things" (*Zh* 2:20). Zhuangzi acknowledges both his difference from and his identity with the other. Both he and the butterfly are indeterminate; rather than generating trepidation, his nebulous confusion leads to a joyous participation in the flux of life.

In Kierkegaard, the radical otherness of God is intended to alert us to the alterity and strangeness of the other, by wresting us from solipsistic encounters. This is in part because the relationship of the self to the self is assumed to be primary, and the relationships with others are derivatives of our self-relationships. God is supposed to release us from the shackles of a stultifying self-relation. However, an other is only viewed as radically other if we remain ensconced in a kind of radical self-enclosure. The radical otherness of God allows us to affirm our neighbor's otherness. While this invests the particular other with the infinite, the need for such mediation suggests that self-overcoming is the necessary prelude to social interaction, which respects particularity. By insisting that we need such radical intervention, Kierkegaard points to the tremendous barriers that bar an encounter with the other that truly respects their particularity. *Dao* does not mediate between individuals in this way, but rather allows for an immediate encounter with the other which spawns the spontaneous transformation of both. Self and other are always already intertwined, because we are who we are in relation to the other.

Self-less Transformations

Both Kierkegaard and Daoist thinkers, although emanating from disparate philosophical and religious traditions, impute a greater value to the particular than many of their philosophical predecessors. Indeed, one could argue that the distrust of traditional ethics toward the particular is what results in their trenchant criticisms of morality. In the case of Kierkegaard, conventional morality marks a mere extension of the self, which fails to appreciate the other as other, and reduces it to the self in order to find common ground. However, even the term "self" used in this context is problematic, for this is not an individualized, personal self but rather a collective, public one. Ethics, from this perspective, becomes an egotistical self-love which guards boundaries and is predicated on self–contempt, because it is closely associated with the desire to erect walls *against* the fluidity that is also at the core of one's being. This in part accounts for the zealous way in which we condemn moral outcasts, who not only violate prescribed codes of ethics, but remind us of the unstable basis that gnaws at the center of our own being. Kierkegaard is aware of the continual pull between the desire to establish boundaries and the need to overcome them. Religious faith allows us to be "at home" in the midst of this instability, by putting our trust in something which we cannot know. It not only catapults us beyond ethics, but also revivifies ethics by severing the connection between an invidious self-love and morality, opening us up to the wonder of difference. The religious ethics that Kierkegaard proposes invites us to embrace the other not on *our* terms but rather on no terms at all. This constitutes both an affront to ethics and a return to it.

A comparison with Daoist philosophy reveals the extent to which Kierkegaard's thought, although engaged in an incessant quest to overcome egoism, is riddled with this very egoism. Because he comes out of a tradition where self-reflection plays such a prominent role, an interaction with the other, which respects the other as other, demands a dramatic wresting of the self from its moorings to heed a call that emanates from the outside. The outside and inside are experienced in stark opposition to each other. Paradoxically, it is the outside that also opens the self up to its own particularity, because it calls upon me as an individual rather than being mediated through concepts and universals.

The outside-inside dichotomy is almost non-existent in Daoist texts because there is no aspiration of the self to be all, nor is there a conscious participation in the art of self-making. Therefore, *Dao* cannot be radically other in the manner of Kierkegaard's God. Zhuangzi's butterfly dream does not propel him toward an existential crisis, and whether he is a butterfly or a man is of no consequence. In fact, it is unimportant that this dream is "merely a dream" because it exemplifies the reality of the transformation of all things. Each thing becomes itself through the interaction with others, and therefore there is no problem of the other as there is in Kierkegaard's thought. This is a non-egoistic self-love that is coterminous with a love of everything, because the self opens itself to the universe:

> To have a human form is a joyful thing. But in the universe of possible forms, there are others just as good. Isn't it a blessing to have these uncountable possibilities! The sage goes where nothing escapes him, and rests contented there with them. He takes pleasure in an early death, in old age, in the origin and in the end and sees them all as equally good—he should be an example to others. (*Zh* 6:50)

However, with its esteem for constant transformation, Daoist thought may underestimate the extent to which the desire on the part of the self to settle, and the comfort that comes from the boundaries of the familiar, are an indelible feature of human existence. When Kierkegaard refers to the ethical realm as an abode, he acknowledges that conventional ethics with its tendency to set the parameters of the human community cannot and should not be overcome completely. The interaction between enclosure and openness attests to the recognition of the multifaceted nature of the self which both longs for constancy and struggles to escape it. In Daoist thought, constancy is not ignored but associated with a spontaneous harmonizing with the other that takes into account the peculiarities of each unique situation. It is harmony rather than sameness and predictability that is to imbue the individual with the serenity of rest.

Nevertheless, Kierkegaard and Daoist thinkers would concur that conventional morality cannot stand on its own without degenerating into its opposite. It is linked to the enterprise of knowledge, which is interpreted in Daoist thought as a kind of acquisitiveness that tries to impose artificial boundaries on the limitless. The problem that Daoist thinkers identify is with the process of reification that takes place when we begin to apply moral labels. As soon as we become attached to a word, there is a tendency to want to define and circumscribe it, and this leads to the codification of moral convention. Human social order becomes predicated on enclosure, and this propensity to impose limits can result in efforts to stamp out the particularity of others. In Daoism, authenticity is patterned on the unending formlessness and openness of *Dao*. If there is a Daoist ethics, it is based on openness and formlessness, which allows each to harmonize with the other. In Kierkegaard, authenticity is also linked to perpetual transformation, but the self is plagued by thoughts of its own indebtedness and incompleteness in relation to an infinite god. Therefore, openness is always associated with anxiety and trepidation because the self longs for the very definition that it rejects. In Daoism, there is no guilt or awareness of shortcomings because there is no longing for a complete identity—indeed, there is no longing for an identity at all. Harmony rather than aesthetic self-creation is the constant goal of the authentic individual. According to Kierkegaard, there can be no carefree wandering, since we are always torn between a yearning for the comfort of boundaries and the unsettling but wondrous openness of the infinite which always throws our identity into turmoil. This dissonance that throttles our very being accounts for the pathos that Kierkegaard would never want to extirpate from our existence.

CHAPTER FOUR

Beyond Good and Evil: Flexible Ethics in Nietzsche and Daoist Thought

Kierkegaard's philosophy sheds light on the limits of ethical systems, which manifest a disturbing discomfort with the stranger and therefore fail to appreciate the diversity of the world. For Kierkegaard, our existence is marked by an intractable and yet rejuvenating paradox. The infinite is both completely other to human beings and deeply embedded in the world within which we live, accounting for both its incomprehensibility and wonder. Difference marks the voice of the infinite within the finite. The urgent need to resuscitate the particular provides a strong link between his thought and that of Daoist thinkers, for whom the oneness of the world is possible not in spite of the world's diversity but rather because of it. However, particularity is very much associated with self-definition, and arises out of the acute awareness that we stand as solitary individuals in a relationship with an infinite and absolute God. This is not a concern shared by Daoist thinkers for whom self-definition is irrelevant. Instead, the self is seen as one particular among many who engage in an ongoing process of mutual creation. This process is not carried out by the self for the self, but rather is a dynamic in which different beings participate with each other.

Nietzsche is another thinker who vituperates against the restrictive conditions imposed by morality. His exhortation to go beyond good and evil has often been associated with an amoral relativism that pushes ethics to the sidelines, in order to make way for an unimpeded creativity or unleash the dynamics of power. In the West, Nietzsche holds the dubious reputation for permitting the worst of moral abuses in his effort to promote the aesthetic and political hero who would revitalize a phlegmatic and moribund social order. While there is some truth to these assumptions, this overlooks the trenchant critique of egoism that pervades his writings, and his assumption that such egoism is the unacknowledged backbone of the moral world we have constructed. A comparison with Daoist philosophy helps to foreground this aspect of Nietzsche's philosophy, since it makes clear that the need to catapult human beings beyond good and evil does not necessarily grow out of a lust for power, but rather serves to keep human ambitions in check. However, unlike the Daoists, Nietzsche would not suggest that egoism can be dispensed with altogether. He is a thinker of contradictions who not only castigates human beings for their obsession with the self, but also dares them to be selfish rather than becoming enslaved to ossified social customs.

There is no doubt that Nietzsche is critical of universal moral prescriptions which are linked to the rabid pursuit of knowledge that attempts to congeal life into timeless categories, providing shelter from the pulsing world around us. For him, morality has little to do with benevolence but entails the mastery of others and nature, in an attempt to render what is fluid predictable. Most moral thinkers recognize that egoism is a threat to morality which must be overcome, but Nietzsche locates it at the hub of the moral system itself, which manifests the desperate attempt of a bounded being to impose boundaries on others. Morality is a kind of fortress emerging out of a collective egoism, which tries to keep the more menacing and overwhelming forces of life at bay and attempts to further demarcate human beings from nature; it is also egotistical because it is primarily concerned with making sure that nobody can outdo me. This demands that we negate not only nature but also nature within ourselves.

Nietzsche's critique of the self-centered and anthropomorphic biases of human beings echoes the words of Daoist thinkers, who also lament the hubris of humanity. Daoist thinkers link morality to a preoccupation with language that impels us to impose an order on the world that may hinder the development of our natural dispositions and potential (*de* 德), and also invite the very egoism it is intended to forestall. From a Daoist perspective, when we begin to define virtues, we begin to focus on *what* we are and *what* we are doing, rather than the process of doing things well. Values are easily turned into things that can be possessed like riches, and such desire to possess leads to an egotistical preoccupation with self, objectifying both itself and others.

There is no doubt that Daoist thinkers are more concerned with the interconnection between beings than Nietzsche, who advocates an opening of the self to the infinite panoply of experiences that the world has to offer, in order to participate and contribute to its creative energy. Meanwhile, Daoist thinkers emphasize the need to foster equilibrium between beings. Morality, rather than making us receptive to the particular virtues of other beings, leads us to superimpose our own blueprint on them, and this is why there are strong ties between traditional ethics and egoism. We turn others into objects that become images of ourselves. Moral orders are needed when human beings fail to be receptive to others and the world around them. According to Daoist thinkers, codes of ethics are symptomatic of ethical failure.

Art and Knowledge

Nietzsche is probably the most virulent critic of Western morality, predicating his attack largely on the Judeo-Christian tradition of mores. Nevertheless, his exhortation to go beyond good and evil has largely been misunderstood and does not constitute an invitation to violence and authoritarianism as is sometimes alleged.

In fact, his vitriol is unleashed largely against the hypocrisy that, he believes, underlies the moral tradition. When morality ceases to have meaning and degenerates into vacuous mimicry, it is no longer moral. This prompts him to ask the unconventional question—what is the value of morality? Although the tenets of moral dogma have been subjected to debate, the value of morality is itself taken for granted: "In all 'science of morals' so far one thing was *lacking*, strange as it may sound: the problem of morality itself; what was lacking was any suspicion that there was something problematic here. What the philosophers called a 'rational foundation for morality' . . . was, seen in the right light, merely a scholarly variation of the common *faith* in the prevalent morality; a new means of *expression* for this faith" (*BGE* 186).[1] Once values are bereft of meaning, they are reduced to empty gestures that are simply parroted because it is easy and comfortable to do so. It is not the positing of values per se that Nietzsche objects to, but rather their ossification.

Nietzsche links morality to a sometimes pernicious anthropomorphism that places human beings at the fulcrum of the cosmos:

> Behind all logic and its seeming sovereignty of movement, too, there stand valuations or, more clearly, physiological demands for the preservation of a certain type of life. For example, that the definite should be worth more than the indefinite, and mere appearance worth less than truth . . . which may be necessary for the preservation of just such beings as we are. Supposing, that is, that not just man is the "measure of things."
>
> (*BGE* 3)

Thus, morality is closely linked to a certain kind of knowledge which attempts to freeze behavior into clearly defined categories, and is ultimately about power and control: "'Knowledge for its own sake'—that is the last snare of morality: with that one becomes completely entangled in it once more" (*BGE* 64). The idea that knowledge has an intrinsic worth is ripe for questioning. For Nietzsche, this quest for knowledge is part of a propensity to entrench ideas and uphold their timelessness and universality. It signals an enormous hubris that refuses to acknowledge our debt to both life and nature: "Even the term 'science of morals' is much too arrogant considering what it designates, and offends *good* taste (*Geschmack*)—which always prefers more modest terms" (*BGE* 186). Nietzsche prefers the term "taste" because it acknowledges the limited nature of our presuppositions which are not universal.

Nietzsche is not suggesting that we dispense with knowledge and wisdom. However, he would like wisdom to be responsive to life, rather than posing as the autocrat who keeps life within bounds. The relationship between them is akin to a kind of dance which plays on both the antagonism and affinity between them. In *Thus Spoke Zarathustra*, this dialogue between Wisdom and Life takes the form of a dance between

---

1 Friedrich Nietzsche, *Beyond Good and Evil*, in *Basic Writings of Nietzsche*, trans. Walter Kaufmann (New York: Modern Library, 1968).

two women. Both are equal partners in movement, and so neither one can be considered the substratum or essence of the other, nor does one try to eclipse the other. The dance requires both commonality and distance between them. Zarathustra cannot distinguish his fondness for wisdom from his fondness for life: "From the heart of me I love only Life—and in truth, I love her most of all when I hate her! But that I am fond of Wisdom, and often too fond . . . because she very much reminds me of Life!" (Z II:10).[2] Life mocks Zarathustra because of his implicit assumption that what he, as a man, cannot understand is unfathomable (*unergründlich*), and for the fact that "you men always endow us with your own virtues" (Z II:10). The problem with morality is that it tries to use wisdom to subjugate life. Life mocks Zarathustra for objectifying women and equating them with a set of values.

When ideas become rigidified, they undercut the responsiveness to nature and prevent us from participating in the ever-changing rhythms of life, rendering truth hollow. The timelessness of ideas, far from bestowing legitimacy on them, robs them of their vitality according to Nietzsche. We begin to take them for granted, and they lose their meaning for us. This is why the death of truth, ushered in by its own success in eternalizing itself, also marks the death of appearance: "We have rid ourselves of the true world: what world are we left with? Perhaps that of appearances? . . . But no! *Along with the true world, we have also rid ourselves of the apparent world*" (*TI* 7).[3] Truth represents a tendency to valorize certain concepts and imbue them with a universal legitimacy. However, the moment they have become too ensconced in our consciousness is precisely when they cease to function as a way of holding a dialogue with life. Their interactive element is moribund and they become the subject of unquestioning and hollow dogma that ceases to have meaning. For Nietzsche, the establishment of a realm of truth is a creative act, and this is why he has great respect for philosophers such as Socrates, despite disagreeing with their ideas.

2 Friedrich Nietzsche, *Thus Spoke Zarathustra*, trans. R. J. Hollingdale (Middlesex: Penguin, 1968).

3 Friedrich Nietzsche, *Twilight of the Idols*, trans. R. J. Hollingdale (Middlesex: Penguin, 1968).

For Nietzsche, all concepts falsify life: "Every concept originates through equating the unequal" (OTF 19).[4] While the concept is a useful and inevitable navigational tool, it should not be adhered to too rigidly, for then it glosses over the complex wonder of nature. Nothing contributes more to the arrogant mastery of nature on the part of human beings than the valorization of concepts, which tempts us to establish a "pyramidal order of castes and grades" that shows "the rigid regularity of a roman columbarium and in logic breathes forth that rigor and coldness which we find in mathematics" (OTF 181–2).

Nietzsche does not deny that the conceptual impetus of human beings is necessary to provide them with some semblance of calm. However, we must recognize that these concepts are merely crutches and should never become substitutes for being. The true artist recognizes that "enormous framework and hoarding of concepts, by clinging to which the needy man saves himself throughout life, is to the freed intellect only a scaffolding and a toy for his most daring feats; and when he smashes it to pieces, throws it into confusion, and then puts it together again ironically, pairing the most alien, separating the closest items, then he reveals that he is no longer led by concepts but by intuitions" (OTF 190). When we wrap ourselves in the cocoons of our concepts, then we assume we have mastered nature, forgetting that we are only ever in dialogue with it. Thus, Nietzsche suggests that the concept itself leads to a bloated human ego, which predicates its relationship to the world on a pattern of consumption.

For Nietzsche, the notion that human beings could utilize logic to "penetrate the deepest abysses of being" thereby not only "knowing being but even of *correcting* it" (*BT* 15)[5] marks the attempt on the part of a finite creature to impose its finitude on the world. The process of conceptualization is often linked to consumption, because it assimilates, consumes, and reduces differences. Thus, the notion that knowledge can

---

4 Friedrich Nietzsche, "On Truth and Falsity in an Extra-Moral Sense," in *Early Greek Philosophy and Other Essays*, trans. M. A. Mügge, *The Complete Works of Friedrich Nietzsche*, vol. 2, ed. Oscar Levy (New York: Russell and Russell, 1964).

5 Friedrich Nietzsche, *The Birth of Tragedy*, in *Basic Writings of Nietzsche*, trans. Walter Kaufmann (New York: Modern Library, 1968).

be disinterested and objective is ludicrous, since knowledge culminates in the domination of all that is unfamiliar:

> The spirit's power to appropriate the foreign stands revealed in its inclination to assimilate the new to the old, to simplify the manifold, and to overlook or repulse whatever is totally contradictory—just as it involuntarily emphasizes certain features and lines in what is foreign, in every piece of the "external world" retouching and falsifying the whole to suit itself. Its intent in all this is to incorporate new "experiences," to file new things in old files—growth, in a word—or more precisely, the *feeling* of growth, the feeling of increased power.
>
> (*BGE* 230)

"Truth" is the decree that anoints the conceptual apparatuses we have created with universal legitimacy. It is appearance masquerading as something that is immune to questioning.

Nietzsche does not condemn the mission of conceptualization entirely, for it is an indelible aspect of our experience, reflected in the Apollonian dimension of ancient Greek art. We seek refuge in the permanent statues of Apollo: "The higher truth, the perfection of these states in contrast to the incompletely intelligible everyday world, this deep consciousness of nature, healing and helping in sleep and dreams, is at the same time the symbolical analogue of the soothsaying faculty of the arts generally, which make life possible and worth living" (*BT* 1). Apollo is the god of calm repose in the midst of the turbulent maelstrom of existence. He is the god of form and the visual arts. Nietzsche makes use of the German word *Schein*, which has the connotation of illusion, appearance, and shining: "In fact, we might say of Apollo that in him the unshaken faith in this *principium* and the calm repose of the man wrapped up in it receive their most sublime expression; and we might call Apollo himself the glorious divine image of the *principium individuationis*, through whose gestures and eyes all the joy and wisdom of 'illusion' together with its beauty, speak to us" (*BT* 1). The link to the *principium individuationis* is important, since Apollo represents the bounded nature of existence, and by resting our gaze on these clearly delineated forms, we are placated by the momentary illusion that our boundaries are secure. Nietzsche also notes that Apollo is the god of morality: "Apollo, as ethical deity, exacts measure of his disciples, and, to be able to maintain it, he requires self-knowledge" (*BT* 4). Furthermore, he argues that we cannot survive without the realm of fantasy that Apollo represents, which buffers us from the harsh realities that surround us: "*Art* approaches a saving sorceress, expert at healing. She alone knows how to turn these nauseous thoughts about the horror or absurdity of existence into notions with which one can live" (*BT* 7).

Nietzsche does not wish to expunge the Apollonian from our existence. On the contrary, he asserts that it is essential in order to preserve meaningfulness since it provides temporary shelter from a surrounding whirlwind. However, the Apollonian can only survive in the presence of its opposite. The very boundaries we delight in must also be disbanded in occasional acts of Dionysian revelry in order to effect a reunion with nature, from which human beings become somewhat alienated while sheltered in their Apollonian abode: "Under the charm of the Dionysian not only is the union between man and man reaffirmed, but nature which has become alienated, hostile, or subjugated, celebrates once more her reconciliation with her lost son, man" (*BT* 1). The contrast between the Apollonian and Dionysian enables us to revel in both. Without one, the other becomes defunct. The elevation of Apollo to such heights that Dionysus is forgotten deprives us of the meaning that derives from the contrast between them. While we are individuated beings, we are also part of the teeming pulse of nature, and should not aspire to live a one-dimensional existence. Jason Kemp Winfree argues that in relation to the Dionysian, Apollo, who has represented the principles of measure and moderation, becomes a principle of "excessive de-marcation."[6] The God who is supposed to provide a panacea against suffering is also revealed as the handmaiden of suffering, when the release offered by Dionysus is denied.

The Dionysian also represents the more unmediated impulses of nature whereby individual boundaries are destroyed and we give expression to our uncensored impulses. Without the opportunity for unleash-

6 Jason Kemp Winfree, "Before the Subject: Rereading *The Birth of Tragedy*," *Journal of Nietzsche Studies* 25 (2003): 58–77.

ing the Dionysian forces, through festivals and the unfurling of sexual energy, there is a danger that it could explode the boundaries of civilization. This is why Dionysus must be tempered, but not squashed, by Apollo or by Apollo gone mad, as Nietzsche believes it has. It is no coincidence that the Apollonian is closely associated with morality. However, a moral system that tries to eradicate Dionysus only opens the door for the turmoil resulting from the repressed fury of the Dionysian. Without giving voice to those urges that the moral system all too readily labels evil, we invite not only moral hypocrisy but also the more destructive aspects of Dionysus. Acts of violence, for Nietzsche, are unleashed by a yearning for oneness and if Dionysus is not provided with an outlet then inexplicable acts of horror are likely to abound.

The Art of Morality

Nietzsche is one of the few thinkers to throw the entire edifice of Western morality under question. Far from offering an invitation to nihilistic violence, he exposes the sinister side of morality in order to demonstrate its violent foundations. For him, morality is part of the process of rendering human beings knowable, which manifests the impulse to conquer by reducing the rich ambiguity and complexity of things into something that can be controlled and owned. He paints what is perhaps the most brutal genealogy of morals in the Western tradition, maintaining that we are the inheritors of a bloodstained and violent history: "How much blood and cruelty lies at the bottom of all good things" (*GM* III:9).[7] Morality is part of the horrific quest to render human behavior predictable and thus permanent: "Our eye finds it more comfortable to respond to a given stimulus by reproducing once more an image that it has produced many times before, instead of registering what is different and new in an impression. The latter would require more strength, more 'morality. Hearing something new is embarrassing and difficult for the ear; foreign music we do not hear well'" (*BGE* 192). Eventually, when violence has

7 Friedrich Nietzsche, *On the Genealogy of Morals*, in *Basic Writings of Nietzsche*, trans. Walter Kaufmann (New York: Modern Library, 1968).

civilized us, we no longer need to have recourse to such drastic methods. The culmination of this process is the creation of the herd mentality, which marks morality's acme yet also the downfall.

There is no doubt in Nietzsche's mind that morality was established as an antidote to nature, which arose out of the need for self-preservation. Initially, the master, ebullient and overflowing with the primal forces of nature, simply conceived of the "basic concept of 'good' in advance and spontaneously out of himself" (*GM* I:11). The master is not immoral but amoral. In contrast to almost all theorists of morality, Nietzsche warns that the good had nothing to do with altruism or selflessness: "It follows from this origin that the word 'good' was definitely *not* linked from the first and by necessity to 'unegoistic' actions, as the superstition of these genealogists of morality would have it" (*GM* I:2). Good was originally not a moral term. The *pathos of distance* marked the genesis of value judgments such as good and bad: "The pathos of nobility and distance, . . . the protracted and domineering fundamental total feeling on the part of a higher ruling order in relation to a lower order, to a 'below'—*that* is the origin of the antithesis of 'good' and 'bad'" (*GM* I:2). Nietzsche claims there is an etymological link between the word "good" and the noble or aristocratic.

What we understand as moral behavior marks the effort to secure social conformity:

> What is essential "in heaven and on earth" seems to be, to say it once more, that there should be *obedience* over a long period of time and in a *single* direction. . . . Consider any morality with this in mind: what there is in it of "nature" teaches hatred of the *laisser-aller*, of any all-too-great freedom, and implants the need for limited horizons and the nearest tasks—teaching the *narrowing of our perspective*, and thus in a certain sense stupidity, as a condition of life and growth. "You shall obey—someone and for a long time: *else* you will perish and lose the last respect for yourself.
>
> (*BGE* 188)

He thereby closely links morality to the pursuit of knowledge, which in turn is linked to the Apollonian dimension of art. However, we are aware of the artistic impulse underlying it, and the power of the Apollonian illusion. The meaning of the Apollonian is provided through its contrast with the Dionysian. Morality, like science, elevates the Apollonian to the status of untouchable truth and it is precisely when its truths are immune to questioning that the process of their decline begins, because they are not part of a lively system of reinterpretation occasioned by the interplay of opposites.

Nietzsche avers that the link between morality and altruism must have originated with those to "whom 'goodness' was shown" (*GM* I:2). The moral system we take for granted today is an invention of the Judeo-Christian religion which,

> with awe inspiring consistency, dared to invert the aristocratic value equation (good = noble = powerful = beautiful = happy = beloved of God) and to hang on to this inversion with their teeth, the teeth of the most abysmal hatred (the hatred of impotence), saying "the wretched alone are the good; the poor, impotent, lowly alone are the good . . . and you, the powerful and noble are on the contrary, the evil, the cruel the lustful, the insatiable, the godless to all eternity; and you shall be in all eternity the unblessed, the accused, the damned." (*GM* I:7)

The shift from "the good versus the bad" to "good versus evil" is significant, for the term "evil" denotes the positing of an intrinsic and absolute worth. When we use the words "good" and "evil," we deny the relativity associated with the words "good" and "bad," which are more commonly held to be value judgments or matters of taste. Morality for Nietzsche consists of value judgments that are then rendered permanent.

Morality is rooted in *ressentiment* or revenge, and it is this wrathful lust that gives rise to the propensity to assimilate in order to survive. Nietzsche does not differentiate morals from the act of moralizing which seeks to debase others: "Slave morality from the outset says No to what is 'outside,' what is 'different,' what is 'not itself'; and *this* No is its creative deed. This inversion of the value-positing eye—this *need* to direct one's view outward instead of back to oneself—is of the essence of *ressentiment*: in order to exist, slave morality always first needs a hostile external world; it needs, physiologically speaking, external stimuli in order to act at all—its action is fundamentally reaction" (*GM* I:10). In order for a moral system to grow, one must find someone to blame, and thus good is a derivative of evil which arises out of the tendency to impute to others the responsibility for one's ailments: "For he desires his enemy for himself, as his mark of distinction; he can endure no other enemy than one in whom there is nothing to despise and very much to honour! . . . He has conceived 'the evil enemy,' '*the Evil One*,' and this in fact is his basic concept, from which he then evolves, as an afterthought and pendant, a 'good one'—himself!" (*GM* I:11). While Nietzsche's account of the birth of morality may be prone to exaggeration, it does expose the fundamental dynamic of egoism, namely the tendency to seek self-affirmation by deprecating those who differ from oneself. The moral edifice would crumble without outsiders against whom one can measure oneself. Morality is intrinsically divisive and is predicated on a seething resentment against an "other."

Nevertheless, Nietzsche would not deny the creativity of the slaves whose actions are continuously blocked by the masters. They draw a sharp distinction between themselves and the external world, because they see their will to power and growth impeded. The masters are not aware of their own boundaries in this way, because their spontaneous flow of energy is untrammeled. Morality is therefore the tactic employed by the weak in order to keep the strong in check. Nevertheless, this manifests a tremendous creativity on the part of the slaves who are willing to survive at all costs, even if they have to turn the entire value structure of human society on its head. They are able to triumph in the world by devaluing it. Unable to affirm life through their own activity, they begin to negate the masters and the world of nature, inventing the notion that their environment is not as it should be: "According to slave morality, those who are 'evil' thus inspire fear; according to master morality it is precisely those who are 'good' that inspire, and wish to inspire fear, while the 'bad' are felt to be contemptible" (*BGE* 260). By denying the world as it is, they are able to transform it into one that they have *chosen*. All that is evil is imputed to the master, while by deduction, the slave is held up to constitute the quintessence of good. This is fundamentally a morality of utility which allows the weak to flourish: "The good human being has to be *undangerous* in the slaves' way of thinking: he is good natured, easy to deceive, a little stupid perhaps, *un bonhomme*. Wherever slave morality becomes preponderant, language tends to bring the words 'good' and 'stupid' closer together" (*BGE* 260).

Furthermore, the repression of natural drives that the slaves achieve through the process of negation is the basis of creativity and art, for it enables human beings to choose the direction their impulses will take. According to Nietzsche, the modern phenomenon of the herd is a culmination of a moral process that has ripened over generations. The metaphysical urge to know the universe and render it predictable is part of the dynamic of a finite creature, not only against others but against the passage of time. Human beings become victims of their own quest for knowledge. Morality has eventuated in a dynamic of extreme self-objectification, by which a measurable standard is externally imposed and then becomes the locus of self-judgment. Nietzsche is fully cognizant of the fact that human beings cannot cope with the multifarious stimuli that intrude upon their psyche every day. This is why he deems that forgetfulness is such an important human instrument in allowing us to experience the world anew:

> Forgetting is no mere *vis inertie* as the superficial imagine, it is rather an active and in the strictest sense positive faculty of repression, that is responsible for the fact that what we experience and absorb enters our consciousness while we are digesting it. . . . To close the doors and windows of consciousness for a time; to remain undisturbed by the noise and struggle of our underworld of utility organs working with and against one another . . . that is the purpose of active forgetfulness, which is like a doorkeeper, a preserver of psychic order, repose and etiquette.
>
> (*GM* II:1)

Forgetfulness facilitates creativity, because it allows the soul to be impregnated with new experiences and sensations.

At the same time, Nietzsche is aware that the idea of being responsible for one's actions is a function of memory, and without this measurement of the self by external standards, we could not become moral creatures who are above all to be made "calculable, regular and necessary" (*GM* II:1). But in order to accomplish this task, human beings had to be capable of making promises. The paradox of morality is that it begins with a fear of the unfamiliar other, whether this other consists of other human beings, nature, or some unknown force. However, to limit the impact of otherness, an extreme othering of the self was necessary so that the process of assimilation could be complete. The fear of the other is also a fear of the unknown within oneself. Nietzsche is not impervious to the virtues of such a process, which he claims also gave birth to the "sovereign individual" who could become the project for his own self-cultivation. To be self-determining, one must first objectify oneself rather than responding spontaneously to any stimulus at hand. The sovereign individual is a double-edged sword: "This emancipated individual, with the actual *right* to make promises, this master of a *free* will, this sovereign man—how should he not be aware of his superiority over all those who lack the right to make promises and stand as their own guarantors—and how this mastery over himself also necessarily gives him mastery over circumstances nature, and over all more short-willed and unreliable creatures" (*GM* II:3). Thus, Nietzsche recognizes that the need for self-control and mastery is necessarily linked to the desire for control over others.

The creature with enough punctiliousness and regularity to make promises was born, in Nietzsche's view, out of the debtor-creditor relationship. The difference between a Confucian moral system, which subscribes to the continuity of custom and recognizes its specificity with respect to location, and the Judeo-Christian mores Nietzsche describes, is that the latter arrogate to themselves the status of universality. This necessitates the imposition of a readily measurable standard, and the numerical values imposed by debts serve this function well: "Have these genealogists of morals had even the remotest suspicion that, for example, the major moral concept *Schuld* [guilt] has its origin in the very material concept of *Schulden* [debts]?" (*GM* II:4). The notion of returning what was owed, or punishment befitting the crime, was predicated on a love of inflicting pain, and Nietzsche points to the creditor's right to cut off a portion of the debtor's body, allegedly commensurate with what he owed. The origins of morality are soiled with blood and could not have developed without a love for cruelty. Furthermore, the monetary relationship between creditor and debtor made it easier for one person to measure himself "against another" (*GM* II:8). Numbers are very effective illusions because they efface their own conceptual heritage. Through repeated use of a fiction, we conveniently forget its metaphorical origins. Numbers permit a relationship with the other that is predicated not on dialogue but on competition. By symbolically linking morality to the creditor-debtor relationship in this way, Nietzsche closely links ethics to possession, not only of the other but of oneself. Both self and other are contained in the concepts that we hold. The German word for "concept," *Begriff*, referring to the act of grabbing, beautifully portrays this phenomenon.[8]

The birth of justice closely parallels the genesis of the concept, which is linked to the reduction of difference to sameness and to the deliberate erasure of origins:

> Setting prices, determining values, contriving equivalences, exchanging—these preoccupied the earliest thinking of man to so great an extent that in a certain sense, they constitute thinking *as such* . . . here, likewise, we may suppose did human pride, the feeling of superiority in relation to other animals have its first beginnings. . . . Perhaps our word "man" (*manas*) still expresses something of precisely *this feeling* of satisfaction: man designated himself as the creature that measures values, evaluates and measures as the "valuating animal as such."
>
> (*GM* II:8)

Values are reified in such a way that we forget they are constructs of the imagination. Because the imaginary origins of our values are banished from memory, we invent the notion that justice is disinterested and fair. The process of universalization, which is an intrinsic part of conceptualization, is also indelibly imprinted on our moral universe. This is why morality always concerns itself with what the other is doing in relation to oneself, and what one is doing in relation to others. The cruelty of tactics used to implement such conformity has waned, only because the self-control exercised has increased exponentially. Mercy becomes possible when this control has become so internalized that power can be more readily exercised, through gratuitous acts of mercy that allow someone who is above the law to transcend the regulations of

---

8 A German word for "understanding" is *begreifen*, which also has connotations of grabbing; *greifen* means "to grab."

the system: "This self-overcoming of justice: one knows the beautiful name it has given itself—*mercy*; it goes without saying that mercy remains the privilege of the most powerful man, or better, his—beyond the law" (*GM* II:11).

Nietzsche's purpose in exposing the dark underbelly of morality stems from his contempt for the hypocrisy of the human being, who believes he is "on his way to becoming an 'angel'" (*GM* II:7) and is easily repulsed by all that he encounters on his journey within himself that is natural and human: "Not only the joy and innocence of the animal but life itself has become repugnant to him—so that sometimes he holds his nose in his own presence and, with Pope Innocent the Third, disapprovingly catalogues his own repellent aspects ('impure begetting, disgusting means of nutrition in the mother's womb, baseness of the matter out of which man evolves, hideous stink, secretion of saliva, urine and filth')" (*GM* II:7). When these primeval urges are turned inward, guilt is born, and it is this division between the social constraints and the instincts they repress that produces not only the conscience but also the soul. From Nietzsche's conjectures, one can assume that the idea that the soul is distinct from the body comes precisely from this fissure between the natural instincts and the straightjacket that the social order thrusts upon us: "All instincts that do not discharge themselves outwardly *turn* inward—this is what I call the *internalization* of man: thus it was that man first developed what was later called his 'soul'" (*GM* II:16). This sentiment that "I am not what I should or could be" is a creative force, but also has the potential to become stifling. Nietzsche writes that the development of an "animal soul turned against itself, taking sides against itself, was something so new, profound, unheard of, enigmatic, contradictory, *and pregnant with a future*, that the aspect of the earth was essentially altered" (*GM* II:16). The fact that the human being is now destined to be malcontent with his or her present form means that there are new horizons opened up for the art of becoming, for it provides a catalyst for being something other than one is. Therefore, morality and the bad conscience are not peremptorily dismissed by Nietzsche, but they are useful only insofar as they contribute to the artistry of creating the human spirit.

Ironically, when morality reaches its acme, it heralds a process of decline from which humanity has never fully recovered. This, according to Nietzsche, would not have been possible without the Christian religion. He points out that even the earliest societies recognize a debt to ancestors and deities: "The conviction reigns that it is only through the sacrifices and accomplishments of the ancestors that the tribe *exists*—and that one has to *pay them back* with sacrifices and accomplishment: one thus recognizes a *debt* that constantly grows greater, since these forebears never cease" (*GM* II:19). The escalation of this process results in the worship of the Christian God who, "as maximum god attained so far, was therefore accompanied by the maximum feeling of guilty indebtedness on earth" (*GM* II:20). The secularization of human society is precipitated by a God that has become so powerful that our debt can never be repaid, and this also eventuates in a "considerable decline in man's feeling of guilt" (*GM* II:20) which spawns the growth of atheism, a "second innocence." Atheism is a direct consequence of an unbearable guilt, which leads us to reject the god who sits in judgment upon us. The resentment that had hitherto been directed inward is now directed against this god, until we end up becoming the ugly men in *Thus Spoke Zarathustra*, who are responsible for the murder of God.

By creating a god that was so powerful, Christian priests had paralyzed humanity with a guilt so debilitating that it could no longer act as a stimulus to existence. Morality had initially been a creative force that had rebelled against and negated the powerful, but with the presence of God, and the birth of the idea that human beings are responsible for their suffering, the ascetic priests have created a monster. The priest avers that we ourselves are to blame for our suffering: "*You alone are to blame for yourself*" (*GM* III:15). Such utter self-contempt requires an antidote and this tremendous guilt generates income for countless doctors of the soul. By not allowing respite from one's guilt, and by encouraging endless self-torture in the form of self-reflection, human beings are exposed to the weight of an overburdened and overgrown ego. The problem with the modern individual is that we cannot flee from ourselves: "A strong and well-constituted man digests his experiences (his deeds and misdeeds included) as he digests his meals, even when he has to swallow some tough morsels. If he cannot get over an experience and have done with it, this kind of indigestion is as much physiological as is the other" (*GM* III:16).

Having introduced this "dominating sense of displeasure" (*GM* III:17), the ascetic priest then begins to provide a numbing comfort, which reduces "the feeling of life to its lowest point" (*GM* III:17). Banality is seen as the ultimate panacea and even "will and desire" are abolished. According to Nietzsche, an "astonishing amount of energy" is invested into sending human beings into hibernation, and they increasingly resemble one another. Mechanical activity is an instance of such narcotic activity which increasingly stupefies us. Despite the rancor that the priest spews onto a now "sullied" existence, Nietzsche maintains that it is only in the priestly form that "man first became an interesting animal, that only here did the human soul in a higher sense acquire depth and become *evil*" (*GM* I:7).

The tendency to expunge contradiction from existence casts a frightening specter over humankind. Nietzsche is not opposed to the tension between the natural and cultural, but the idea that the sensual is to be eradicated is a sickness that philosophers and moralists share. This manifests an intolerable degree of hubris, as the philosopher affirms "*his* existence and *only* his existence" to the point where he is willing to "let the world perish" as long as there is philosophy and he begins to worship only himself (*GM* III:7). Thus, Nietzsche equates a profound egoism with the desensualization and denaturalization of existence, for the senses and nature remind us that we are part of a larger whole: "Our whole attitude toward nature, the way we violate her with the aid of machines and the heedless inventiveness of our technicians and engineers is *hubris*, our attitude toward God as some alleged spider of purpose and morality behind the great captious web of causality is *hubris* . . . our attitude toward ourselves is *hubris*" (*GM* III:9). Nietzsche, like the Daoists, and many religious and moral thinkers, believes that the time has come to cure humanity of its exaggerated egoism. Morality is the most profound egoism which, if unchecked, eventuates in the desertification of human beings. The philosopher "easily forgets and easily despises" (*GM* III:8). Although Nietzsche in no way condones the eradication of the lust for power, insisting that it is an irrevocable aspect of growth and development, he insists with asceticism that it has gone mad, engulfing the entire planet: "For an ascetic life is a self-contradiction: here rules a *ressentiment* without equal, that of an insatiable instinct and power-will that wants to become master not over something in life over life itself, over its most profound, powerful and basic conditions" (*GM* III:11).

However, the ascetic ideal encompasses more than the denial of the body and nature. One falls victim to the ascetic ideal whenever one considers any system intrinsically good and self-justifying to the exclusion of others, and therefore denies the interconnectivity of life. Asceticism is linked to an egoism which attempts to expunge influences that elude its control: "Every spirit has its own sound and loves its own sound" (*GM* III:8). In short, the ascetic ideal manifests a hostile desire to purify the world of *other* sounds. This is why Nietzsche is so keen to point out that moralizing and the ascetic ideal manifest the will to power. While appearing to ward off meaninglessness, the ascetic ideal ends up willing nothingness. It fervently hopes to escape change, becoming ultimately its own death, but in the process of doing so dries up the wellspring of its own creativity.

Redemption from Morality

In Nietzsche's view, the devastation wrought upon humanity by morality also laid the groundwork for a creative rebirth of the artistic impulse: "This secret self-ravishment, this artists' cruelty, this delight in imposing a form on oneself as a hard, recalcitrant, suffering material—eventually this entirely *active* 'bad conscience'—you will have guessed it—as the womb of all ideal and imaginative phenomena, also brought to light an abundance of strange new beauty and affirmation" (*GM* II:18). Nietzsche hopes that the moral era will be superseded by a new aesthetic era in which the multiplicity of life can be actively affirmed. He uses aesthetics to point out that there is an alternative to a way of life focused on epistemological concerns. While he may reject the categorical imperative, he subscribes to an aesthetic imperative which demands a continuous responsiveness and transformation of the world that we inhabit. His famous proclamation in *The Birth of Tragedy* that it is only as an "aesthetic phenomenon that existence and the world are eternally *justified*" (*BT* 5) is a refrain that reverberates throughout his entire corpus. This is a statement suffused with irony, because it implies that our existence must be justified anew at every moment and for every individual, because the world resists ready justification. Meaninglessness spurs the quest for meaning but in order to find it, we cannot simply shape the world in our image. We must recognize that we are a part of the teeming, creative, and throbbing pulse of life and as such, are part of the "artistry of nature." Art is not just something that human beings contribute to the world; it is a way of participating in the creative energy of the cosmos. If Nietzsche elevates the artist to unparalleled levels of significance, it is also important to recognize that he objects to the hubris in insisting that artistry is a human phenomenon, without recognizing that its roots lie deeply embedded within the realm of nature.

According to Nietzsche, our relationship to the world is expressed primarily through metaphors that do not capture reality but rather symbolize and express it, and therefore depend upon a certain distance from the world that we inhabit. Metaphor is seen as a way of entering into a dialogue with the cosmos, rather than as a means of capturing it. The paradox of being at one with the cosmos, and yet not at one with it, is what allows us to contribute to the proliferation of its creative energy. Nietzsche holds up music as the most poignant medium of expression in this regard. This is significant and has moral repercussions because, in music, the self occasionally succumbs to oblivion whereby its own boundaries become more fluid: "The willing individual that furthers his own egoistic ends can be conceived of only as the antagonist, not as the origin of art. Insofar as the subject is the artist, however, he has already been released from his individual will, and has become, as it were, the medium through which the only truly existent subject celebrates his release in appearance" (*BT* 5). Nietzsche declares that melody is the most "primary and universal" art form which "generates the poem out of itself" (*BT* 6). The paradox of music is an important one because it is universally understood but remains shrouded in mystery: "All phenomena, compared with it, are merely symbols: hence *language*, as the organ and symbol of phenomena can never by any means disclose the innermost heart of music; language in its attempt to imitate it, can only be in superficial contact with music" (*BT* 6). Sarah Kofman notes that music is the most appropriate symbolic art form because it most aptly affirms the diversity of life.[9] It yields multiple and endless interpretations, and it is impossible to state with any credibility that one interpretation supersedes them all. Music demands both the surrender and expression of one's individuality. By elevating metaphor and music to such an eminent status, Nietzsche inverts the traditional philosophical hierarchy which accords unquestioned primacy to the concept.

Nietzsche's pessimistic views on morality which attribute to human beings sinister intentions prompt many to consider him an immoralist par excellence, who would revel in a world where the strong prevail and the weak deservedly perish. While this is undoubtedly a facet of his thought, his plea to go beyond good and evil also serves as a reminder to human beings that they are not the fulcrum of the universe. The moral fortress cuts human beings off from the wellspring of life. Perhaps nowhere is this most evident than in his work *Thus Spoke Zarathustra* wherein Zarathustra wanders in pursuit of an affirmative posture toward life, hoping to find companions for his voyage beyond good and evil. It is no coincidence that Zarathustra is the Persian God who was largely responsible for the bifurcation between good and evil that also seeped into Christian doctrine. By using this same figure as the symbol of renewal, Nietzsche is illustrating that we should not be scarred by resentment for past mistakes.

Zarathustra hopes to instill in his people a taste for creativity and overcoming, so that they will be able to cast their moribund values aside: "Virtue to them is that which makes modest and tame: with that they have turned the wolf into a dog and man himself into man's best domestic animal" (Z III:5). The ability to overcome also depends upon the ability to be overcome: creativity demands a delicate balance between arrogance and humility. Yet, Nietzsche recognizes that genuine humility is the more difficult virtue to cultivate. The humility instilled in human beings by Christianity is, in his view, a false humility. Despairing over

9 Sarah Kofman, *Nietzsche et la métaphore* (Paris: Editions Galilée, 1972), p. 23.

the fact that people are becoming "smaller and smaller . . . *due to their doctrine of happiness and virtue*" (Z III:5), he laments that they do not know how to love with a great love and great contempt (Z III:5). Love and contempt are correlative because their interrelationship acknowledges a willingness to recognize that all things come into being and pass away. However, as the story of Zarathustra reveals, he not only has difficulty sowing the seeds of genuine humility, but also has trouble cultivating it within himself.

The challenge facing Zarathustra is to find a way of affirming life that is not dependent on his control, and he must come to recognize that he is an infinitesimal speck in an infinite landscape. This means that he must learn to affirm life unconditionally, not simply on his own terms; it is this point which proves to be the most difficult, for it demands recognition that the self is perishable. This is why Zarathustra moves through the depths of despair. Learning to affirm what eclipses the self is the most difficult aspect of Zarathustra's lesson, both for himself and for his disciples.

Zarathustra begins his journey on an arrogant note, wondering where the sun would be if it did not have those for whom it would shine (Z P:1). Speaking to the sun, he notes that "you have come up here to my cave for ten years: you would have grown weary of your light and of this journey, without me, my eagle and my serpent" (Z P:1). Having tasted solitude, he now longs to spread his overflowing wisdom in the valleys below, where those who suffer from moral putrefaction reside. Like the sun, he too must go under: "For that I must descend to the depths, as you do in the evening when you go behind the sea and still bring light to the underworld, you overrich star" (Z P:1).[10] At this juncture, Zarathustra fails to recognize that his going under does not just involve descending to the level of those beneath him, but demands a willingness to go under himself.

10 Laurence Lampert notes that the modern Zarathustra depicted here differs from the ancient Zarathustra, who "prayed to the sun as a god." Zarathustra expresses gratitude to the sun but assumes that the sun is dependent upon his gratitude. See Lampert, *Nietzsche's Teaching: An Interpretation of Thus Spoke Zarathustra* (New Haven: Yale University Press, 1986), p. 14.

Zarathustra's own generosity and gift-giving are problematic because he cannot easily accept gifts from others: "The danger of those who always give is that they lose their sense of shame; and the heart and hand of those who always mete out become callous from always meting out" (Z II:9). Self-overcoming is not just a matter of catapulting oneself to ever greater heights, but rather invites recognition that one's voice may be eclipsed by others. Zarathustra must learn to be at ease in the night, which awakens the songs of lovers because it erases individual boundaries: "Night has come; now all foundations speak more loudly. And my soul too, is a fountain. Night has come; now all the songs of lovers awaken. And my soul too is the song of a lover" (Z II:9). Yet, Zarathustra has trouble welcoming nightfall: "Forgive me my sadness. Evening has come; forgive me that evening has come" (Z II:9). Zarathustra is drawn to the self-dissolution that night offers him, but also trembles with fear at this prospect.

The lesson of humility is one that Zarathustra finds hardest to learn. In one episode, a child holds up the mirror to Zarathustra and he interprets the devil's grimace he sees there to mean that his disciples have not mirrored his teachings faithfully: "My *teaching* is in danger; weeds pose as wheat. My enemies have grown powerful and have distorted my teaching till those dearest to me must be ashamed of the gifts I gave them" (Z II:1). Yet, in the same parable, he speaks of an outpouring of love, which embraces his friends as well as his enemies. He loves his enemies because they catapult him to new heights, and thus they are part of his transformation: "The spear which I throw at my enemies! How I thank my enemies that at last I can throw it" (Z II:1). At the same time, he recognizes the nature of his misplaced longing, which seeks to single-handedly transform the world, and is unwilling to grant a place for interlocutors. Because he keeps his own company, he has forgotten how to listen: "Too long have I belonged to loneliness; thus have I forgotten how to be silent" (Z II:1). His failure to be silent attests to his inability to provide an opening for the words of others. The love he proclaims from the mountaintop is self-love which seeks to envelop the world: "I have become nothing but speech and the tumbling of a brook from high rocks: I want to hurl my words down into the valleys" (Z II:1).

Zarathustra continually exists on the cusp of extreme arrogance and humility as demonstrated in a chapter entitled "The Wanderer," which follows the peregrinations of his tormented soul. He begins by reflecting upon his solitary wanderings and "how many mountains and ridges and peaks he had already climbed" (Z III:1). Zarathustra's soul is frenetic, and he is constantly drawn to the heights unable to abide the depths: "I am a wanderer and a mountain climber, he said to his heart; I do not like the plains and it seems I cannot sit still for too long" (Z III:1). Comforting himself with the thought that he will reach his ultimate peak, he discovers at the "height of the ridge" that the night was cold. At the same time, he knows that the ability to appreciate his smallness *is* his ultimate peak: "Indeed to look down upon myself, and even upon my stars, that I alone I should call my *peak*; that has remained for me as my *ultimate* peak" (Z III:1). It is his preoccupation with himself that has filled his heart with such agonizing longing: "One must learn to *look away* from oneself in order to *see much*: this hardness is necessary to every climber of mountains" (Z III:1). His ascent to the mountains is significant, because it is in the mountain climber that the ambiguity of the ego becomes manifest. The sight on a mountain peak forces one to recognize one's smallness in the face of a vast landscape; meanwhile, the success in reaching the peak also imbues him with feelings of conquest and the sense that he is standing on top of the world.

While Zarathustra's soul is overflowing with love, it is a desirous love that seeks to fill a void within himself: "You have wanted to pet every monster. A whiff of warm breath, a little soft tuft on the paw—and at once you were ready to love and lure it. Love is the danger of the loneliest; love of everything if only it is alive. Laughable, verily, are my folly and my modesty in love" (Z III:1). The fact that he seeks a panacea for his loneliness through others attests to both his modesty and his hubris. He recognizes that his being is intimately linked to others, while at the same time, harnessing others for himself. This is why Zarathustra, like Christ, becomes a caster of nets that attempts to reel in the multicolored creatures of the sea: "My happiness itself I cast out far and wide, between sunrise, noon, and sunset, to see if many human fish might learn to wriggle and wiggle from my happiness until, biting at my sharp hidden hooks, they must come up to *my* height—the most colorful abysmal groundlings to the most sarcastic of all who fish for men . . . thus men may now come *up* to me" (Z IV:1). Nietzsche exposes the egotistical underbelly of the universality of love which manifests the desire to bring everything under his fold. He mocks himself for his desire to climb the high mountains to catch fish, recognizing that men have never caught fish on high mountains. Fishermen do not assertively pursue their prey, but wait for it to come to them.

It is significant that the chapter on Zarathustra's summit fever and wandering is followed by the vision of the eternal return. Here, eternity is portrayed as an eternal repetition of the same, rather than depicting an ever-increasing fullness. It is important not to understand this metaphor too literally. It implies that there is no peak or climax that Zarathustra will attain, which will satiate a soul in quest of the ultimate fullness. At each moment, we are at a gateway or crossroads that arbitrarily divides the eternal lane running into the future from that leading towards the past. These two paths appear to be in opposition to each other, but only because the gateway of the moment marks them in this way. The moment is suspended between past and future; without it, the past and future would be one continuous line. We bear the insignia of the moment because we are finite beings, behind whom lies the infinity of the past and before whom spreads the infinity of the future. The modern individual who rushes headlong toward the future, assuming that he has accomplished a dramatic feat of self-overcoming, really has not moved anywhere at all.

Only the human being sees past and future as opposed and Zarathustra suggests that if one were to "follow them further and further and even further," the opposition between the lines might be diminished (Z III:178). All things are "bound fast together in such a way that this moment draws after it all future things? Therefore, draws itself too" (Z III:179). From an "infinite" perspective, time utterly collapses and everything that will happen in the future has already happened. Only the finite being experiences time parceled up into moments. Everything that exists is interconnected and so every event is a reconfiguration of things that have already happened, thus constituting a repetition of the same.

Nietzsche utters the seemingly nonsensical words that the current moment also "draws after it all future things" (Z III:2) to reinforce the idea that from the perspective of the whole, time is irrelevant.

This notion of repetition seems to fly in the face of the hymns of praise Nietzsche sings for the process of perpetual self-overcoming. However, one must remember that self-overcoming also refers to the overcoming of the self that locates itself at the center of existence. We can only overcome the self if we accept "outside" influences that catapult us to new horizons. However, these are only new for us, not for the cosmos at large. Therefore, self-overcoming reinforces rather than undermines the eternal return of the same. The eternal recurrence reminds us that we are not simply *causa sui*, but beings who are acted upon.

The eternal return is poisoned by the voice of its cynical mouthpiece, the spirit of gravity, who proclaims that "everything straight lies" and "all truth is crooked, time itself is a circle" (Z III:2), revealing the illusory nature of progress. He also insists that every stone one throws must fall, undermining the belief that we can shed our mortal coils. This creature derives pleasure from smashing the idols that prop up our worldview. He reminds us that we are irrevocably tied to the earth, which he hopes will unleash a gloomy chorus of despair. His contemptuous tone is indicative of the fact that we still lament the loss of the Platonist and Christian worldview which we are beginning to abandon.

Nietzsche does not object to the veracity of the spirit of gravity's utterance, but rather to the attitude of mockery he represents. His pessimism and boredom are the direct consequences of an exaggerated Platonism that derogated the earth. Zarathustra admonishes the dwarf, not to "treat this too lightly" (Z III:2). Even if he insists upon the pallor of transcendent truth, the dwarf is unable to take the earth seriously, instead taking nothing seriously. The spirit of gravity is a symptom of the contemporary age, which through its nihilism, and ultimate sense of meaninglessness, finds it impossible to affirm but only to deny. It is important to recognize that the German term for the spirit of gravity is *der Geiste zum Trotz*. *Trotz* implies scorn for the sake of scorn. We are still the victims of the totalizing age of transcendent truths, because we turn absolute faith into an absolute denial. For this reason, we are barred from the enchantment of the world.

The stark contrast to the scornful nature of the dwarf can be seen in the reaction of the peasant with the serpent coiled in his throat. This depicts the particularly human response to the cyclical nature of the eternal recurrence. The shepherd writhing in agony prompts Zarathustra to urge him to bite his head off, in such a way that "all his horror, hate, disgust, pity and good and evil cried out of him with a single cry" (Z III:2). His response affirms the necessity of destruction for creation and creation for destruction. The peasant takes his life very seriously, being ready to defend it and yet emerges out of the situation "a transformed being, surrounded by light, *laughing*!" (Z III:2). The peasant is able to recognize the paradox of the significance and insignificance of his life. Mark Weeks maintains that Nietzsche's thought advocates a kind of super-laughter that defies the temporality of becoming by enticing individuals to "laugh over themselves." [11] This is certainly one aspect of Nietzschean laughter that becomes part of the project of self-overcoming. However, the peasant's laughter is also an example of the kind of laughter that accepts the temporality of the seasons and the possibility of his own death. This laughter occurs after he has experienced the fragility of his own existence. His conquest over death is only temporary and it is this recognition that causes him to erupt in laughter. Upon hearing the peasant's laughter and the transformation wrought by it, Zarathustra is once again filled with the life-giving longing rather than mere defiance: "No longer shepherd, no longer human—one changed, radiant *laughing*! Never yet on earth has a human being laughed as he laughed! O my brothers, I heard a laughter that was no human laughter; and now a thirst gnaws at me, a longing that never grows still. My longing for this

11 Mark Weeks astutely points out that Nietzschean laughter is fuelled by desire. It marks temporary destruction, which is directed at the future and is an indelible part of the process of self-overcoming. See Weeks, "Beyond a Joke: Nietzsche and the Birth of Super-Laughter," *Journal of Nietzsche Studies* 27 (2004): 1–17. However, Zarathustra's interpretation of the peasant's laughter may also be a testament to Zarathustra's own inability to truly revel in the moment and accept its finitude. At this point in the parable, there may be a disjunction between the peasant's laughter and Zarathustra's interpretation of it. Zarathustra sees laughter as a means for overcoming the gravity of life, and the peasant's laughter may represent a kind of joyous release from the perspective that each moment is a means to another.

laughter gnaws at me, how do I bear to go on living! And how could I bear to die now!" (Z III:2). A being that is able to revel in his own finitude must be divine. Paradoxically, by making this laughter the object of his striving, Zarathustra diminishes the possibility of attaining it. The peasant's laughter is possible because at that moment, he ceases to strive and revels in the immediate pleasure of his life.

Laughter is the most important weapon against the mocking tone of the spirit of gravity, because it constitutes a denial that is at once an affirmation. The transformed peasant renews his relationship with the earth and all that surrounds him. It is an egoless laughter while the spirit of gravity's consumptive laughter is that of the egoist, who must lash out against everything else in order to inflate his insidious subjectivity.

In the next section, Zarathustra sings a hymn of praise to the open sky which is no longer seen simply as that which transcends the earth, but reflects the openness that not only makes life on earth possible but shelters and fills it with wonder. The juxtaposition of opposites is striking in this passage: "O heaven above me, pure and deep! You abyss of light! Seeing you, I tremble with godlike desires. To throw myself into your height, that is *my* depth. To hide in your purity, that is *my* innocence" (Z III:3). The silence of the sky represents a nonjudgmental openness that does not bequeath value onto any single doctrine: "We do not speak to each other, because we know too much; we are silent to each other, we smile our knowledge at each other" (Z III:3). Because the sky does not speak, it allows for the appreciation of things as they are, without subjecting them to the chains of necessity. Zarathustra speaks of his contempt for the drifting clouds that prey on the sky's unbounded openness: "I loathe the drifting clouds . . . these mediators and mixers, the drifting clouds that are half-and-half and have learned neither to bless nor to curse from their heart" (Z III:3). These clouds represent for Zarathustra the values which do not allow human beings to either affirm or negate, but rather freeze him in the position of eternal spectator to life. Good and evil are among them: "For all things have been baptized in the well of eternity and are beyond good and evil; and good and evil themselves are but intervening shadows and damp depressions and drifting clouds" (Z III:3). Good and evil attempt to block the openness of the sky which neither commands nor ordains. Instead, its blessing is conferred in the form of silence, revealing a gentle, affirmative humility: "Your love and your shyness are a revelation to my roaring soul" (Z III:2).

The moment of the sky's journey that enchants Zarathustra is the moment before sunrise, which is between light and darkness. This moment neither banishes darkness nor obfuscates light. It recognizes the fragility of all that exists, and celebrates the transitory nature that accounts for the beauty of this moment. Twilight and dawn encapsulate the brevity, beauty, and significance of the moment.

The path to redemption necessitates a healthy love of oneself, which is not an egotistical love intent on devouring all that lies in one's path. Each being must celebrate its own particularity, which is why the relativity of morality must be acknowledged in Nietzsche's view. "This is *my* good and evil" (Z III:11). In a parody of Jesus, who claims to have found *the* way, Zarathustra retorts: "This is *my* way; where is yours?"—thus I answered those who asked me 'the way.' For *the* way—that does not exist" (Z III:11). Nietzsche hopes for an unconditional affirmation of all that exists, which includes evil as well as good: "Everything that the good call evil must come together so that one truth may be born" (Z III:11).

Zarathustra's redemption depends upon an attunement with the natural world. It is significant that the animals play a central role in his convalescence. The pervasive nihilism of the modern age infects us to the extent that nothing can be taken seriously. When this thought fills Zarathustra with horror, he is able to begin his recovery: "One morning, not long after his return to the cave, Zarathustra jumped up from his resting place like a madman, roared in a terrible voice, and acted as if somebody else were still lying on his resting place who refused to get up" (Z III:13). After this episode, he falls asleep and his animals awaken him from his slumber after seven days, telling him that the "world awaits him like a garden" (Z III:13). Only after a complete numbing of the senses can he delight in the wonders of the world. In response to their plea, Zarathustra is able to revel in the beauty of their words, whose newness he savors: "How lovely it is that there are words and sounds! Are not words and sounds rainbows and illusive bridges between things which are eternally apart" (Z III:13). The animals relay to him that all things minister to him. But whereas the animals see the world as an enclosed garden, he sees an indeterminate openness that allows the play of language to weave new worlds: "Have not names and sounds been given to things that man might find things refreshing? Speaking is a beautiful folly: with that man dances over all things. How lovely is all talking, and all the deception of sounds! With sounds our love dances on many-hued rainbows" (Z III:13). Zarathustra is able to return to the art of naming, instead of relying upon stale concepts that are divorced from the mystery of life.

The animals respond by chanting homage to the eternal return. Immersed in the moment, they do not lament but rather celebrate its repetition, which is like a joyful chorus that all participate in:

> To those who think as we do, all things themselves are dancing: they come and offer their hands and laugh and flee—and come back. Everything goes, everything comes back; eternally rolls the wheel of being. Everything dies, everything blossoms again; eternally runs the year of being. Everything breaks. Everything is joined anew, eternally the same house of being is built. Everything parts, everything greets every other thing again; eternally the ring of being remains faithful to itself. In every Now, being begins; round every Here rolls the sphere There. The centre is everywhere. Bent is the path of eternity. (Z III:13)

The animals present a nonteleological conception of time, wherein every moment is interconnected with every other, and every being welcomes every other being. However, the animals, who live in the moment, do not understand human beings whose gateways of the moment leave them suspended between past and future. From a nihilistic perspective, thoughts of eternal repetition correspond to boredom and despair, which cannot easily endure the possibility that the highest must perish and the lowliest will rear their heads again and again. Human beings cannot live in the moment; each moment is a crossroads weighed down by the burden of decision. Nevertheless, while human beings must choose and will their future, this does not elevate them on a pedestal supervising the rest of creation. Learning that one is both great and small is rejuvenating, like the laughter of the peasant:

> The soul is as mortal as the body. But the knot of causes in which I am entangled recurs and will create me again. I myself belong to the causes of the

> eternal recurrence. I come again, with this sun, with this earth, with this eagle, with this serpent—*not* to a new life or a better life or a similar life: I come back eternally to this same, selfsame life, in what is greatest as in what is smallest, to teach the eternal recurrence of all things, to speak again the word of the great noon of earth and man, to proclaim the overman again to men. The hour has now come when he who goes under should bless himself.
>
> (Z III:13)

Ethics and Language

In the previous chapter, I began to discuss the discomfort that Daoist philosophy exhibits toward the reification that occurs when morality is closely wedded to language. In this section, I will build upon this analysis, highlighting the themes that Daoist thinkers share in common with Nietzsche, who illuminates the more sinister purpose of language that manifests a human desire to control the world and reduce it to utilitarian use. This is a perspective shared by Daoist thinkers, who suggest that language makes it possible for us to treat nature as an object. For this reason, they try to open up possibilities for a new kind of language, which is deliberately nebulous in an attempt to keep the process of human domination in check.

Like Nietzsche, Daoist thinkers subscribe to a perspectivism of knowledge, which has profound ethical implications. *Dao* is boundless, and it is considered dangerous "to use what has a boundary to pursue what is limitless" (*Zh* 3:22) since this undermines the harmonizing rhythm of the cosmos. Conventional morality, which operates through the medium of language and often mistakes a single perspective for a universally valid one, is considered perilous for this very reason. We become ensnared by the words we use, and then find ourselves unable to return to the root of *Dao* which manifests endless openness. The order that ensues cannot be equated with harmony and, more often than not, is predicated on assimilation.

To see that many Daoist writers heap condemnation upon the dictums of morality is not to say that their thought is devoid of moral intention. Instead, Daoist thinkers voice caution in linking morality too closely to speech and knowledge, for this can easily degenerate into mindless ritual or ossified behavior. This is why the "grandest forms of virtue follow only the way" which is described as vague and "indefinite" (*DDJ* 21). There is no center to *Dao*; it both withdraws and appears, returns and sneaks away. Language must imitate the "slippery" nature of *Dao*. Zhuangzi prefers the use of vague labels. Moral virtues such as *ren* 仁 and *yi* 義 can become reified and, as a result, are all too easily closely allied to convention. When Zhuangzi is asked about *ren*, he responds: "Tigers and wolves are benevolent" (*Zh* 13:118). The irony of this response should not go unnoticed, for *ren* and *yi* are considered to be quintessentially human virtues. He then goes on to state that perfect *ren* is of the highest order, but that words like "'filial piety'" cannot describe it (*Zh* 13:118). The *Zhuangzi* both ridicules Confucius as a moral pedant and cultural conservative, and affectionately invokes him as the mouthpiece of *Dao*, refusing to reify even this historical figure. In one passage, Confucius regrets having sent his pupil Zigong to mourning rituals, because he comes back maligning the friends of the deceased for singing in the presence of the dead body and accusing them of being "uncouth." Confucius responds, "They have truly become one with the Maker of all and now wander as the original breath of Heaven and Earth. . . . They begin and cease without knowing what is beginning or ceasing. Unaware they wander beyond the mundane world and stroll in the world of non-action. Why should they have to worry about proper conduct just to please ordinary people" (*Zh* 6:55). Confucius has learned to go beyond his own codes of custom in order to embrace the openness of *Dao*.

When reason is used too confidently, it simply steamrollers over the nuances of situations and we lose attentiveness to the kind of specificity that makes proper judgment possible. In one episode of the *Zhuangzi*, Huizi is given seeds that produce gourds but because he is mired in his own mindset that gourds are used only as ladles, he smashes them. Zhuangzi teasingly responds, "Now, Sir, you had a gourd big enough to hold five bushels, so why didn't you use it to make big bottles which could help you float down rivers and lakes, instead of dismissing it as useless? Because, dear Sir, your head is full of straw!" (*Zh* 1:6). The kind of thinking employed by Huizi manifests the dominance of the conceptual mental apparatus, which bars him from opening himself to the opportunity offered by novel experiences. Doing things well is closely connected to treating others well. In a more sinister example, Bo Le boasts that he knows how to train horses and proceeds to brand them, cut their hair and their hooves, bridle them, and confine them to stables. He uses fear to compel them to race, killing more than half the horses in the process (*Zh* 9:72). Instead of respecting and responding to the nature of the horses, he tries to impose his idea of the horse onto them, and destroys them as a result.

Like Nietzsche, Daoist thinkers would assert that the need to deliberately inculcate virtue is a testament to the limitations of human beings, who desperately try to invent mechanisms of survival by imposing their own standards on the cosmos as a whole. Zhuangzi notes that at the time of perfect virtue, "people live side by side with birds and beasts, sharing the world in common with all life. No one knows of distinctions such as nobles and the peasantry" (*Zh* 9:73). There is no doubt that language plays a powerful role in the dynamic of division by attaching labels. However, a thinker such as Zhuangzi is also profoundly attuned to linguistic paradox that makes him cognizant of the potential of language: "Supposed words constitute nine-tenths of discourse, quotes make up seven-tenths and flowing words are brought forth every day, refined by the influence of Heaven" (*Zh* 27:244). *Yuyan* 寓言 (supposed words; *Zh* Ch 27:381) can also be translated as "residence words," implying that the meaning of these words has started to congeal, functioning as an objective yardstick in addition to being wedded to a particular place. Thus, they are implicitly linked to convention and a kind of stasis. Of the "supposed words" only seven-tenths are considered "quotes," or heavy words (*zhong yan* 重言 or *chong yan*, which means repeated words; *Zh* Ch 27:381), dripping from the tongues of important people. The ambiguity of the term "heavy" and important is used here, for heavy words are also cumbersome. This provides a contrast with *zhi yan* 卮言 (wine-goblet words; *Zh* Ch 27:381) that take their shape according to the container they are in, undergoing metamorphosis in response to situations, not stubbornly fixed in their meaning.

Most people use language in order to judge the world by their own standards: "Thus they say that whatever agrees with them is right, but whatever they dislike they call wrong" (*Zh* 27:244). Supposed words or "residence words" are used for the sake of "objectivity" and are like outsiders being brought in: "Supposed words which constitute nine-tenths are similar to people who are brought in from outside. For example, no father is used as a reference for his son, for the father cannot be as objective as someone not in the family" (*Zh* 27:244). The Chinese text states that no father could be as competent a matchmaker for his own son as an outsider. The meaning of this passage is deliberately ambiguous. On one hand, these words can serve to broaden the perspective of the family, because they serve as an external reference point; on the other hand, these words are also meant to impose an external standard which may not take into account the personality of the son, with which the father would be more intimately familiar.

The most dangerous words, according to this passage, are the heavy and/or repeated words attributed to sagacious elders, who are assumed to hold positions of moral prominence. Their words often serve to end arguments, but their antiquity is not necessarily the badge of wisdom. Words invested with this kind of authority disrupt the flow of language: "However, those who are old but have not grasped the warp and weft, the root and branch can't be quoted as sagacious elders" (*Zh* 27:244). Entrenched codes of conduct generate an army of sycophants: "But you parade profit and righteousness before us, and your likes and dislikes, and what you approve and disapprove and you produce nothing more than servile agreement" (*Zh* 27:245). It is clear that the preference expressed is for "wine-goblet" words, which attune to the chorus of the cosmos spontaneously and remain in agreement as long as nothing is said about them: "Words are in agreement but agreement is not in words" (*Zh* 27:244). An agreement that is secured through words is externally imposed and does not necessarily constitute a genuine harmony. Wine-goblet words preserve the openness of language which allows others to speak. The power of silence shelters language, by both keeping it modest and providing the open abode into which it can enter. If language fills all empty spaces, then it becomes meaningless chatter because its meaning depends upon the melody created by the alternation between appearance and withdrawal. Words must echo the dynamic of the cosmos: "All forms of life arise from the same base and in their diverse forms they succeed each other. They begin and end like an unbroken circle and none can say why. This is the influence of Heaven. This influence of Heaven is the harmony of Heaven" (*Zh* 27:245).

The flowing nature of words is maintained by not worrying too much about their meaning. We must not engage in a frenetic hunt for certainty. Here the shadow that mirrors the movements of its outline has an important lesson to teach because he is not worried about his identity. His form changes due to his interaction with others:

> The outline asked the Shadow, "A few minutes ago you were looking down, now you are looking up; a few minutes ago your hair was piled up, now it is hanging down; a few minutes ago you were sitting down, now you are standing up; a few minutes ago you were walking, now you are standing still. Why?" Shadow said, "Petty, petty! Why do you ask me about all this? This is all true to me, but I haven't a clue why I do it. I am like the shell of a cicada or the shed skin of a snake: something which seems real but is not. In the sunlight I appear, in darkness I disappear. However do you think I arise from these? For they are themselves dependent upon others. When it comes, I come also. When it goes, I go with it. If they arise from the mighty yang, so do I. However, there is no point in asking about the mighty yang!"
>
> (*Zh* 27:247)

The shadow is led in a multitude of directions and does not mind. Because it is shapeless, it can assume many shapes.

Zhuangzi also uses language to undo some of its effects. The *Zhuangzi* begins with complicated wordplay and juxtaposition of opposites: "In the darkness of the north there is a fish whose name is Kun. . . . It also changes into a bird, whose name is Peng, and its back is I don't know how many thousand miles across. When it rises in the air, its wings are like the clouds of Heaven. When the seas move, this bird too travels to the south darkness, the darkness known as the pool of Heaven" (*Zh* 1:1). The interaction between *yin* and *yang* here is reminiscent of the interplay between Apollo and Dionysus in Nietzsche. The bird, a *yang* creature, could also be deemed Apollonian. However, it moves into the southern darkness and the pool of heaven, which juxtaposes water, a *yin* element, with heaven, traditionally associated with *yang*. *Yin* transforms into *yang* and *yang* into *yin*. The boundaries between them are fluid. Although the bird flies to the south, traditionally associated with *yang*, this particular south is dark and becomes more *yin*-like. The opening of this text bears an uncanny resemblance to Zarathustra's journey, who begins by going down from the heights, embarking on a descent from the *yang* realm close to the sun on the mountaintop, to the *yin* valley that lies below. However, there is a marked, important contrast between Nietzschean and Daoist understandings. The tension between Apollo and Dionysus is imperative for Nietzsche since Dionysus tears asunder Apollonian structures, while Apollo reacts to the chaos of Dionysus by returning to a semblance of order. In the *Zhuangzi*, there is no reference to violent destruction of boundaries, which instead metamorphize into each other.

Zhuangzi also deliberately confounds our perspective since *kun* 鯤 (*Zh* Ch 1:3), the name of the gigantic fish, in itself means fish roe. The smallest and biggest are juxtaposed. Zhuangzi uses language to remind us that our evaluations are simply a matter of perspective. Compared to the expanse of heaven, the fish is miniscule, whereas from our more limited vantage point, it is huge. If we become attached to the name for the fish (*kun*), we might not appreciate its true nature. However, in this passage, the name in combination with the description for this creature reminds us that our judgments are not absolute. Language is used to broaden rather than narrow one's perspective.

For Zhuangzi, it is important to bear in mind that the words used to explain concepts are merely pointers, and we should be careful not to become ensnared by the language we use. Without recognizing this, we fail to speak and become mired in what Heidegger refers to as idle talk, where we are reduced to a simple parroting of others, having completely lost track of what we are speaking about: "Words are used to express concepts but once you have grasped the concepts, the words are forgotten. I would like to find someone who has forgotten words so I could debate with such a person" (*Zh* 26:242). It is the gap, between the words and that which they hope to convey, that makes speech possible. Without recognizing that the stimulus to language lies beyond the scope of language, one is unable even to have a conversation. Language cannot be left to stew in its own juices.

The division of the world through the name which occasions judgment is responsible for the limitations of morality, according to Daoist thinkers, and also makes morality necessary: "The great Tao has no beginning and words have changed their meaning from the beginning, but because of the idea of a 'this is' there came to be limitations. I want to say something about these limitations. There is right and left, relationships and their consequences, divisions and disagreements, emulations and contentions. These are known as the eight Virtues" (*Zh* 2:15–6). The process of labeling something also separates it from other things. Morality is then needed to harmonize what has been divided. Yet we become trapped in a vicious cycle because we use words to give shape to this morality, and thus the schism between beings is widened in the very attempt to close it. Nietzsche also links morality to a process of labeling. Good and bad were initially simply words that were used to distinguish the powerful from the powerless. But the words "good" and "bad" eventually led the powerless on a struggle to appropriate the label "good" for themselves by inverting its meaning. In the end, we clamor for the appropriation of a label which can be arbitrarily applied to anyone or anything. Even *yin* and *yang* turn out in Zhuangzi's text to be labels that cannot be so easily pinned down. Sunlight can be as blinding as darkness.

When Nietzsche exhorts us to make the leap beyond good and evil, he is not enjoining us to enter a world where anything goes and only power relationships hold sway. Rather, he is enticing us to venture into terrain beyond language by encouraging us to affirm everything even though language may impose restrictions. This is why he extols the night, a realm of silence and boundarylessness that allows the songs of lovers to awaken. The darkness of the night, which appears to be negation of existence and seems representative of nothingness and negation, becomes a symbol of the most poignant affirmation. However, there is also a profound and perhaps unsettling difference between Nietzsche and Zhuangzi's approach. While Nietzsche also exhorts us to celebrate openness, it leads to love and harmony, as well as agonistic conflict which are interdependent. Although Zarathustra is on a desperate mission to find friends, he wishes to entice those who are also prepared to be his enemies, because he considers this the only means to furthering the growth of all. The agonism is both inevitable and fruitful according to Nietzsche, since the establishment and reformation of boundaries is part of the cycle of existence. Flourishing not only derives from complementary harmony, as in the Daoist vision, but from struggle and excess.

For Daoists, division is not natural and is attributed primarily to conceptualization and language. Silence is invoked in order to balance the more divisive aspects of speech. Speech informed by silence is portrayed as providing the greatest potential for a deeper harmony. The *Liezi* provides an account of this transition to a new kind of language:

> Three years after I began to serve the Master and befriend a certain man, my mind no longer dared to think of right and wrong, my mouth no longer dared to speak of benefit and harm and it was only then that I got so much as a glance from the Master. After five years, my mind was again thinking of right and wrong, my mouth was again speaking of benefit and harm, and for the first time the Master's face relaxed into a smile. After seven years, I thought of whatever came into my mind without any longer distinguishing between right and wrong, said whatever came into my mouth without any longer distinguishing between benefit and harm; and for the first time the Master pulled me over to sit with him on the same mat. After nine years, I thought without restraint of whatever came into my mouth without knowing whether the right and wrong, benefit and harm, were mine or another's, without knowing that the Master was my teacher and the man I have mentioned was my friend. (*Lie* 36)

Initially, Liezi is aware of the difficulties with language and, fearing the disapproval of his master, simply refrains from speaking. Later on, he is able to return to the language of right and wrong but is more flexible in its usage. Only after many years of disciplined conditioning is he able to use words in such a way where he does not worry about approval or disapproval, and no longer depends upon concepts of right and wrong. He is able to use language in a flexible way, without being attached to the words he uses. The language becomes part of the process of life, rather than an instrument for its control. At this point, the hierarchical relationships between master and student also dissolve because a more profound harmony has been attained.

Conceptual labeling can occasion an ethics of utility which is condemned by Zhuangzi, since it forecloses the possibility of opening oneself to the potential of another being. Instead, it reduces everything to the narrow parameters of the human vision: "You have to understand what is useless, then you can talk about what is useful. . . . Heaven and Earth are vast indeed and yet human beings only use the tiny part of the universe on which they tread. However, if you dug away beneath your feet until you came to the Yellow Springs, could anyone make use of this" (*Zh* 26:240). One must learn not to incessantly superimpose human meaning onto things in order to enjoy different layers of experience. Zhuangzi relates the story of the big tree whose gnarly and knotted surface repelled carpenters and whose uneven branches resisted measurement. He advises, "Now you, Sir have a large tree, and you don't know how to use it, so why not plant it in the middle of nowhere, where you can go to wander or fall asleep under its shade? No axe under heaven will attack it, nor shorten its day, for something which is useless will never be disturbed" (*Zh* 1:6). The most useful things are the useless, which force human beings to expand the repertoire of their experience. An ethics of utility cannot accommodate diversity but repudiates it. Joseph Grange remarks that Zhuangzi's story of the gnarled tree "steadfastly refuses to accept usefulness as the definition of the real." [12] Nietzsche also warns human beings of their profound anthropomorphism, reducing everything to an ethics of utility which forces all to dance to a single tune.

Unity imposed by human beings upon diversity produces strife. For Zhuangzi, the problem with an ethical worldview is that it substitutes unity for interconnection: "Now, however, because of the multitudinous varieties of species and the ethical codes of humanity, things certainly aren't what they were! There is unity only in order to divide; fulfilment only in order to collapse" (*Zh* 20:168). This is why one must be highly sensitive to the limits of language and recognize the need to go beyond it by learning to savor its "meaninglessness," so that the spontaneity of the moment can be appreciated: "Day and night follow each other and we have no idea why. Enough, enough! Morning and night exist; we

12 Joseph Grange, "Zhuangzi's Tree," *Journal of Chinese Philosophy* 32, no. 2 (2005): 171–82.

cannot know more about the Origins than this. Without them, we don't exist, without us they have no purpose. This is close to our meaning but we cannot know what creates things to be thus. It is as if they have a Supreme guidance, but there is no grasping such a One" (*Zh* 2:10). Rather than locating meaning in a world which can be known, it is to be found in the interconnection between things:

> Heaven and earth have great beauty but no words.
> The four seasons follow their regular path but do not debate it.
> All forms of life have their own distinct natures but do not discuss them.
> The sage looks at the beauties of Heaven and earth and
> Comprehends the principle behind all life.
> So the perfect man does without doing
> And the great sage initiates nothing,
> For, as we say, they have glimpsed heaven and earth.
>
> (*Zh* 22:189)

The centrality that language assumes in occasioning moral judgment attests to a troubling anthropomorphism, and texts like the *Zhuangzi* repeatedly draw upon animals as mouthpieces in order to remind us that our vision of the cosmos is not the only one. Zarathustra too is accompanied by his eagle and serpent who remind him that the world is a garden waiting to be explored. But the use of these animal companions is also ironic. In these texts, animals speak and become caricatures of human beings. Animals can only be said to hold alternate perspectives when their activity is relayed to us in *human* terms. They are thereby transformed into metaphors for the human experience.

Nonetheless, there is a notable sensitivity toward nonhuman life and its flourishing in the *Zhuangzi*. A horse trainer is repudiated for whipping and mistreating his horses. The Earl of Lu carried the seabird to an ancestral shrine where he made offerings to it and played the Nine Shao music in apparent gestures of veneration, but the bird refused to eat and eventually died: "The problem was trying to feed a bird on what you eat rather than what a bird needs" (*Zh* 18:153). Human beings are reminded that they are merely part of the cycle of *Dao*, rather than being its masters: "Sheep come together in intercourse with bamboo that has not put forth any shoots for years and they give birth to Green Peace plants.

These give birth to leopards, leopards give birth to horses, horses give birth to humans, humans eventually sink back to what was in the beginning. All the multitudes of life arise from the mystery of the beginning and return there" (*Zh* 18:154).

The proliferation of perspectives, including the recognition that there is life beyond the human realm, keeps us humble and allows us to use words without becoming too attached to them. Karyn Lai points out that Zhuangzi is not chasing the truth, but rather hopes to invite a plurality of views which lend themselves to negotiation instead of domination.[13] Zhuangzi notes that there is no single correct vantage point which we can assume:

> The understanding of the small cannot be compared to the understanding of the great. A few years cannot be compared to many years. How do we know this? The morning mushroom does not know of the waxing and waning of the moon. The cicada does not know of spring and autumn. For theirs are but short lives. To the south of Chu there is a vast creature for whom five hundred years is but a spring and five hundred years is but an autumn. In the ancient antiquity there was a giant tree called Chun for whom spring was eight thousand years and for whom autumn was eight thousand years. Yet Peng Zi is the only man renowned for his great age, something envied by many people, which is rather pathetic?
>
> (*Zh* 1:2)

The *Daodejing* distinguishes the sage from others by the knowledge of her limitations which allows awareness to grow:

> To know yet to think that one does not know is best;
> Not to know yet to think that one knows will lead to difficulty.
> It is by being alive to difficulty that one can avoid it.
> The sage meets with no difficulty.
> It is because he is alive to it that he meets with no difficulty.
>
> (*DDJ* 71)

The Chinese text referring to the sage reads: 聖人不病，以其病病，是以不病 (*sheng ren bu bing, yi qi bing bing, shi yi bu bing*; *DDJ* Ch 71). This could also

13 Karyn L. Lai, "Philosophy and Philosophical Reasoning in the *Zhuangzi*: Dealing with Plurality," *Journal of Chinese Philosophy* 33, no. 3 (2006): 371.

be translated as: "The sage has no limitations. Because he recognizes limitations as limitations, he has no limitations." Because the sage acknowledges his own boundaries, they can also be transformed into possibilities and he will then be open to diverse encounters. Language is such a limitation. Once it is recognized as such, we can begin liberating it from itself.

Oneness and Self-Forgetting

Perhaps one of the features that distinguishes Daoist philosophies most profoundly from that of Nietzsche is the importance placed on oneness. The oneness of *Dao* always exists due to the interconnections of all things, which can never be undermined by human behavior. Even our transgressions and departures from *Dao* end up being part of its inexorable rhythm, embracing all opposites. Daoist philosophy is not simply a kind of "back to nature" movement, because human beings must *learn* to attune themselves to this oneness, and it is here that the image of a Daoist ethics begins to emerge. Human beings consciously harmonize with *Dao* by deliberately trying to undo the chains of their own consciousness. If they are to accomplish this, they must learn to forget themselves in order to be themselves. According to Zhuangzi, one must be released from the trappings of convention in order to harmonize with *Dao*, but it is very difficult to do this without first moving *through* conventional ethics. Yan Hui, one of Confucius's most revered disciples, is encouraged to free himself of his Confucian education. On the first day, he notes that he is improving because he has forgotten benevolence and righteousness; the next day, he forgets rites and music. Finally, he proclaims: "My limbs are without feeling and my mind is without light. I have ignored my body and cast aside my wisdom. Thus, I am united with *Dao*. This is what sitting right down and forgetting is" (*Zh* 6:58). Significantly, the art of *forgetting* benevolence and righteousness is not tantamount to renouncing them completely. They do make one aware of the need for harmony, albeit bounded. Only by recognizing their bounded nature is Yan Hui able to move beyond them. He is capable of moving to the next phase of forgetting, because he is practiced in these virtues. After all, he is Confucius's best student. By recognizing both the possibilities and limits of these virtues, he is able to "forget" them. This is an active rather than a passive forgetting. His sincerity and skill allow him to go beyond Confucianism to attain oneness with *Dao*. Once he has forgotten himself in this way, an open relationship with others is made possible.

Oneness as forgetting is closely related to the central role of nothingness in Daoist philosophy:

> There is something which exists, though it emerges from no roots, it returns through no opening. It exists but has no place; it survives yet has no beginning nor end. Though it emerges through no opening, there is something which tells us it is real. It is real but it has no permanent place: this tells us it is a dimension of space. It survives, but has no beginning nor end: this tells us it has dimensions of time. It is born, it dies, it emerges, it returns, though in its emergence and return there is no form to be seen. This is what we call the Heavenly Gate. The Heavenly Gate is non-existence, and all forms of life emerge from non-existence. That which exists cannot cause things to exist. They all arise from non-existence. Non-existence is the oneness of existence. This is the hidden knowledge of the sages.
>
> (*Zh* 23:205)

The fact that non-existence constitutes the oneness of existence underscores the fact that the formlessness and openness, which are at the heart of things, allow one thing to metamorphize into another. Oneness is seen as something that emerges *between* things and, at the same time, allows for their appearance and their dissolution. Just as there is no absolute presence, there is no absolute absence. Oneness does not facilitate the transcendence of the temporal reality, but rather enables one to rest within its midst. Yan Hui in the aforementioned passage is so at one with his world that he no longer notices his limbs, because there is no felt difference between him and his environs.

The importance of nothingness offers an interesting counterpoint to the thought of Nietzsche, because Zarathustra must also experience the depths of nothingness in order to be redeemed. Yet, according to Nietzsche, the most abysmal thought which becomes the sinister prelude to his redemption at first sends him into the grip of paralyzing despair, because it means that everything one has known is torn asunder. This is indicative of the extent to which the bounded world is the primary locus of meaning. Nihilism brings about a fragmentation that is unsettling to Zarathustra and unleashes a maelstrom of ominous visions, many of which are distorted versions of his own that he encounters when the coffins are thrust open and all sorts of demons arrive on the scene. Because nothingness is associated with nihilism, it leads to an explosion of unrelated and disconnected images. This corresponds to a kind of dissolution into the many, which Zarathustra is ill-equipped to deal with. Yan Hui does not go through a psychotic breakdown when he sheds the trappings of Confucian thought, precisely because of his understanding that there is an emptiness that connects everything and is the source of oneness. While Daoist thinkers insist on a kind of harmonious oneness that connects all beings, Nietzsche would insist that one cannot simply eradicate the strife and conflict that characterizes our existence. The world which embraces me is also my enemy, symbolized by the serpent's coils that threaten to asphyxiate the peasant. My oneness as an individual is at least partly defined *against* the world. The circular nature of the eternal return is not only a vision of harmony, but also one of destruction, against which one must vigorously assert one's identity, just as the peasant must bite off the serpent's head. The serpent in the text figures both as an enemy and as a companion, in keeping with the interrelationship between friends and enemies that Zarathustra is so keen to highlight.

From a Daoist perspective, the kind of nothingness Zarathustra encounters constitutes negation. For Nietzsche, renewal can only begin in the aftermath of an apocalyptic experience that rattles the self to its foundations. Zarathustra must be violently freed of his ego-self by being reminded of the fragility of his conceptions, just as Abraham is asked to make the ultimate sacrifice in order to divest himself of his ego. The Daoist process of forgetting is not traumatic because nothingness in Daoism is related to a kind of homecoming and return to the oneness of *Dao*, rather than a demolition of all that is familiar. It does not constitute a powerful and terrifying negation or the experience of loss.

Ossified structures and the egotistical leanings of Zarathustra are blasted with the pellets of nihilism because nothingness is seen as the opposite of being, and thus allows for its renewal and regeneration. In

Daoism, nothingness is at the heart of all beings rather than constituting their negation, and thus is the complement of existence instead of the sledgehammer that chisels away at its foundations. While Daoist thought stresses the complementary nature of being and nothingness, Nietzsche underlines their necessary opposition and the concomitant alternation between them. My own individual existence matters, and without a self willing to erect boundaries in addition to relinquishing them, there would be no diversity. According to Daoist thinkers, each being is a composite of shape and shapelessness, being and nothingness. The difference is that, from a Daoist perspective, these opposites are above all complementary, while Nietzsche wishes to retain their combative relationship. It is because the peasant fears his death and assiduously struggles against it, rather than accepting it, that he is able to emerge laughing. A life-and-death struggle is the prelude to his redemption.

The *Daodejing* stipulates that things cannot be born merely out of existence, because it constitutes the boundary between things. The priority accorded to nothingness affirms the centrality of interconnection in Daoist thinking: "'Non-existence' I call the beginning of Heaven and Earth. 'Existence' I call the mother of individual beings. Therefore does the direction towards non-existence lead to the sight of the miraculous essence, the direction towards existence to the sight of spatial limitations" (*DDJ* 1). Existence complements nothingness because it constitutes the differentiation between things that allows for their interaction. Only the combination of nothingness and existence produces flowing movements.

The cultivation of nothingness also surfaces in the state of sleep which dissolves the boundaries between things and, in so doing, dissolves the self. Different kinds of dreams are portrayed in the Daoist literature. There is the anxiety-ridden dream that replays the worries of the day. According to the *Liezi*, dreams that intrude upon our psyche manifest the anxiety of our waking existence: "The spirit chances on it, and we dream; the body encounters it, and it happens. Hence by day we imagine and by night dream what spirit and body chance upon. That is why, when someone's spirit is concentrated, imagination and dreaming diminish of themselves" (*Lie* 67).

On the other hand, Zhuangzi gives an account of the famous butterfly dream which manifests receptivity to the changing nature of reality, leaving him unable to decide whether he is a butterfly dreaming he is a man, or a man dreaming he is a butterfly (*Zh* 2:20). Nothingness functions in a variety of ways. On one hand, there is no difference between him and the butterfly, and the distinction between the waking and sleeping states as well as between the subject and its world is collapsed. At the same time, nothingness is the space between him and the butterfly, which makes him aware that there is "some sort of difference" between them. Zhuangzi does not have to choose between the reality and fiction of his dream, nor does he have to decide whether he is indeed a butterfly or a man. He is the butterfly and yet is not the butterfly. He recognizes the distinction between himself and the butterfly, and also acknowledges the irrelevance of this distinction. His experience of the transformation into a butterfly also is symbolic of the oneness of all things. Furthermore, his apparently fictional "butterfly self" also elucidates the fictional nature of his "normal self."

The *Liezi* also recounts a famous story of King Mu who was visited by a sorcerer from the West. Wanting to bestow the greatest hospitality upon him, he built luxurious towers and palaces, bursting with delectable food, and providing expansive views of the sky and Mount Kunlun. However, much to his chagrin, all of this left his visitor thoroughly unimpressed. Consequently, King Mu was invited to travel into the spirit world with the sorcerer and, upon seeing such opulence, realized that to his guest, his own palaces must seem like a mean hovel. He then awakens from a dream, sitting on his chair in the same position as before. The sorcerer relays words of wisdom to him: "Your Majesty has been on a journey of the spirit. Why should your body have moved? Why should the place where you lived be different from your own palace, or the place of our excursion different from your own park? Your Majesty feels at home with the permanent, is suspicious of the sudden and temporary. But can one always measure how far and how fast a scene may alter and turn into something else?" (*Lie* 63). The dream threw into question the permanence of King Mu's abode and exposed him to the fragility of his own reality by providing an alternate one. The irony of this passage is that the King has not moved from his place and yet feels vertigo as a result of his journey. From the perspective of *Dao*, he has not moved at all, and there is no fundamental difference between the palaces he has visited and the one that is his home. The reason he has experienced the dream encounter with such shock is because of the value he had mistakenly placed on his own palace. As Nietzsche pointed out in his discussion of the birth of values, such positing of value is necessarily divisive since it automatically bestows dignity on some things by demeaning others. Recognizing the oneness of all things also demands an ability to affirm them without bestowing value on them. It also means being able to acknowledge realities that may not be immediately our own. Rather than drawing a sharp distinction between fiction and reality, the dream is represented as an alternate reality in which the boundaries of the self are more fluid. Robert Allinson suggests that Zhuangzi's anecdotes remind us that the "waking I" is part of a "dream-like illusion." [14]

The relationship between the one and the many is also highlighted in an interesting passage in the *Daodejing* which draws important connections between the one and the three: "The way begets one; one begets two; two begets three; three begets the myriad creatures" (*DDJ* 42). The "one" in Chinese is denoted by 一 (*yi*), a straight line. Because the one only makes sense in relation to its two sides, it already houses the seeds of the two that it begets. Furthermore, the line is singular thanks to the empty spaces that surround it. Thus, the being of the one could not exist without the nothingness that encircles it. The two produces the three as a result of the oneness in their midst that allows them to interact. It does not constitute a splitting apart from oneness, but rather signifies the movement of oneness at work within it. Indeed, the Chinese character for three 三 (*san*) houses both the one and the two. According to Nietzsche, oneness cannot exist without opposition to other beings, who also aspire to circumscribe their boundaries in this way. He might argue that the singular line of the one marks its presence against the encircling nothingness instead of with it.

According to a Daoist perspective, traditional morality may repre-

---

14 Robert E. Allinson, "On Chuang-tzu as a Deconstructionist with a Difference," *Journal of Chinese Philosophy* 30 no. 3–4 (2003): 493.

sent a misguided attempt to maintain oneness through possession (*you* 有) by defining its parameters. When we do so, we seek to render behavior amenable to comprehension and speech. According to this position, conventional morality and selfishness share a common tendency, which is to obtain oneness within a demarcated milieu which one then strives to protect. From Zhuangzi's perspective, beyond the defined benevolence is the benevolence without limits which is harder to achieve:

> Perfect benevolence is of the highest order, and words such as "filial piety" cannot describe it. . . . When a traveller goes south and then turns to face north, when he has reached Ying he cannot see Ming mountain. Why is this? Because it is far away. There is the saying: filial piety arising from respect is easy, filial piety arising from love is hard. If filial piety from love is easy, then to forget your parents is hard. It is easy to forget your parents, but it is hard to make my parents forget me. It is easy to make my parents forget me, but it is hard to make me forget the whole world. It is easy to forget the whole world, but it is hard for the whole world to forget me.
>
> (*Zh* 13:118)

With each sentence in this paragraph, Zhuangzi describes a broadening conception of love and *ren*. Forgetting here is not a flippant disregard and a process of erasing my memory, but rather letting go of others as possessive attachments for myself. The whole world cannot "forget me" because it does not *have* me as a possession. It is also difficult for me to make myself so invisible through harmonious interaction that the world can forget me.

Daoist thinkers distinguish between traditional morality and *de* 德: "Filial piety, mutual respect, benevolence, righteousness, loyalty, integrity, resoluteness and purity, all of these can be of service to virtue [*de*] but they are not worthy in themselves" (*Zh* 13:118). *De* cannot easily be pinned down, for my specificity develops in interaction with others. *De* refers to the active capacities of beings that are in keeping with the formlessness of *Dao*:

> At the great Origin there was nothing, nothing, no name.
> The one arose from it; there was One without form.
> In taking different forms, it brought life and became known as Virtue.
> Before any shape was given, their roles were assigned,

varied and diverse but all linked to one another.
This was their lot.
The forces worked on and things were created,
They grew and took distinct shapes, and these were called "bodies"
The bodies contained spirits,
each distinct and mortal.
This is what we call the innate nature.
Train this innate nature and it will return to Virtue;
Virtue at its best is identical with the Origin.
Being of the One is to be ultimately formless, and this formlessness is vast.
This is like the opening and shutting of a bird's beak,
where the opening and shutting is like Heaven and Earth united.
This unity is chaotic and disorderly;
it looks stupid or foolish.
This is known as Mysterious Virtue,
being, without knowing it, part of the great Submission.

(*Zh* 12:97)

Virtue, in Daoist thought, is closely associated with the particularity of all beings. Their particular shape (*xing* 形) is the marker that distinguishes things but, for this reason, also lures them towards the one. The character for *xing* consists of the radicals for "beginning," and "etchings" or "markings." Thus, the uniqueness of a particular being is described in terms of the movement marking its singularity, rather than in terms of a static essence. Its form can only be expressed in relation to formlessness, as is signified by the opening and closing of the bird's mouth. It opens itself to the world while maintaining its shape by closing its mouth. Each being has its own particular way of returning to *Dao*, which is why virtue appears mysterious and disorderly. It cannot be encapsulated in words or forced into the framework of knowledge.

By cultivating oneness, a panoply of virtues unfolds, which expresses the particularities of different things. There is no single way of cultivating the one:

Of old, these came to be in possession of the One:
Heaven in virtue of the One is limpid;
Earth in virtue of the One is settled;
Spirits in virtue of the One have their potencies;

> The valley in virtue of the One is full;
> The myriad creatures in virtue of the One are alive;
> Lords and princes in virtue of the One become leaders of the Empire.
>
> (*DDJ* 39)

Later Daoist texts, such as the *Zhuangzi* and the *Liezi*, view the oneness between things as the reason for spurning hierarchy. Liezi himself lives anonymously in a game park and remained unnoticed for forty years. Even nobles and "high officials of state regarded him as one of the common people" (*Lie* 17). The *Daodejing* is more accepting of hierarchy but notes that apparent opposites are actually interdependent:

> Hence the superior must have the inferior as the root; the high must have the low as base.
> Thus lords and princes refer to themselves as "solitary," "desolate," and "hapless." This is taking the inferior as the root, is it not?
> Hence the highest renown is without renown,
> Not wishing to be one among many like jade
> Nor to be aloof like stone.
>
> (*DDJ* 39)

Lords and kings hold their high posts only by virtue of the many who sustain them. Those whom they are inclined to demean constitute their power base.

At some level, the oneness of *Dao* is inescapable, because even differentiation opens up the possibility of a return to *Dao* and a concomitant reaffirmation of oneness. Zhuangzi looks back with nostalgia on a time when knowledge did not yet exist: "In the beginning they did not know that anything existed; this is virtually perfect knowledge, for nothing can be added. Later they knew that some things existed but they did not distinguish between them. Next came those who distinguished between things, but did not judge things as 'being or not being.' It was when judgements were made that *Dao* was damaged, and because *Dao* was damaged, love became complete" (*Zh* 2:14). Lack of knowledge is perfect knowledge, because it implies things are simply interconnected without the division occasioned by the concept. With the advent of judgment, *Dao* is divided and desire is born. Yet at the same time, this departure from *Dao* is part of the process of *Dao*'s movement because it generates the love for the return to *Dao*. We could not return to the one without the sense of having departed from it, like the bird that opens its mouth because it has shut it, and shuts it because it has opened it. The misguided pursuit of oneness through bounded structures constitutes a movement away from the one, but all the while, the one flows through these edifices, beckoning us to return to it.

The oneness of all things also means that even right and wrong are connected and part of *Dao*. When it is said that the sage "manages to harmonize right and wrong" (*Zh* 2:14), this is not a prescription for a kind of moral relativism in which anything goes; rather, it means that from a standpoint which regards things as nondifferentiated, the distinction between good and evil is eclipsed. If I upset the balance now by harming you, eventually the pendulum may correct things by shifting in the opposite direction, restoring equilibrium. However, this is of little comfort to most human beings. Zhuangzi is not implying that the sage is completely indifferent to the course of events. Because he recognizes that things are both differentiated from each other and *not* differentiated from each other, he must *harmonize* between right and wrong instead of dispensing with morality entirely. As differentiated beings, we can inflict harm as well as do good toward one another; as undifferentiated beings, everything we do is merely part of *Dao*'s rhythm. Our actions will usually benefit some and harm others, and partake of both good and evil. Furthermore, recognizing when we do harm to others allows us to see possibilities for goodness. For example, we can learn from the action of the emperors of the north and south seas who drill holes into Hundun in an effort to repay his kindness, instigating his death. They inflict harm on him in the effort to do good. At the same time, Zhuangzi uses this story to teach us a moral lesson so that we learn to be more responsive to the different needs of different beings. Unadulterated goodness is beyond our reach. The sage realizes this, and recognizing human limitations tries to ensure that as much harmony as possible prevails. Furthermore, sages recognize that the categories of right and wrong are not always neatly disentangled. Often, we assume we are doing good when we treat them in ways that we would want to be treated, like the emperors who think they are helping Chaos, or the Duke of Lu, who venerates the seabird but inadvertently causes it to die in its captivity. Thus, Zhuangzi would deny the possibility that good can ever completely triumph over evil, because neither good nor evil is absolute: "With regard to what is right and wrong, I say not being is being and being is not being. . . . But let us not get caught up in discussing this. Forget about life, forget about worrying about right and wrong. Plunge into the unknown and the endless and find your place there" (*Zh* 2:20). Recognizing that right and wrong are somewhat arbitrary distinctions allows us to pay attention to the moral nuances of situations and see the connections between right and wrong. What is good for me is not self-evidently good for somebody else.

The good and the bad are united in the oneness of *Dao*. Both cherish *Dao* and the *Daodejing* uses wordplay to underline their similarity. The good man treasures *Dao* (*shan ren zhi bao* 善人之寶) while the bad man tries to hold onto it and preserve it (*bu shan ren zhi suo bao* 不善人之所保; *DDJ* Ch 62). The phonetic *bao* is the same in both cases. Evil is thus related to goodness. The bad man does not repudiate *Dao* but rather tries to contain it and, in so doing, reduce it to a possession:

> The Tao is the innermost recess of all things
> It is what the good man cherishes
> As well as what the bad man wants to keep.
> With the Tao, beautiful words can buy respect;
> Beautiful deeds can be highly regarded.
> How can the bad man desert the Tao.
>
> (*DDJ* 62)

The last line in this passage in Chinese reads *ren zhi bu shan, he qi zhi you* 人之不善，何棄之有 (*DDJ* Ch 62). It asks how it is possible for the bad man to abandon possession particularly when language is intent on bestowing value, such as beauty on things. Thus, the bad man is part of a system which is insistent on imputing worth: "How can I know that what I saw I know is not actually what I don't know? Likewise, how can I know that what I think I don't know is not really what I do know? I want to put some questions to you: If someone sleeps in a damp place, he will ache all over and he will be half paralysed but is it the same for an eel? If someone climbs a tree he will be frightened and shaking, but is it so for a monkey? . . . As I see it, benevolence and righteousness, also the ways of right and wrong, are completely interwoven. I do not think I can know the difference between them" (*Zh* 2:17).

Wuwei

Affirming the oneness of things is also closely connected to the skillful nurturing of the art of *wuwei* 無為, which is often translated as non-action, or more recently "effortless action." [15] In the *Daodejing*, the art of *wuwei* is outlined in relation to the sage-ruler. Minimal amount of explicit interference is to be exercised by the ruler, who is to remain largely invisible so that people's virtues can develop in accordance with their dispositions. This does not imply that the ruler does nothing, but she is to be so adroit in teasing out the harmonious potential of others, that her rule goes largely unnoticed: "The best of a ruler is but a shadowy presence to his subjects" (*DDJ* 17). This is not a virtue unique to Daoism, for Confucius also refers to *wuwei* in describing the ideal reign of Shun: "If anyone could be said to have effected proper order while remaining nonassertive, surely it was Shun. What did he do? He simply assumed an air of deference and faced due south" (*A* 15:5). Although the Confucian ruler is to rule noncoercively, he is to remain a model for virtuous behavior that others can follow: "Governing with excellence can be compared to being the North Star: the North Star dwells in its place, and the multitude of stars pay it tribute" (*A* 2:1). Zhuangzi mocks such behavior: "That would ruin Virtue. If someone tries to govern everything below Heaven in this way, it's like trying to stride through the seas, or cut a tunnel through the river, or make a mosquito carry a mountain" (*Zh* 7:61). The Daoist sage-ruler is to draw out the virtues of others while remaining inconspicuous, so that all have the sense that their behavior comes naturally. Even striving to be moral and coordinating the behavior of citizens to be harmonious is suspect, for it results in an external imposition of moral codes which, according to the *Daodejing*, means that morality eventually degenerates into an ethics of utility. Both the *Daodejing* and the *Zhuangzi* suggest that if one concerns oneself with acting

15 Slingerland, *Effortless Action*, p. 6.

well, one must not concern oneself with what one does. In other words, one's activity is not to be subordinated to objectified goals, because this can easily slide into a utilitarian ethic where one's actions become means to an end. *Wuwei* is to ensure that no activity is instrumentalized: "In the pursuit of learning one knows more every day; in the pursuit of the way one does less every day. One does less and less until one does nothing at all, and when one does nothing at all there is nothing that is undone" (*DDJ* 48). The decrease that is being referred to here is not a loss, but rather means that one does not attempt to accumulate by "earning" anything, including the accolades of one's fellow human beings or the label of moral person.

This does not mean that the *Daodejing* advocates passive quietism. Instead, it refers to activity without purposefulness that tries to do away with intention and willing. The ruler appears to be a conduit for a transition to a self-governing system:

> I take no action and the people are transformed of themselves;
> I prefer stillness and the people are rectified of themselves;
> I am not meddlesome and the people prosper of themselves;
> I am free from desire and the people of themselves become simple like the uncarved block.
>
> (*DDJ* 57)

Because each action is seen as an interaction and responsiveness, it cannot be conceived of as the subject's activity. The ruler does nothing because he is not acting alone for all actions are performed *with* others. The high premium placed on *wuwei* indicates that *how* actions are performed is closely related to their virtue (*de*). Edward Slingerhand remarks that "any self-conscious attempt to cultivate *wuwei* undermines one's ability to achieve the desired state."[16] In ethical terms, when *wuwei* is practiced, there is no need for demonstrative rituals and rules associated with traditional virtue:

> A man of the highest virtue does not keep to virtue and that is why he has virtue. A man of the lowest virtue never strays from virtue and that is why he is without virtue. The former never acts yet leaves nothing undone. The latter acts but there are things left undone. A man of the highest benevolence acts,

16 Ibid.

> but from no ulterior motive. A man of the highest rectitude acts, but from ulterior motive. A man most conversant in the rites acts, but when no one responds rolls up his sleeves and resorts to persuasion by force.
>
> Hence when the way was lost there was virtue; when virtue was lost there was benevolence; when benevolence was lost there was rectitude; when rectitude was lost there were the rites.
>
> The rites are the wearing thin of loyalty and good faith and the beginning of disorder; . . .
>
> (*DDJ* 38)

The opening of this passage in Chinese reads: 上德不德，是以有德 (*shang de bu de, shi yi you de*; *DDJ* Ch 38), which suggests that the virtuous man has virtue because he is not virtuous. While *ren* can still be practiced through the art of *wuwei*, the passage appears to suggest that justice (*yi* 義) cannot. As I pointed out in Chapter One, *yi* is very much associated with appropriate behavior, which must take into account the customs and rituals of a society. *Ren* is broader because it refers to a general openness to other human beings that is not necessarily tied to a specific milieu.

The notion of *wuwei* would be spurned virulently by Nietzsche. In fact, he connects emptiness to a kind of drugged state and a loss of pathos, which reflects a "narcotic state of disgust with oneself" (*WP* 29).[17] Nonetheless, his will to power also valorizes activity describing a constant impetus for growth and overcoming although it is not, as is commonly assumed, always simply an appetite for naked power and struggle for dominance. The German term *Wille zur Macht* plays on the word *machen* which also means to make and create: "Willing seems to me to be above all something complicated, something that is a unity only as a word" (*BGE* 19). The will cannot necessarily be imputed to the subject, even though it acts "against resistances" (*WP* 659). It is also a teeming life force that ripples through us, a pathos which does not always lie within our realm of control: "Suppose all organic functions could be traced back to this will to power" (*BGE* 36). We do not just will, we are part of the process of willing.

---

17 Friedrich Nietzsche, *The Will to Power*, trans. Walter Kaufmann and R. J. Hollingdale (Middlesex: Penguin, 1968).

Nietzsche would concur with the distrust of intention that the philosophy of *wuwei* exhibits. He views purposiveness as an act of interpretation which prioritizes some things to the detriment of other things: "From time immemorial we have ascribed the value of an action, a character, an existence, to the *intention*, the *purpose* for the sake of which one has acted or lived: this age-old idiosyncrasy finally takes a dangerous turn. . . . The purpose and means are interpretations whereby certain points are emphasized and selected at the expense of other points. Every purposive action is like the heat the sun gives off: the enormously greater part is squandered, a part hardly worth considering serves a 'purpose' has 'meaning'" (*WP* 666). Intention forces our activity into a straightjacket, and does not allow for random spontaneity, which is a necessary aspect of the creative evolution of human beings.

However, the restless momentum of the will to power could not differ more sharply from the notion of *wuwei*, which denotes a kind of activity that incorporates the stillness of motionlessness with the spontaneity of movement. It is engaged in without willing or self-overcoming and thus is subject-less activity. In Confucian philosophy, there is a pronounced emphasis on self-cultivation and becoming the moral person. Although Confucius also implies that with increasing age, one's actions become effortless, the Daoist conception of *wuwei* goes even further because it does not posit explicit goals. The individual who participates in the art of *wuwei* is concerned neither with her subjectivity nor her morality. *Wuwei* not only dispenses with the subject-object dichotomy, but also with intersubjectivity which would depend on the mutual recognition of subjects. It is devoid of intention and willing altogether, instead modeling itself on nature which operates in a balanced manner, without recourse to principles or definition of purpose.

Through *wuwei*, sages provide an opening through which the *de* of others can appear, and they in turn provide an opening for the sages. Sages are secure in who they are because their identity is irrelevant to them. Preoccupation with one's identity leads to a perennial discomfort with one's existence. Because the sage remains invisible, she is not engaged in an ego-driven struggle for recognition. The performance rituals of Confucianism depend, in large degree, on the respect accorded to the personality of the sage, who is responsible for their continuity.

The Daoist sage is a foil to the Confucian sage for he is not to be emulated. This is why the *Zhuangzi* introduces a kaleidoscope of social outcasts, who are unlikely to attract a following. Each of them manifests his *wuwei* in the manner that is appropriate to the task at hand such as Cook Ding, who is able to respond to the contours of his meat in order to perfect the art of butchery. One would not emulate the cook if one were a pianist. The fisherman is another favorite example in Daoist texts. Because fishermen are adept at the art of waiting for the fish to come to them, their activity is assumed to be imbued with a strong Daoist flavor. An old fisherman lectures Confucius on the limits of virtues: "You, Sir, try to distinguish the spheres of benevolence and righteousness, to explore the boundaries between agreement and disagreement, to study changes between rest and movement, to pontificate on giving and receiving, to order what is to be approved of and what disapproved of, to unify the limits of joy and anger, and yet you have hardly escaped calamity" (*Zh* 31:283).

The sage does not aspire to become a model that others can use as a moral beacon. From a Daoist perspective, the exaltation of role models smacks of an insidious egoism, which triggers the construction of defensive walls and unleashes a spiral of competition. Instead, the emphasis is placed on responsiveness, which does not resist but rather adapts behavior to the situation at hand. This does not mean that one merely acquiesces and allows oneself to be overrun. It is like the action of an adept canoeist who, in order to skillfully run rapids, must use the current to her advantage rather than paddling with all her might against it and exhausting herself in the process. According to Daoist philosophy, morality which imputes a large role to performance is bound to eventuate in great disorder, because it will unleash a competition not only for recognition, but treats moral virtues as possessions. Furthermore, because the cosmos is a loosely woven web of thousands of beings, by laying down codes of conduct, one may unwittingly hinder the growth of others. Rituals disrupt this mutual process of flourishing. By prescribing moral rules, Daoism insists that traditional moral philosophy creates the very egoism it purports to overcome. The true sage, on the other hand, attempts to draw out the other in unique and perhaps unpredictable ways, allowing a port of entry for the unknown. Without the construction of moral walls, there is no reason to become immoral. When one draws up a blueprint for correct behavior, one also shapes the immoral behavior that emerges in an attempt to resist these prescriptions.

Wuwei is a skillful activity. In order to provide an opening for other beings, one must be attuned to their *de*. It is akin to the improvisational artistry of a musician who has mastered her instrument to such a degree that her playing seems effortless. He can respond to the harmonies of others without silencing them. In the "Art of Rulership" chapter of the *Huainanzi*, it is said that "non-action does not mean being completely inert, but rather that nothing is initiated from the ego-self" (*AR* 51).[18] The Daoist sage is in such accord with his surroundings that nothing perturbs him: "He does not feel the heat of the burning deserts nor the cold of the vast waters. He is not frightened by the lightning which can split open mountains, nor by the storms that can whip up the seas. Such a person rides the clouds and mounts upon the sun and moon and wanders across and beyond the four seas. Neither death nor life concerns him, nor is he interested in what is good and bad!" (*Zh* 2:18). Furthermore, the Daoist sage has no objectives: "Practice having no thoughts and no reflections and you will come to know *Dao*. Only when you have no place and can see no way forward will you find rest in *Dao*. Have no path and no plans and you will obtain the *Dao*" (*Zh* 22:187). The sage is able to see things as "simply things" and therefore does not share in their limited nature (*Zh* 22:194). Limitlessness is not attained by grasping more and more for oneself, but rather by releasing oneself from the grip of desire and anxiety: "The sage rests, truly rests and is at ease. This manifests his calmness and detachment, so that worries and distress cannot affect him, nothing unpleasant can disturb him, his Virtue is complete and his spirit is not stirred up" (*Zh* 15:130).

Roger Ames notes that in order to understand the complexity of *wuwei*, one must be familiar with the basic presuppositions of Daoism.

18 Huainanzi, *The Art of Rulership: A Study in Ancient Chinese Political Thought*, trans. Roger T. Ames (Honolulu: University of Hawaii Press, 1983).

First of all, the "organismic and holistic" conceptions of reality must be understood. I cannot possibly understand the whole, not because I am a finite creature standing before an omnipresent infinite, but because the whole as well as the particulars are produced out of the varied and interlocking activities of finite beings. Chasing after my own subjectivity in this environment is like trying to contain a river in a box wherein I shut myself off from the multidimensional world I inhabit.

The kind of effortless activity that the *Zhuangzi* extols also renders sages completely comfortable in their own skin, precisely because they are blissfully unconcerned with their identity. Cultivation of the body is such an integral part of Daoist activity. However, the use of the term *shen* 身 rather than *ji* 己 is deliberate, because it is a nonreflective aspect of the self that does not demarcate soul from body, nor mind from self. The body is seen as a locus of interaction, and thus in cultivating one's body, one also cultivates the world. Zhuangzi suggests that someone who loves her body as she loves the world is a fit ruler and then, in the same passage, wonders where such a person would find the time to govern the world. The best way to govern the world is not to govern it, but rather to let it arise in the process of becoming. The individual who loves his body as the world is content with it the way it is at each moment, whether it sprouts willow trees or dead ashes. Only such a person can be entrusted with governance. Who he is will depend upon where he is at any given point in time. At every moment in his life, he is complete:

> So it is that the noble master who finds he has to follow some course to govern the world will realize that actionless action is the best course. By non-action he can rest in the real substance of his nature and destiny. If he appreciates his own body as he appreciates the world, then the world can be placed in his care. He who loves his body as he loves the world can be trusted to govern the world. . . . If he is unconcerned and engaged in actionless action, his gentle spirit will draw all life to him like a dust cloud. How can such a person have time to govern the world?
>
> (*Zh* 11:83–4)

The *Zhuangzi* also notes that only *wuwei* permits one to judge right and wrong, because the sensitivity to context allows one to put things into perspective:

> The whole world is incapable of judging either right or wrong. But it is certain that actionless action can judge both right and wrong. Perfect happiness is keeping yourself alive, and only actionless action can have this effect. This is why I want to say: "Heaven does without doing through its purity, Earth does without doing through its calmness." Thus, the two combine their actionless action and all forms of life are changed and thus come out again to live! Wonder of wonders, they have not come from anywhere! All life is mysterious and emerges from actionless action. There is the saying that Heaven and Earth take actionless action, but yet nothing remains undone. Amongst the people who can follow such actionless action.
>
> (*Zh* 18:150)

Because the sage is purposeless, right and wrong are not invested with any particular interest, and thus only he or she is able to judge their efficacy. This efficacy in terms of harmonious interaction is of more importance to the sage than meeting some objective standard.

Unearthing Egoism

A comparison between Nietzsche and Daoist thought helps to illuminate the fact that Nietzsche's movement beyond good and evil is not simply a call for untrammeled freedom of expression, or the desire for the domination of the powerful. There are several problems endemic to morality according to these thinkers. First of all, by objectifying values, they are turned into virtues one can acquire, and thus our behavior becomes increasingly instrumentalized. Although Confucian thinkers would never advocate a value system based on the reification of values, such reification is inevitable according to Daoist thinkers, as soon as one begins to delineate them. The creative opportunities of the moment are lost and we begin to lose the ability to do things well. From a Daoist perspective, if one focuses on doing things well and harmoniously at each and every moment, there is no need to posit moral goals. Thus, as a counterpart to morality, they emphasize *wuwei*, which focusses on doing things without intention, in order to draw out the potential of others. If one lets go of the need for recognition, as well as the desire of the subject to leave its imprint on the world, then there is no need for explicit virtues.

For Nietzsche, the main concern is not with harmony, but rather with constant creativity and overcoming which for him is tantamount to the flourishing of life. This means that we must abandon our obsession with purposiveness and also allow ourselves to *be overcome* in order to *overcome*. He does not see this as an egotistical journey because the ego is concerned with the establishment and protection of boundaries that are acknowledged by others. In order to let go and allow for the constant transformation that he extols, the attachment to the individual subject must be relinquished. Creativity is not just something we do; it is something that also happens to us.

Furthermore, for both Nietzsche and Daoist thinkers, human anthropomorphism has resulted in a dangerous violence against nature. The tendency of human beings to position themselves at the pinnacle of existence is troubling. Nature is not seen as a realm that is other to us—we are in nature. The *Zhuangzi* reflects with longing upon a time when humans lived side by side with the birds and beasts. For Nietzsche, the tendency to locate human beings at the pinnacle of existence closes off the life-giving forces of nature. Thus, "those who do not require any extreme articles of faith" and "can think of man with a considerable reduction of his value without becoming small and weak on that account" (*WP* 55) are proven to be the strongest.

Both Nietzsche and Zhuangzi identify one major problem with traditional forms of morality, that they manifest a profound hubris on the part of human beings toward their environment. In both cases, the overvaluation of the concept and the reification of language are the primary motors behind the development of the moral system. While it is acknowledged that language development is a necessary and fruitful aspect of human experience, one can become so entranced with concepts that one forgets what these concepts are intended to respond to. Language, like the chirruping of chicks that Zhuangzi describes, must remain spontaneously responsive to the world and part of what Nietzsche would describe as the aesthetic impulse. However, when language ceases to be part of a dialogue with the cosmos and becomes the substitute for immersing ourselves in it, it assumes a dangerous bent. We begin to replace the boundless with the bounded, and reify Apollo without recognizing that Dionysus is his necessary companion. A reified

Apollo loses many of the traits that make him alluring, for it is his partnership with Dionysus that creates art. Nietzsche objects to an overly Apollonian morality that does not recognize its debt to Dionysus. Morality's refusal to acknowledge anything outside itself and arrogate to itself the supreme worth is what makes it so dangerous. Contradiction fuels life and morality in its attempt to expunge all contradiction signs its own death warrant, for it then loses the wellspring of its own meaning.

From the perspective of Daoist thinkers, it is not contradiction but harmony that reflects the rhythm of the cosmos. While Nietzsche readily acknowledges the tension between opposites, Daoist thinkers focus almost exclusively on their complementary nature. Daoists link the reificiation of language to egoism, seeing it as a form of possessiveness which tries to bring everything into a single orbit. The incessant deconstruction of language is necessary in order to remind us of its fragility and also acknowledge what rests at its periphery. Therefore, one could argue that there is a moral reason underlying this playful tendency to destabilize words. Enforcing moral dogma represents a desire to enclose the boundless within the realm of the bounded, thereby fostering egoism rather than eliminating it. The combination of Daoist with Nietzschean insights is helpful here. Nietzsche alludes to the creature racked with homesickness for the wild, as a result of the tension produced between natural impulses and the straightjacket of morality. This tension results in a proclivity to focus on the self and the cultivation of an ego identity. One becomes aware of one's own boundaries when one confronts an external limit to the self. Because morality blocks natural impulses, it intensifies the focus on the self, and thus fosters selfishness and demands that we be concerned with others. The seeds of good and evil are planted simultaneously. Furthermore, morality makes the individual dependent on the approval of others and thus invites a glaring hypocrisy which contributes to its demise. The need to solicit the approbation of others results in treating the self as an object, which is a primary aspect of egoism. Egoism is the obsession with an objectified self, not with the self that Zhuangzi describes as *shen* 身 that becomes a locus of interaction with other beings and the world.

Both Nietzsche and Daoist thinkers argue that openness is the balm for a world inflicted with a suffocating moral code. Zhuangzi's sage must wander with no objective and free herself from all intentions so as to avoid imposing her will on others. Nietzsche too insists that self-overcoming demands a readiness to be overcome by others and also cherishes silence, so that the multicolored world can be invited to speak. Self-identity in Daoism is best achieved in oneness with *Dao*, and therefore the nonself is the most authentic self. Here, the difference between Nietzschean and Daoist thought comes to the surface. For Nietzsche, boundedness and boundarylessness are equally significant dimensions of our existence and we cannot entirely avoid the trappings of egoism. He takes it for granted that the boundaries of the self will be ferociously defended, particularly when threatened with annihilation like the serpent coiled in the peasant's throat. He does not believe, like the Daoists, that death should be greeted with equanimity. Nevertheless, this gravity needs to be counterbalanced with playfulness and the recognition that one's individual life is only part of an infinite and eternal cosmos, which should be affirmed in its entirety. This is why the shepherd who forcibly bites off the serpent's head also emerges laughing, seemingly unfazed by the near brush with death. For Nietzsche, affirmation without negation is not possible. Dionysus is occasionally violent, since the individuated children of Apollo are not always content to be tamed. Thus, the process of ego formation and ego deconstruction will always be in interplay. From a Daoist perspective, egoism is always problematic and nothingness should be cultivated at all times. The sage wanders aimlessly, and thus he is always at home and able to create a home for others. In so doing, he mirrors the limitless and perpetually creative dynamic of *Dao*. Openness for Nietzsche is always in interplay with enclosure, while Daoist thinkers urge us to try to sustain a kind of boundless openness.

CONCLUSION

Morality is integrally connected with the notion of what it means to be a human being. However, this does not imply that the moral path is an easy one. On the contrary, thinkers such as Kant, Confucius, Mencius, and Rousseau assert that it requires unceasing effort and dedication, suggesting that human beings are not part of the world in the same manner as other creatures. According to Confucian thinkers, human beings are continuous with nature, but they must continuously extend and cultivate themselves to ensure that this continuity is nurtured, for it can never be taken for granted. Even though nature is viewed neither as mechanistic nor separate from human beings, it is reflected upon in order that we may participate in the moral order of *tian*. Confucius is more pessimistic than Mencius about the possibility of attaining the unspoken harmony of nature, because *li* and the human artifice associated with it are difficult to incorporate into one's being so that their execution becomes effortless. Mencius, on the other hand, is more confident about the possibility of human harmony with nature, but this may be because he describes a *cultivated* nature that already bears a strong imprint of human beings. We may feel an affective and natural unity with the ox to be slaughtered or the child that falls in the well, but these sentiments are like scaffolding that must be built upon and purposefully cultivated, so that they go beyond our most immediate environs (*M* 1A7). The ox or the cicada do not undergo such a process of continuous extension, and do not reflect upon the organic whole of the cosmos. Human beings must actively foster and nurture their consanguinity with nature.

This process of reflection, both upon the cosmos and upon oneself, is where the dangers of morality lurk, according to Daoist thinkers. Zhuangzi does not object to Confucian virtues such as *ren* and *yi* in and of themselves, but worries about the danger of their objectification and reification, which turn them into properties to acquire rather than processes that we are to participate in. Although Confucian philosophy never claims that these virtues are attributes to be possessed, from a Daoist perspective this "degeneration" begins when role models are established and when morality is predicated on performance that depends upon public recognition (see *DDJ* 66). The egotistical self is one that objectifies itself, seeing the self and the world as items for possession, and is often preoccupied with the perception others hold of it. We see ourselves as objects through the eyes of others and, only under their gaze, begin to attempt to acquire an identity for ourselves. Conventional morality can foster such behavior by placing a high premium on proper roles, a social hierarchy, and the image one projects to others. The Daoist sage is therefore a direct foil to the Confucian sage, and undoes the effects of conventional morality because she is to remain inconspicuous, drawing on the potential of human beings, without acting as the shining polestar to which all are drawn. Instead of being a beacon, the sage becomes a translucent mirror who does not have an identity of her own and is hardly noticed at all. Because of this, she is able to draw out the potential of others without imposing her will on them.

Neither the *Daodejing* nor the *Zhuangzi* imply that we should dispense with the process of reflection; instead, they suggest that we undo or even counterbalance some of its effects by engaging in the meditative processes of forgetting, whereby even our bodily limbs no longer seem to belong to us. This is an exceedingly challenging task because we gradually are to let go of our self-identity. Being invisible in the manner of the sage, and acting in such a way that one is hardly noticed, is a tremendously difficult undertaking. The Confucian moral and extended self is still an agent, while the Daoist sage engaged in *wuwei* becomes almost agentless. The Daoist virtues such as *de* and *wuwei* are meant to be even more amorphous than Confucian ones. If the Confucian is engaged in the cultivation of the self, the Daoist sage participates in the cultivation of the nonself. Once we no longer experience ourselves as subjects, eventually morality is no longer necessary because we are completely integrated into the world that we inhabit.

Strenuous efforts to become a moral person may cast an ominous shadow, because I often covet the recognition of others in doing so. Daoist thinkers object to the role that recognition plays in the moral system because this focus on who one is can easily slide into egotism, when the gaze of others becomes eminently important to me. I may end up acting morally in order to please others. This is why they mock Confucius for actively soliciting the attention and approval of his political superiors (see *Zh* 29:265). The Daoist sages quietly go about their business without worrying about social standing. People are drawn to them without knowing why.

The role that public recognition plays in moral processes may mean that the stranger is difficult to accommodate within the walls of the moral fortress. Although Confucius in no way advocates a kind of moral stasis, he does insist that such skills as learning and wisdom must always be accompanied by *li* which ensures that we accommodate ourselves to the customs and patterns of behavior of the society we live in. Transformation is possible but it must be incremental. Zhuangzi would deny that his order could accommodate the social outcasts who are his exemplars of the sage. These are people who are attuned to the natural rhythm of *Dao* in unexpected ways. Among them are fishermen, cripples, and butchers, none of whom enjoy a secure position in the upper echelons of society. They are society's rejected and/or overlooked, but are able to harmonize with the world around them without worrying about *li* or moral dogma, and draw people to them despite their apparent blemishes. Indeed, their disabilities and/or ostracism prevent them from simply parroting social norms and open up possibilities for unique attunement to *Dao*. Continuity with nature often demands a radical overturning of social convention.

The continuity with nature that both Confucians and Daoists seek would be anathema to thinkers such as Kant, for whom the demarcation of humanity from nature is very important. Kant remarks that morality elevates human beings above nature, because it allows us to assert ourselves against heteronomous desires and impulses (*FMM* 278).

Furthermore, it imbues us with the freedom to posit the universal laws that guide human behavior. However, this not only marks humanity's defiance against nature, but also its imitation of it, since Kant insists that moral laws are patterned along the lines of natural laws and he advocates a kind of chosen inevitability. In his later work, *Critique of Judgment*, Kant notes that the totalizing tendencies of reason can undermine the natural balance of nature. Thus, ironically, morality becomes means by which reason guides human behavior and be kept in check, which in his view makes morality possible in the first place. It is important to note that the ambiguity at the heart of Kantian ethics does not undermine his ethical posture, but makes ethics alluring. The tension that tugs at our being is precisely what makes the capacity to choose the moral law meaningful. The will becomes the centerpiece of Kantian moral philosophy because we are beings divided within ourselves.

For a thinker such as Rousseau, there is at the center of ethics an intractable paradox—the same processes which enable human beings to become moral also make it necessary to become moral. This suggests that morality and immorality may share a common heritage, and thus may be generated in tandem. Fantasies of ridding the world of evil are bound to result in failure, for good and evil are congenitally intertwined. According to Rousseau, the departure from our natural moorings makes ethics necessary, and morality is a process of becoming part of communities in order to compensate for the oneness found within our lost natural home. We are beset by pangs of nostalgia for the self-sufficient bliss of the protohuman who is at one with nature. However, the re-created social oneness can never replace the lost natural oneness of the protohuman. This tension provides a constant thorn in the side of our moral sheath, but at the same time constitutes the wellspring of our perfectibility and freedom because it impels us to keep reconstituting ourselves. Ironically, Rousseau takes as his yardstick for morality an asocial protohuman creature who had very little interaction with others. Once human beings begin to form societies, their ineluctable fall from protohuman serenity has begun. Like Kant, he insists that even though our imperfections frustrate us, they are the source of our freedom.

According to Rousseau, selfishness can never be eradicated. He would maintain that our longing for the protohuman state while in the midst of society may awaken the desire to be complete unto ourselves, especially when competition spawns a rising insecurity. The comparative understanding of ourselves unleashed by *amour-propre* raises within us the specter of insufficiency, and imbues us with fantasies of independence (*DOI* 64). Ironically, he tries to minimize the effects of egoism by accommodating it within the social order thereby transforming it. By suggesting that each member of the society must legislate for the entire community, the self is universalized. This appeals to our egoism because I, as an individual, am the whole. Meanwhile, it keeps our egoism in check because each other person is also the whole, and thus, ideally, no one could erode the freedom of another. Since every citizen is equal, no one citizen has claims to dominate another and Rousseau hopes that in this way, centripetal tendencies might be staved off. The problem that plagues his formulation of a society run by the general will is that it is impossible to legislate a community into existence, when the existing society is comprised mainly of atomized individuals.

Rousseau constantly refers to nature, but sees social development as a departure from it. Mencius, unlike Rousseau, stresses that we are naturally social beings housing the four sprouts of virtue deep within us. He also remarks that social conventions can submerge these innate social dispositions if they do not heed natural rhythms. Artifice can eclipse nature, and it is this warning that finds echoes in the philosophy of a thinker such as Rousseau. Selfishness can be likened to a kind of disharmony with nature because it undercuts the flowing nature of *qi* (see *M* 2A2). Like Rousseau, Mencius invokes natural sentiments such as pity and affection to ensure that convention does not go astray. A reflection upon these sentiments can impel us to extend our moral horizons to those who are not our immediate companions. Such extension of the care for others contributes to the flowing movement of *qi*, and thus becomes the means by which we fit into the balanced dynamic of nature.

Despite Mencius's emphasis on harmony, he also acknowledges that dissonance or the failure to fit into the social order is a catalyst to morality. The awareness that one may be a stranger to the community is a powerful stimulant for moral development, as exemplified by the important role that Mencius imputes to shame (see *M* 6A10). However, as Rousseau points out, shame is a double-edged sword since it spawns feelings of incompleteness that can foster the misguided attempt to become complete unto ourselves, unleashing seemingly unstoppable spirals of egoism. The fear of being an outcast suggests that the force of morality rests in part upon the threat of social ostracism.

Having a place to which one belongs is important in the Confucian understanding. The family is the central node from which moral feelings develop and radiate outward. From a Daoist perspective, this is too exclusive and does not allow one to be genuinely open to others. This is why being able to travel anywhere is important in Daoism, and there are stories of marvelous transformations and journeys that take one to unfamiliar places. Moral systems by their nature diminish multiplicity and therefore disrupt the process of open harmonizing. A genuine openness would eliminate the need for moral structures.

Because language is inclined toward an acknowledgement of the familiar, Daoist thinkers insist on the importance of cultivating silence and nothingness as counterweights to language. Silence, in its radical openness, can welcome any being. While they would not suggest that we dispense with language, silence is a means of recognizing the inherent interconnection of all beings, and that the boundaries between things are artificial. This in turn allows for a transformation of language, which becomes flowing like wine-goblet words that are open to different sounds. Moral systems are predicated on the formation and recognition of boundaries. This is why Daoist texts vociferously resist definitions of virtues and also try to counterbalance the linguistic propensity to define by cultivating nothingness, which is the openness within each thing that connects it to other beings, as well as the space between beings that both maintains their difference and allows them to interact. In Daoist philosophy, sameness is not opposed to difference but rather dependent upon it. Things are the same because they interact, and not because they can recognize themselves in each other. The mirror, a potent symbol in Daoist thought, does not reflect identical images but rather difference. Anyone can see himself or herself in a mirror. The heart of the sage or the genuine person is like a mirror because anyone can see his or her reflection in it. Language is to become a kind of mirror which invites different responses to the world, rather than a container which tries to hold it in place.

I would like to reiterate that Daoist philosophies do not spurn behavior that we would commonly consider ethical: openness and concern for the wellbeing of others. Zhuangzi notes that he has no problem with *ren* but does not like its association with certain defined forms of action, such as filial piety (see *Zh* 13:118). Moral systems cannot function without moral evaluation. The good is posited against the bad. As the *Daodejing* notes, holding up paragons of virtue and goodness heightens the temptation to transgress, in an attempt to break down the boundaries that can be stifling, particularly if one does not easily fit into the prescribed mold. Furthermore, boundaries whet our appetite for transgression (see *DDJ* 19). This has some pernicious effects, because it deliberately undermines the openness which can accommodate the diversity of the ten-thousand things.

Nietzsche shares the Daoist suspicion of morality and more forcefully links it to our addiction for language and knowledge. He insists that its main objective is to render the world and ourselves amenable to human comprehension. Knowledge and possession are intricately linked, since both are predicated on the demarcation of things from one another. This means that moral systems rest on the ostracism of the stranger who symbolizes the unknown, and cannot so easily be embraced within prevailing paradigms.

Nietzsche warns of a world that is excessively Apollonian because this can easily spill into Dionysian excess, which is then preoccupied with the need for disindividuation rather than with oneness between nature and human beings (see *BT*). Boundaries are torn down in destructive frenzy and no thought is given to their reconstitution. The desire for openness, if too constrained by a rigid morality, can become destructive. By holding up morality as a guiding beacon, we perhaps inadvertently issue invitations to act in immoral ways.

For Nietzsche, the birth of morality is also closely linked to the ossification of the concept. The process of making oneself into a knowable subject accounts for the creative vigor of morality. Thus, morality is at its most creative during the formative stages. Once it becomes increasingly pervasive, a herd mentality is produced and morality starts on its steady downward spiral of stagnation and nihilism (see *GM* III). Like many *moral* thinkers, Nietzsche remarks that morality that becomes too easy has lost its potency. Ironically, animal impulses have to be kept alive to do battle with, otherwise morality degenerates into pale mimicry.

While it is undoubtedly problematic for Nietzsche that the will of the weak has prevailed, there is more to his moral philosophy than simply a lament for the downfall of the strong. Morality is predicated on division, and denies the powerful unity of all life and human beings. Music and metaphor become alternative ways of living in Nietzschean thought, because they are responses to life rather than concepts which try to capture and consume it. Furthermore, the Dionysian aspect of music expresses the primordial oneness of existence, and allows for an affirmation of life in its dizzying totality (*BT* 6). Music cannot be known; it can merely be participated in, since change and transformation are part of its dynamic.

The connection between morality and language also comes across very powerfully in Kierkegaard's writing. He repeatedly underscores that ethics is universalizable and hence must be spoken, while Abraham cannot speak of his act of faith (*FT* 112). Because morality is so closely connected to what can be recognized publicly, it is unable to accommodate the irreducible nature of the particular individual. Kierkegaard does not suggest that we abandon morality entirely but that its limitations be revealed through faith. God, as radically other, wrests the individual from all attachments, as the command issued by Abraham to sacrifice Isaac demonstrates. Abraham receives Isaac anew not as his, but as a particular individual that is irreducible to another. The encounter with the particular allows the knight of faith to revel in the wonder of his daily existence.

For Kierkegaard, the primary problem with morality is that it depends upon assimilation of the diverse and unfamiliar. This is why the ability to love a stranger puts ethics to its most exacting test. Love is meant as an alternative to conventional ethics since it necessitates faith. The stranger cannot be welcomed into our fold because he suits us. In fact, he may not fit in at all. Kierkegaard's *Works of Love* focuses on the neighbor, who is both close and far. It is this nearness and distance that is significant. The neighbor lives in proximity but also a stranger to us. For this reason, the neighbor becomes a metaphor for all of humanity. Furthermore, the fact that our encounter with neighbors is accidental rather than chosen suggests that we have responsibility toward someone who simply stumbles across our path, regardless of their relationship to us.

Kierkegaardian love shares some similarities with the Daoist notion of *wuwei* in the sense that it represents an openness not encumbered by the ego and is a response to another, rather than an imposition of norms. However, there is also a profound and significant difference between the approaches of Daoist writers and Kierkegaard. *Wuwei* is an activity devoid of intention, meaning that it is unencumbered by the will (*DDJ* 63). However, this does not necessitate supreme humility or the surrender to another. The Daoist sage is secure in her identity because it is irrelevant to her. Thus, she provides an opening for the other to express his or her particular virtue, while the other in turn provides such an opening for her. There is no notion that one is incomplete or infinitesimally small when confronted with an infinite God. By contrast, the Kierkegaardian encounter with God demands extreme humility and sacrifice. Abraham is called upon to sacrifice his son who is deeply interwoven with his identity. The love of the neighbor necessitates God as intermediary and is indicative of the iron grip that egoism has on the psyche (*WL* 106). Only God who is radically other can effect this change, in Kierkegaard's view, and bring us to acknowledge the other who is also the same. This notion of radical otherness is not part of Daoist ways of thinking, since it only makes sense if the separation between individuals is assumed to be primary. Even *Dao* itself is never radically other, but only hiding and appearing. Unlike Kierkegaard's God, *Dao* is transcendent only because it is immanent, not because it makes us aware of an immeasurable distance between the finite and the infinite. The finite is the infinite because of its immeasurable diversity. Therefore, the sage is complete because he does not worry about completeness. There is no infinite that he desires to become, or God that he is not.

The primary difficulty, according to those thinkers who seem to impugn moral systems, is that it operates within the realm of the bounded.

This does not imply that morality ought to be dispensed with. Like language, it may be an indelible aspect of the human condition. It is no coincidence that Yan Hui, versed in Confucian morality, is able to eventually let it go, and along with it, his own identity (*Zh* 6:58). Even Confucius is presented both as a moral pedant and as a Daoist sage. This suggests that traditional morality is a stage most of us must go through before nurturing the skills of a deeper harmonizing that no longer relies on the guidelines provided by *li*. The critics of morality do not invite us to wantonly tear asunder all moral edifices, leaving us drifting and perpetually rudderless in the midst of a Dionysian tempest. By highlighting the more pernicious aspects of ethics, they remind us that it is important to be humble about moral constructions, which are not immune from our all-too-human limitations. Insisting that morality is unassailable may be the height of humanist egoism, and can lead to a utilitarian exploitation of others and our world. Nietzsche and Daoist thinkers invite us to accompany them on a journey beyond morality. By revealing the unethical underbelly of ethics, they may be suggesting that in order to ensure that ethics does not don the straightjacket of the ego, there may be times when we must be prepared to go beyond it. Only in this way can we keep it alive.

BIBLIOGRAPHY

Primary Sources

Confucius. *The Analects of Confucius: A Philosophical Translation*. Trans. Roger T. Ames and Henry Rosemont. New York: Ballantine Books, 1998.

Daodejing 道德經. Beijing: Beijing daxue chubanshe, 1995.

Huainanzi. *The Art of Rulership: A Study in Ancient Chinese Political Thought*. Trans. Roger T. Ames. Honolulu: University of Hawaii Press, 1983.

———. *Huainan honglie jijie* 淮南鴻烈集解. Beijing: Zhonghua shuju chubanshe, 1989.

———. "The Taoism of Huai-nan Tzu." Trans. Wing-Tsit Chan. In *A Sourcebook in Chinese Philosophy*. Princeton: Princeton University Press, 1963.

———. *Yuan Dao: Tracing Dao to Its Source*. Trans. Roger T. Ames and D. C. Lau. New York: Ballantine Books, 1998.

Kant, Immanuel. *Critique of Judgment*. Trans. J. H. Bernard. New York: Hafner Publishing Company, 1968.

———. *Critique of Practical Reason*. Trans. H. J. Paton. New York: Harper and Row, 1964.

———. *Foundations of the Metaphysics of Morals*. In *Kant Selections*. Ed. Lewis White Beck. New York: Macmillan Publishing Company, 1988.

———. "Idea for a Universal History from a Cosmopolitan Point of View." In *Kant Selections*. Ed. Lewis White Beck. New York: Macmillan Publishing Company, 1988.

———. *Kritik der praktischen Vernunft*. Köln: Könemann Verlagsgesellschaft mbH, 1995.

———. *Kritik der Urteilskraft*. Köln: Könemann Verlagsgesellschaft mbH, 1995.

———. *Lectures on Pedagogy*. In *On Education*. London: Kegan Paul, 1897.

———. *The Metaphysical Principles of Virtue*. New York: Bobbs-Merrill and Company, 1964.

———. *Die Metaphysik der Sitten*. Köln: Könemann Verlagsgesellschaft mbH, 1995.

———. *Die Religion innerhalb der Grenzen der blossen Vernunft*. Köln: Könemann Verlagsgesellschaft mbH, 1995.

———. *Religion within the Bounds of Bare Reason*. Trans. Werner S. Pluhar. Indianapolis: Hackett Publishing Company, 2009.

Kierkegaard, Søren. *The Concept of Anxiety: A Simple Psychologically Orienting Deliberation on the Dogmatic Issue of Hereditary Sin*. Trans. Reidar Thomte. Princeton: Princeton University Press, 1981.

———. *Concluding Unscientific Postscript to Philosophical Fragments*. Trans. Howard V. Hong and Edna H. Hong. Princeton: Princeton University Press, 1992.

———. *Either/Or Part I*. Trans. Howard V. Hong and Edna H. Hong. Princeton: Princeton University Press, 1987.

———. *Either/Or Part II*. Trans. Howard V. Hong and Edna H. Hong. Princeton: Princeton University Press, 1987.

———. *Fear and Trembling*. Trans. Howard V. Hong and Edna H. Hong. Princeton: Princeton University Press, 1983.

———. *The Sickness Unto Death: A Christian Psychological Exposition for Upbuilding and Awakening*. Trans. Alastair Hannay. Princeton: Princeton University Press, 1980.

———. *Training in Christianity and the Edifying Discourse Which Accompanied It*. Trans. Walter Lowrie. Princeton: Princeton University Press, 1944.

———. *Works of Love*. Trans. Howard V. Hong and Edna H. Hong. Princeton: Princeton University Press, 1998.

Liezi. *The Book of Lieh-tzu: A Classic of Tao*. Trans. A. C. Graham. New York: Columbia University Press, 1990.

Mencius. *Mengzi*. Trans. Bryan W. Van Norden. Indianapolis: Hackett Publishing Company, 2008.

———. *The Works of Mencius*. In *The Chinese Classics*. Taipei: SMC Publishing, 1988.

Nietzsche, Friedrich. *Also Sprach Zarathustra*. In *Friedrich Nietzsche: Das Hauptwerk*. Bd. III. München: Nymphenburger Verlag, 1990.

———. *Beyond Good and Evil*. In *Basic Writings of Nietzsche*. Trans. Walter Kaufmann. New York: Modern Library, 1968.

———. *The Birth of Tragedy*. In *Basic Writings of Nietzsche*. Trans. Walter Kaufmann. New York: Modern Library, 1968.

———. *Die Fröhliche Wissenschaft*. In *Friedrich Nietzsche: Das Hauptwerk*. Bd. II.

München: Nymphenburger Verlag, 1990.
———. *Die Geburt der Tragödie*. In *Friedrich Nietzsche: Das Hauptwerk*. Bd. III. München: Nymphenburger Verlag, 1990.
———. *On the Genealogy of Morals*. In *Basic Writings of Nietzsche*. Trans. Walter Kaufmann. New York: Modern Library, 1968.
———. *Jenseits von Gut und Böse*. In *Friedrich Nietzsche: Das Hauptwerk*. Bd. III. München: Nymphenburger Verlag, 1990.
———. *Thus Spoke Zarathustra*. Trans. R. J. Hollingdale. Middlesex: Penguin, 1968.
———. "On Truth and Falsity in an Extra-Moral Sense." In *Early Greek Philosophy and Other Essays*. Trans. M. A. Mügge. *The Complete Works of Friedrich Nietzsche*, vol. 2. Ed. Oscar Levy. New York: Russell and Russell, 1964.
———. *Twilight of the Idols*. Trans. R. J. Hollingdale. Middlesex: Penguin, 1968.
———. *The Will to Power*. Trans. Walter Kaufmann and R. J. Hollingdale. Middlesex: Penguin, 1968.
Rousseau, Jean-Jacques. *Du Contrat Social*. In *Du Contrat Social: Oeuvres Choisies de Jean-Jacques Rousseau*. Paris: Editions Garnier Frères, 1962.
———. *Discours sur l'Inégalité*. In *Du Contrat Social: Oeuvres Choisies de Jean-Jacques Rousseau*. Paris: Editions Garnier Frères, 1962.
———. *Discourse on the Origins of Inequality*. In *The Basic Political Writings*. Ed. Peter Gay. Indianapolis: Hackett Publishing Company, 1987.
———. *Emile*. Trans. Allan Bloom. New York: Basic Books, 1979.
———. *Emile, ou l'Education*. Paris: Garnier Flammarion, 1966.
———. *On the Social Contract*. In *The Basic Political Writings*. Ed. Peter Gay. Indianapolis: Hackett Publishing Company, 1987.
Tao Te Ching. Trans. D. C. Lau. London: Penguin Books, 1963.
Zhuangzi. *The Book of Chuang-tzu*. Trans. Martin Palmer. New York: Vintage, 1968.
———. *Zhuangzi duben* 莊子讀本. Taipei: Sanmin shuju, 1998.

Secondary Sources

Allinson, Robert E. "On Chuang-tzu as a Deconstructionist with a Difference." *Journal of Chinese Philosophy* 30, no. 3–4 (2003): 487–500.
Ames, Roger T. "Knowing in the *Zhuangzi*: From Here on the Bridge Over the River Hao." In *Wandering at Ease in the Zhuangzi*, ed. Roger T. Ames, pp. 219–230. Albany: State University of New York Press, 1998.

Ames, Roger T., and David Hall. *Thinking from the Han: Self, Truth and Transcendence in Chinese and Western Culture*. Albany: State University of New York Press, 1998.

———. *Thinking Through Confucius*. Albany: State University of New York Press, 1987.

Ames, Roger T., and Peter D. Hershock. *Confucian Cultures of Authority*. Albany: State University of New York Press, 2006.

Ames, Roger T., and Henry Rosemont. "Introduction." In *The Analects of Confucius*, ed. Roger T. Ames and Henry Rosemont, pp. 1–70. New York: Ballantine Books, 1998.

Beabout, Gregory. *Freedom and Its Misuses: Kierkegaard on Anxiety and Despair*. Milwaukee, Wisconsin: Marquette University Press, 1996.

Behuniak, James, Jr. "Disposition and Aspiration in the *Mencius* and *Zhuangzi*." *Journal of Chinese Philosophy* 29, no. 1 (2002): 65–79.

Birdwhistell, Joanne D. *Mencius and Masculinities: Dynamics of Power, Morality and Maternal Thinking*. Albany: State University of New York Press, 2007.

Burgelin, Pierre. *La Philosophie die l'Existence de Jean-Jacques Rousseau*. Paris: Presses Universitaires de France, 1952.

Caputo, John. *Against Ethics: Contributions to a Poetics of Obligation with Constant Reference to Deconstruction*. Bloomington: Indiana University Press, 1993.

Carr, Karen, and Philip J. Ivanhoe. *Senses of Anti-Rationalism: Religious Thought of Zhuangzi and Kierkegaard*. New York: Seven Bridges Press, 1999.

Chalier, Catherine. *What Ought I to Do?: Morality in Kant and Levinas*. Trans. Jane Marie Todd. Ithaca: Cornell University Press, 2002.

Chang, Chung-Yuan. "The Philosophy of Taoism according to Chuang-tzu." *Philosophy East and West* 27, no. 4 (1977): 409–422.

Cheng, Chung-Ying. *New Dimensions of Confucian and Neo-Confucian Philosophy*. Albany: State University of New York Press, 1991.

Ching, Julia. "Chinese Ethics and Kant." *Philosophy East and West* 28, no. 2 (1978): 161–172.

Froese, Katrin. *Nietzsche, Heidegger and Daoist Thought: Crossing Paths In-Between*. Albany: State University of New York Press, 2006.

Gardner, Daniel. *Zhu Xi's Reading of the Analects*. New York: Columbia University Press, 2003.

Grange, Joseph. "Zhuangzi's Tree." *Journal of Chinese Philosophy* 32, no. 2 (2005): 171–182.

Guo, Qingfan. *Zhuangzi jijie* 莊子集解. Beijing: Zhonghua shuju, 1961.

Hall, Amy Laura. *Kierkegaard and the Treachery of Love*. Cambridge: Cambridge University Press, 2002.

Hannay, Alastair. *Kierkegaard*. London: Routledge, 1991.

Hansen, Chad. "Freedom and Moral Responsibility in Confucian Ethics." *Philosophy East and West* 22, no. 2 (1972): 169–186.

Hegel, G. W. F. *Phenomenology of Spirit*. Trans. A. V. Miller. Oxford: Oxford University Press, 1979.

Horowitz, Asher. *Rousseau, Nature and History*. Toronto: University of Toronto Press, 1987.

Ivanhoe, Philip J. "Confucian Self Cultivation and Mengzi's Notion of Extension." In *Essays on the Moral Philosophy of Mengzi*, ed. Xiusheng Liu and Philip J. Ivanhoe, pp. 221–241. Indianapolis: Hackett Publishing Company, 2002.

Ivanhoe, Philip J., and P. Kjellberg. *Essays on Skepticism, Relativism and Ethics in the Zhuangzi*. Albany: State University of New York Press, 1996.

Jacobs, Brian, and Patrick Kain, eds. *Essays on Kant's Anthropology*. Cambridge: Cambridge University Press, 2003.

Jones, W. T. *Kant and the Nineteenth Century*. New York: Harcourt Brace Jovanovich, 1975.

Kofman, Sarah. *Nietzsche et la métaphore*. Paris: Editions Galilée, 1972.

Kohn, Livia. *Early Chinese Mysticism: Philosophy and Soteriology in the Taoist Tradition*. Princeton: Princeton University Press, 1992.

———. *Taoist Mystical Philosophy: The Scripture of Western Ascension*. Albany: State University of New York Press, 1991.

Kohn, Livia, and Michael LaFargue, eds. *Lao-Tzu and the Tao-Te-Ching*. Albany: State University of New York Press, 1996.

Kroner, Richard. *Kant's Weltanshauung*. Chicago: University of Chicago Press, 1956.

Lai, Karyn L. "Confucian Moral Thinking." *Philosophy East and West* 45, no. 2 (1995): 249–271.

———. "Philosophy and Philosophical Reasoning in the *Zhuangzi*: Dealing with Plurality." *Journal of Chinese Philosophy* 33, no. 3 (2006): 365–374.

Lampert, Laurence. *Nietzsche's Teaching: An Interpretation of Thus Spoke Zarathustra*. New Haven: Yale University Press, 1986.

Liu, Xiaogan. "An Inquiry into the Core Value of Laozi's Philosophy." In *Religious and Philosophical Aspects of the Laozi*, ed. Mark Csikszentmihalyi and Philip J. Ivanhoe, pp. 211–238. Albany: State University of New York Press, 1999.

Louden, Robert. *Kant's Impure Ethics: From Rational Beings to Human Beings*. New

York: Oxford University Press, 2000.

Löwith, Karl. *Nietzsches Philosophie der Ewigen Wiederkehr des Gleichen*. Stuttgart: Kohlhammer, 1956.

Lukács, Georg. "The Foundering of Form Against Life: Søren Kierkegaard and Regine Olson." In *Søren Kierkegaard*, ed. Harold Bloom, pp. 5–18. New York: Chelsea House Press, 1989.

Man, Eva Kit-Wah. "Contemporary Feminist Body Theories and Mencius's Ideas of Body and Mind." *Journal of Chinese Philosophy* 27, no. 2 (2000): 155–169.

Moeller, Hans-Georg. *The Philosophy of the Daodejing*. New York: Columbia University Press, 2006.

Mooney, Edward. *Knights of Faith and Resignation: Reading Kierkegaard's Fear and Trembling*. Albany: State University of New York Press, 1991.

Morgenstern, Mira. *Rousseau and the Politics of Ambiguity: Self, Culture and Society*. University Park: Pennsylvania State University Press, 1996.

Müller-Lauter, Wolfgang. *Nietzsche: Seine Philosophie der Gegensätze und die Gegensätze seiner Philosophie*. Berlin: Walter de Gruyter, 1971.

Nishitani, Keiji. *Religion and Nothingness*. Berkeley: University of California Press, 1982.

Paton, H. J. *The Categorical Imperative*. London: Hutchinson, 1967.

Pattison, George. *Kierkegaard, Religion and the Nineteenth-Century Crisis of Culture*. Cambridge: Cambridge University Press, 2002.

Perkins, Franklin. "Mencius, Emotion and Autonomy." *Journal of Chinese Philosophy* 29, no. 2 (2002): 207–226.

Robinet, Isabelle. "The Diverse Interpretations of the Laozi." In *Religious and Philosophical Aspects of the Laozi*, ed. Mark Csikszentmihalyi and Philip J. Ivanhoe, pp. 127–160. Albany: State University of New York Press, 1991.

Saurette, Paul. "Kant's Culture of Humiliation: Politics and Ethical Cultivation." *Philosophy and Social Criticism* 28, no. 1 (2002): 59–90.

Schipper, Kristofer. *The Taoist Body*. Berkeley: University of California Press, 1993.

Schwartz, Benjamin. *The World of Thought in Ancient China*. Cambridge: Harvard University Press, 1985.

Shang, Geling. *Liberation as Affirmation: The Religiosity of Zhuangzi and Nietzsche*. Albany: State University of New York Press, 2006.

Shun, Kwong-Loi. "*Ren* and *Li* in the *Analects*." In *Confucius and the Analects: New Essays*, ed. Bryan V. Norden, pp. 53–72. Oxford: Oxford University Press, 2002.

Slingerland, Edward. *Effortless Action: Wuwei as a Conceptual Metaphor and Spiritual Ideal in Early China*. New York: Oxford University Press, 2003.

Stambaugh, Joan. *Nietzsche's Thought of Eternal Return*. Baltimore: John Hopkins University Press, 1972.

———. *The Other Nietzsche.* Albany: State University of New York Press, 1994.

Sullivan, Roger J. *Immanuel Kant's Moral Theory*. Cambridge: Cambridge University Press, 1989.

———. *An Introduction to Kant's Ethics*. Cambridge: Cambridge University Press, 1994.

Tan, Sor-Hoon. *Confucian Democracy: A Deweyan Reconstruction*. Albany: State University of New York Press, 2003.

———. "Imagining Confucius: Paradigmatic Characters and Virtue Ethics." *Journal of Chinese Philosophy* 32, no. 3 (2005): 409–426.

Taylor, Charles. *Sources of the Self: The Making of Modern Identity*. Cambridge: Cambridge University Press, 1989.

Tu, Weiming. *Confucian Thought: Selfhood as Creative Transformation*. Albany: State University of New York Press, 1985.

———. "Probing the 'Three Bonds' and 'Five Relationships' in Confucian Humanism." In *Confucianism and the Family*, ed. Walter H. Slote and George A. De Vos, pp. 121–136. Albany: State University of New York Press, 1998.

———. "Selfhood and Otherness in Confucian Thought." In *Culture and Self: Asian and Western Perspectives*, ed. Anthony J. Marsella, George A. De Vos and Francis L. K. Hsu, pp. 231–251. New York: Tavistock Publication, 1985.

Wang, Bi. *Commentary on the Lao-Tzu*. Trans. Ariane Rump and Wing-Tsit Chan. Honolulu: University Press of Hawaii, 1981.

Wee, Cecilia. "Descartes and Mencius on Self and Community." *Journal of Chinese Philosophy* 29, no. 2 (2002): 265–289.

Weeks, Mark. "Beyond a Joke: Nietzsche and the Birth of Super-Laughter." *Journal of Nietzsche Studies* 27 (2004): 1–17.

Winfree, Jason Kemp. "Before the Subject: Rereading *The Birth of Tragedy*." *Journal of Nietzsche Studies* 25 (2003): 58–77.

Wood, Allen. *Kant's Ethical Thought*. Cambridge: Cambridge University Press, 1999.

Wu, Kuang-Ming. *The Butterfly as Companion*. Albany: State University of New York Press, 1990.

———. "Zhuangzi de zixiang maodun" 莊子的自相矛盾. *Taida zhexue lunping* 臺大哲學論評 12 (1989): 313–323.

Xu, Shen. *Shuowen jiezi* 説文解字. Beijing: Zhonghua shuju, 1963.

Yu, Jiyuan. "The Moral Self and the Perfect Self in Aristotle and Mencius." *Journal of Chinese Philosophy* 28, no. 3 (2001): 235–256.

Zhang, Longxi. "Qian Zhongshu on Philosophical and Mystical Paradoxes in the *Laozi*." In *Religious and Philosophical Aspects of the Laozi*, ed. Mark Csikszentmihalyi and Philip J. Ivanhoe, pp. 97–126. Albany: State University of New York Press, 1999.

INDEX